Shakespeare and the Popular Voice

Shakespeare and the Popular Voice

Annabel Patterson

Basil Blackwell

First published 1989

Basil Blackwell Inc.
3 Cambridge Center
Cambridge, MA 02142, USA

Basil Blackwell Ltd
108 Cowley Road, Oxford, 0X4 1JF, UK

Library of Congress Cataloging in Publication Data

Patterson, Annabel M.
Shakespeare and the popular voice/Annabel Patterson.
p. cm.
Bibliography: p.
Includes index.
ISBN 0-631-16872-9 – ISBN 0-631-16873-7 (pbk.)
1. Shakespeare, William, 1564–1616 – Criticism and interpretation.
2. Literature and society – Great Britain. 3. Popular culture.
I. Title.
PR2976.P38 1990 89-32246
822.3'3. – dc20 CIP

British Library Cataloguing in Publication Data

A CIP catalogue record for this book is available from the British Library.

Typeset in 10 on 12 pt Sabon
by Setrite Typesetters
Printed in Great Britain by T. J. Press Ltd., Padstow

Contents

Acknowledgements

My first acknowledgement must be to the students at the Bread Loaf School of English, who encouraged my early forays into Shakespeare criticism. The thought that these arguments of mine might be useful in *their* classrooms has helped me to confront, without being intimidated, the monumental institutions of Shakespeare studies that began construction in the early nineteenth century and have grown more forbidding, to the ordinary reader, ever since. If a group of dedicated high-school teachers – many of whom taught with immense fortitude in underprivileged communities – could see in my lectures the rough outline of a Shakespeare their students could latch onto, possibly the time had come for the fences around the Shakespearean shrine to be levelled. In his own day London's most popular playright, Shakespeare might conceivably become popular again; though one will need to read the book to discover precisely (or inclusively) what 'popular' means.

Beyond this early encouragement, I am grateful to Duke University (especially Dean Richard White, Provost Phillip Griffiths, and my two chairmen, Frederic Jameson and Stanley Fish): not for giving me the time to write, for most of that has been stolen, but for providing the intellectual environment, along with the everyday resources, that render one's iconoclasm a little less scary to oneself.

But because it remains iconoclasm, I am more than usually conscious of the inestimable value of the collegial helping hand. Brian (R. B.) Parker, David Berington, George Williams, Theodore Leinwand, Gary Taylor, Richard Helgerson, Margot Heinemann, F. J. Levy all read substantial parts of this book, and their responses, selflessly detailed, have saved me many a mistake and provided me with many a confirmatory fact or reference. Frederic Jameson, Peter Stallybrass, David Lawrence and again George Williams lent me crucial books at crucial moments. Derek Hirst generously helped me to mount my case against him in respect to the Midlands Rising.

Lloyd Davies was a research assistant of exceptional patience and resourcefulness. And above all my husband and colleague Lee Patterson listened constructively, averted his eyes from domestic errors and omissions, saved me on countless occasions from the demons of doubt, hybris and hypertension, and generally made the project companionable.

Earlier versions of chapters 1, 3 and 4 have previously appeared in *New Literary History*, *Renaissance Papers* and *Renaissance Drama*. I am grateful to the editors of these journals for giving my work preliminary circulation, and for permission to reproduce those parts of the arguments that have not been substantially revised.

This book is dedicated to my sister,
Miranda De Souza, whose work for
the Citizens' Advice Bureau is
the real, unmediated, thing.

Foreword: Hindsight

the Plebeian Impe from lofty throne,
Creates and rules a world.

I.M.S. commendatory poem,
Second Folio of Shakespeare's *Works*

But Shakespeare, the Plebean Driller, was
Founder'd in's *Pericles*, and must not pass.

John Tatham, 1652

This book has three goals. The first is to alter common opinion on a perennially interesting, perennially troubling question: what were Shakespeare's social assumptions and, in particular, what was his attitude to the ordinary working people inside and outside his plays? Common opinion (which is, of course, not really common, but the product of a tiny fraction of the reading public) has for a long time held that Shakespeare's attitude to the 'common' people (who were by far the majority of the population) ranged from tolerant amusement to contempt. This opinion, which was not in circulation until the early nineteenth century, is actually counter-intuitive. Common sense suggests, conversely, that a popular dramatist, himself the son of a country glover, and whose livelihood depended on the huge and socially diverse audiences for the London public theater, was unlikely to have unquestioningly adopted an anti-popular myth as his own.

It is not, of course, possible to read off Shakespeare's social attitudes simply from his social origins. We know that John Shakespeare became a substantial citizen in Stratford, serving as constable, juror, alderman, a member of the civic council, and that by 1568 he had achieved the position of high bailiff, the equivalent of mayor; we also know that a few years later his career was on a downward slide, that he was in major financial difficulties, and by 1586 was deprived of his alderman's gown. We know that Shakespeare himself became a wealthy man, part-owner in his successful theatrical company, the proceeds of which were invested in land and property in Stratford. In this he was fully representative of a stage in English social history that, all historians agree, was then unprecedented in its degree of social mobility. We also know that in 1596 Shakespeare applied on behalf of John Shakespeare, yeoman, for a gentleman's coat of arms: 'Gold, on a bend sables, a spear of the first steeled argent,' with a motto, 'Non Sanz Droit,' not without right.[1] But we cannot be sure what this deeply symbolic gesture means, whose aspirations were at stake. Nor can the evidence of Shakespeare's real estate deals in later life, along with those ambiguous records relating to enclosures, justify our drawing the conclusion that a man who moves upwards on the social scale is inevitably proud of that move, to the point of invariably defending the class divisions in his society and denigrating what he has left behind. Modern playwrights do not make that elementary mistake. Even Edward Bond, whose *Bingo* may be taken to represent the sharpest reproach of a socialist critic for such an assumed defection, imagined a Shakespeare with a bad conscience, and one whose ability to perceive what was wrong with his society was out of all proportion to his ability to alter it.[2]

But if psychologically there can be no simple answers as to how Shakespeare's social loyalties would have been constructed or redirected, we know that in some broad sense he must have regarded himself, certainly when he began his career as actor and playwright, as one of that largest of all possible groupings in England at that time – those below the rank of the landed aristocracy or gentry. While social historians today are quick to point out that terms like 'the commons', 'the commonalty', 'the people' or populace' were and are blanket terms that conceal large social and economic differences, and while the ranks of the gentry and even the aristocracy were not in practice impermeable, the fact remains that there was a clear line drawn conceptually (ideologically) between the gentry and everyone below, whether successful yeomen or merchants, wage laborers, apprentices, or, at the bottom of the scale, the rural poor.[3]

A crucial component of this thinking was, moreover, political rather than vocational or economic, in the sense that it supported a restricted franchise. From the late 1590s there were a few signs that the extension of voting rights was being considered, invariably as a local issue; by 1610, when Shakespeare returned to Stratford, some members of the House of Commons were beginning to conceive of their responsibilities to represent 'the commons' in a larger sense; and by the 1620s they were hesitantly formulating theories of a general right of male inhabitants to the franchise, while in practise the vote was gradually being extended, both through the effects of inflation on the old economic barrier (40 shilling freehold) established in 1430, and also by enlightened electoral practice in the larger cities outside London (Lincoln, Northampton, Leicester, Exeter).

A few statistics, however hypothetical, will help to sharpen the picture. The population in England as a whole in 1600 was approximately four million. Of those four million persons, fewer than sixty were peers, and the gentry made up between two and three per cent of the population. As for the electorate, historians vary widely in their estimates of how far the expansion in the reign of Charles I went in altering the social balance, one claiming that at the peak of this development, the early months of the Long Parliament, the potential electorate was between twenty-seven and forty per cent of the adult male population, another that it was only 4.7 per cent by the end of the seventeenth century. One must suppose that, like all other interpreters, historians see in part what they wish to see.[4] In 1643 Sir John Spelman, anxious to discredit the Long Parliament, claimed that eligible voters 'cannot be above a tenth part of the Kingdome'.[5] But even if we accept the most generous estimate for the later period, the situation as Shakespeare saw it (and reflected on it in *Coriolanus*) was far more restrictive. At least ninety-five per cent of the population, commonly known as 'the commons', were excluded by law and practice from any voice in the major affairs of the state. As I shall later argue, *Coriolanus* stands as Shakespeare's meditation, late in his career, on an alternative political system – the early Roman republic – where the plebeians, both through their tribunes and directly, did have a voice in government; and, as is so often the case, his capacity to imagine an alternative was prophetic, in a way that we are only now, perhaps, fully able to appreciate.[6]

But if common sense suggests that Shakespeare would have placed himself and his fellow-actors in the category of 'the commons', it provides a far stronger incentive to reconsider what it meant to be a popular dramatist. Cognate with 'the people' and 'populace', the term 'popular' was in wide and complex use in Shakespeare's day. It connoted, usually pejoratively, anything or anyone with wide appeal to the common people; for example, the populist strategies of the second earl of Essex, who was subsequently executed for them; democratic forms of government; or, as in the phrase 'Vox Populi', sometimes found in the titles of pamphlets, the voice of the people themselves. Given what we know of Shakespeare's status as the most popular playwright at a time when the theater was popular as never before or since – at its peak the London theater attendance ranged between 8,000 and 10,000 per day – it seems folly to assume that his plays, by assuming an elitist social perspective, knowingly insulted a large proportion of their audience. Some of that foolishness derives, I contend, from a misunderstanding of *Hamlet*, our best guide to Shakespeare's own sociology of the theater; yet Hamlet's contemptuous remarks on the subject of the popular audience – the 'groundlings' – would, like his preference in plays, have made him a disastrous failure in the Elizabethan commercial theater. My first chapter, accordingly, situates Shakespeare materially in his profession, and, by way of Hamlet's extensive commentary on that profession, confronts the conditions of Shakespeare's success: the economic and political postulates of the secular, public theaters, the social construction of the audience, the extent and effects of court patronage and surveillance and, most important, the problems of the *uncommon* playwright in defining his social goals, the intellectual's everlasting dilemma.

My second task is to frame the question of Shakespeare's social goals in today's thought about popular culture and popular protest, a concern that connects history, political theory, anthropology, sociology and such subfields as ethnomethodology, with sporadic inroads into literary criticism and theory. Certain procedural problems endemic in all of these approaches to the popular are magnified for Shakespeare's period. For a time for which the archives seldom record the sound of the popular voice, how are we to reconstruct its messages? If modern anthropology has succeeded in transcribing both sides of the social dialectic as it occurs in other geopolitical regions at a comparable stage of development, how much conceptual transferability can we assume? Can we define the term 'popular' with historical rigor, as it was in fact used, and used frequently, in Shakespeare's society? How, especially, do we avoid contamination by later historical experience of the failures of democracy, the commercialization of culture, and the hideous versions of populism deployed by fascist and totalitarian regimes? These and other problems of theory and method are raised in or by my second, third and sixth chapters, the second dealing with popular protest and resistance, the third with festival practices, and the sixth with classical republicanism, the only conceptual system known to Shakespeare for incorporating the popular, by formal representation, into the state.

My third and most elusive objective, is to align both the Shakespearean project and its social frame with the contemporary debate on humanism – that is to say, with the stated arguments and underlying assumptions of those who have discarded humanism as a useful category of thought, and those who believe, for whatever motive, that we cannot do without it. It will be already apparent from these opening statements that this book calmly reinstates certain categories of thought that some have declared obsolete: above all the concept of authorship, which itself depends on our predicating a continuous, if not a consistent self, of self-determination and, in literary terms, of intention. It is disingenuous, at best, to substitute for the concept 'Shakespeare', someone who certainly existed (however inadequate our biographical account of him) the concept of 'the text', something which, thanks to the revisionist bibliography of the past two decades, we now recognize *never* existed as a stable entity. And it is an ironic comment on the literary institution that those who have been most anxious to align Shakespeare with their own ideas of social hierarchy have happily attributed intentions to him; whereas those who deplore the alignment have feared, because of the avant-garde proscriptions against talking about authors or intentions, to meet them on their own ground. Being an author of sorts myself, and accustomed to having my intentions elucidated in critical reviews, I have no difficulty in positing Shakespeare as a writer whose intentions, if never fully recoverable, are certainly worth debating.

Although the humanist assumptions of this study are usually to be met with subliminally, my fifth chapter starts by looking rather sharply at certain fashionable forms of anti-humanism which have seriously inhibited our capacity to talk sensibly about literature, not least because of their own secret elitism. This chapter returns to *Hamlet*, as a play whose emphasis upon subjectivity has made it peculiarly vulnerable to psycho-analytic criticism, which in its late (Lacanian) phase has occluded the play's social meaning; and it pairs with *Hamlet*, through the linked topics of voice, social criticism and responsibility, *King Lear*, a play whose focus on 'unaccomodated man' certainly requires understanding in terms of a new and theoretically self-conscious humanism.

Since the early nineteenth century, conservative critics from Coleridge to Tillyard, democrats like Hazlitt or Whitman, and even contemporary Marxist critics like Terry Eagleton, if they agree in nothing else, have converged in believing that Shakespeare accepted without question contemporary social hierarchy and its self-justifications. This consensus is so ubiquitous that Eagleton could begin with the statement, 'Even those who know very little about Shakespeare might be vaguely aware that his plays value social order and stability.'[7] It followed from this premise that the Elizabethan underclasses were deliberately represented in the plays as ignorant groundlings castigated by Hamlet, licensed, dependent clowns in courtly households, and unsavory crowds in the street. Of course there were some exceptions. Eminent critics would develop excuses for Shakespeare, comb the canon for counterarguments or, in the wake of postmodern theories of language, argue that the *texts* have a political unconscious inaccessible to Shakespeare himself and 'at odds with his political ideology.'[8] But virtually nobody seems to have doubted that the heart of Shakespeare's social theory resided in his hostile treatment of the crowd when noisy, protesting, or (worst of all) in open riot or rebellion.

Nobody, that is, since the early nineteenth century. There is barely a trace of this opinion among Shakespeare's contemporaries or later in the seventeenth century, when critical commentary on his plays began to emerge. It does not appear where one would expect to find it, in Dryden's *Essay of Dramatic Poesy*, or John Dennis's *Impartial Critick*, or Samuel Johnson's 'Preface to Shakespeare', where a theory of *generic* regulation involves a critique of the irregular English theater, with its comic inserts into tragedy, a concession, it is implied, to the popular audience. That is to say, Shakespeare erred by being popular himself. 'Our Poets,' wrote Dryden in 1668, 'present you the Play and the farce together; and our Stages still retain somewhat of the Original civility of the Red-Bull.' The Red Bull in Shakespeare's London and subsequently in Dryden's was proverbial for catering to the rowdiest audiences; and Dryden's ironic 'civility' is explained to the educated reader by a quotation (in Latin) from one of Horace's epistles (2:1:185–86): '*Atque ursum & pugiles media inter carmina poscunt*' (they call in the middle of the play for a bear or for boxers).[9] For Dryden, Shakespeare is the native master whose errors in decorum are not interrogated at the level of his social theory (though Dryden's is certainly evident); Shakespeare will be rescued as the supreme native dramatist despite that barbarous 'civility', not by attributing to him Dryden's own commitment to social stability. And even John Milton, as one of the defeated revolutionaries who faced the revival of the Restoration stage with extremely complex emotions, reiterated this neoclassical position: tragedy requires vindication

> from the small esteem, or rather infamy, which in the account of many it undergoes at this day with other *common* Interludes; happ'ning through the Poet's error of intermixing Comic stuff with Tragic sadness and gravity; or introducing *trivial and vulgar persons*, which by all judicious hath been counted absurd; and brought in without discretion, corruptly to gratify the people.[10]

In the early nineteenth century, however, this shared belief in a populist Shakespeare had to be done away with; and the chief agent of its demise was Samuel Taylor Coleridge. For Coleridge, the question of Shakespeare's social theory was crucial, and not only because there was need for a paradigm shift if a new generation of literary critics were to replace those neoclassical authorities. In the postwar crisis after Waterloo, Coleridge was deeply embroiled in an anti-radical polemic, conducted in his *Lay Sermons* and in the journalistic press. He was also delivering literary lectures in London. In December 1818 he declared of *The Tempest:*

> In this play [and especially in the conspiracy between Stephano, Trinculo and Caliban] are also shown the springs of the vulgar in politics...In his treatment of this subject, wherever it occurs, Shakspere is quite peculiar. In other writers we find the particular opinions of the individual; in Massinger it is rank republicanism; in Beaumont and Fletcher even *jure divino* principles are carried to excess; – but Shakspere never promulgates any party tenets. He is always the philosopher and the moralist, but at the same time with a profound veneration for all the established institutions of society, and for those classes which form the permanent elements of the state – especially never introducing a professional character, as such, otherwise than as respectable. If he must have any name, he should be styled a philosophical aristocrat, delighting in those hereditary institutions which have a tendency to bind one age to another, and in that distinction of ranks, of which, although few may be in possession, all enjoy the advantages.

And gratuitously (since the topic is only the troublesome conspiracy of three in *The Tempest*) Coleridge proceeded to his view of Shakespeare's treatment, in general, of the 'mob':

> You will observe the good nature with which he seems always to make sport with the passions and follies of a mob, as with an irrational animal. He is never angry with it, but hugely content with holding up its absurdities to its face; and sometimes you may trace a tone of almost affectionate superiority, something like that in which a father speaks of the rogueries of a child.[11]

This lecture was taken by his contemporaries as proof, if more proof were needed, that Coleridge was an apostate from his early radicalism and an anti-Jacobin reactionary.[12]

The point, however, is not, with Hazlitt, to reproach Coleridge for having turned his coat, still less (again like Hazlitt) to deplore the contamination of 'literary' lectures by politics. The point is to see where our critical commonplaces came from. Here historical irony reigns: for the critic who single-handedly created for the English-speaking world the credo of Shakespeare's disinterestedness, or transcendental freedom from the historical conditions of his time,[13] *also* created the credo of Shakespeare's philosophical conservativism; and Coleridge had undoubtedly arrived at that position in response to a contemporary law-and-order crisis. From 1816 through 1819, when Coleridge was consolidating his thoughts on Shakespeare, the sociopolitical scene in England was marked by agricultural distress, hunger marches, the suspension of Habeas Corpus, political censorship and demands for electoral reform. The conclusion of Radical agitation was the 'Peterloo Massacre' of August 1819, and the Six Acts which, among other repressive measures, created a tax on newspapers and pamphlets that effectively placed them out of reach of a 'popular' readership. Coleridge was already anxious to dispose of the neoclassical postulate that Shakespeare was a disorderly playwright because 'he wrote for the mob,'[14] an interesting restatement of Dryden's critique of Red-Bull civility; the tensions of 1816–18 gave that anxiety a precisely contemporary edge;[15] and the result was a disinterested, yet firmly aristocratic Shakespeare, with whom we have been dealing ever since.[16]

In one sense, however, Coleridge's opinions were as much a symptom as a cause. Hazlitt, facing the same social conditions, saw the same, or a darker, treatment of the crowd in *Coriolanus*, though he did not, of course, find his own interpretation reassuring. And the inference that a conservative Shakespeare was a nineteenth-century construction has other support. It has gradually become clear that the false problem of the plays' authorship – the industry that developed in presenting the rival claims of Bacon, the earls of Oxford, Rutland and others – was motivated in part by the belief that so important a literary inheritance as 'Shakespeare' could not descend from a yeoman's son from Stratford. As R. C. Churchill scathingly demonstrated, most of the rival theories of authorship, almost all of which were formulated in the nineteenth century, derive from a single assumption, that 'the works of Shakespeare could have been written only by an aristocrat or with aristocratic assistance.'[17]

A similar story, though chronologically asynchronic, has been told of Shakespeare's reception in the United States. As Lawrence Levine tells it, early nineteenth-century America, still alive with democratic fervor, provided a very different environment for Shakespearean interpretation than did counter-revolutionary England. Shakespeare began as America's most popular playwright, in the sense of appealing to a large proportion of the population, his plays constantly performed before mixed audiences in a partly acknowledged egalitarian rite of shared architectural space. The plays too were treated with democratic freedom, in the sense that they were cheerfully mutilated, parodied or interpolated with circus-like amusements, a return of that 'civility of the Red-Bull' that Dryden wished away. But by the end of the nineteenth century 'Shakespeare' had become a cultural icon, the property only of the 'legitimate theater', if indeed of the theater at all; for his plays had been effectively transferred into an academic safety-deposit. Charles Lamb, visiting the United States, declared that the plays were unsuited for performance, especially to a mass audience, because they were 'so deep that the depth of them lies out of the reach of most of us'; A. C. Wheeler argued that the theater 'materializes Shakespeare, and doing so vulgarizes him. Intellectual good taste outside of the theatre spiritualizes him.' And A. A. Lipscomb, writing in 1882, declared Shakespeare's ascent 'to a new and higher sphere in the firmament of intellect'; for, since to understand him required above all *training*, he was 'destined to become the Shakespeare of the college and university, and even more the Shakespeare of private and select culture.'[18]

The language of these critics makes evident how quickly the cultural ambience of the new republic had been infiltrated by European class prejudice; while the theater itself dramatically marked that development in its own spatial terms, by gradually segregating the intelligentsia into playhouses of their own. Nothing underlined that development more sharply than the Astor Place riot of 1848, provoked by ideological rivalry between the English actor William Macready and the American actor Edwin Forrest, the former contemptuous of popular audiences, the latter playing for popular appeal. The riot outside the Astor Place Opera House, where Macready had unwisely agreed to perform, involved 1,800 working men, about 22 of whom were killed by the militia; and as the *Philadelphia Public Ledger* commented, this disaster revealed 'a feeling that there is now in our country, in New York City, what every good patriot hitherto has considered it his duty to deny – *a high and a low class*.'[19]

It is therefore less surprising that the Coleridgean position reached its logical conclusion in North American academic discourse. Brents Stirling's *The Populace in Shakespeare* was, in effect, an extended gloss on Coleridge's theory of Shakespeare and the 'mob', though innocent of the perception that that *was* Coleridge's theory. Surveying the critical tradition between Coleridge and himself, and defining most of his predecessors, including Coleridge, as apologists for Shakespeare's hostility to the crowd (which had now assumed the status of a fact) Stirling proposed to advance the inquiry by way of a historicist approach; for he assumes in Shakespeare pressing *reasons* for that hostility – the very opposite of aesthetic disinterestedness – reasons specific to Shakespeare's historical environment:

> the problem is not whether Shakespeare had contempt for mobs (there can be little doubt of that), but whether there were reasons for public interest in theatrical mob scenes, and whether there were causes for dramatic portrayal of popular movements in the guise of mob anarchy, mob stupidity, or mob terror.[20]

From his own textual analysis of the plays Stirling concluded that in them 'massed humanity is simian' (p. 88); and from his assessment of their historical environment he deduced a cause – an intense public concern, from the 1580s onward, with public order, occasioned by Puritan critiques of the system but maintained and exacerbated by 'conservative propaganda' (p. 107). This concern Shakespeare adopted as his own, so Stirling's argument goes, and in his hostility to the crowd was merely speaking the official language of the day, including its biases and distortions.

For Stirling, his account of Shakespeare's social attitude was superior to those of his predecessors because he had uncovered what we now call ideology, an 'influential mythology' of class relations to which Shakespeare, unlike his clear-sighted critic, would have been fully vulnerable. In his conclusion, Stirling compared this anti-democratic mythology, which consistently stigmatized the idea of the 'popular' by equating it with revolutionary impulses, to contemporary attacks on American liberalism as 'dominated by extremist forces,' (p. 190). He thus situated himself both as liberalism's defender and as one whose own thought was immune from manipulation.[21] But why should social mythology be penetrable by an academic critic of the 1950s, and completely impenetrable to a great writer of the 1590s and onwards? This question clearly interrogates, as well as Stirling, much postmodernist criticism of Shakespeare, whether Marx or Freud or some combination of the two is dominant in its genealogy. Conversely, this book grants as much perspicaciousness to Shakespeare as is now assumed by his most sophisticated readers.

I take the position that Shakespeare was one of our first cultural critics, in the sense of being capable of profound, structural analysis. I assume that he, as well as we, was capable of grasping not only the relation between the material conditions of life and those of its intelligibility (human self-consciousness), but also the function of all those practices that for want of precise definition we loosely denote as aspects of 'culture': reading, writing, theater-going, philosophizing, formal education, legal and constitutional rule-making. And nothing, in Shakespeare's experience, was more clearly in the cultural arena than the public theaters, whose unprecedented development, both in physical space and social organization, encouraged a social critique. The public theaters clearly heightened consciousness of class distinctions, both in what they staged and what, as a social heterocosm, they stood for; and other events of the 1590s and onwards, whose shadows appear in the plays, provided a powerful stimulus to extend such thinking outward.

Shakespeare's career can, therefore, be seen as a life-long meditation on the structure of English society, during which, not surprisingly, his social attitudes altered. If he began with a wary belief in the Elizabethan settlement, in the chance for a unified nation, and hence in the need to support the conventional structures and institutions of the world into which he was born, he was never a philosophical aristocrat. If the early plays are nervous of the point at which popular culture becomes organized resistance to the status quo, they also register problems on the other side of the social dialectic: manipulation of or condescension to the 'people', which connects with the problem of political representation (who shall speak on behalf of the unrepresented) and the power/literacy dynamic.

As the Elizabethan moment waned, and Shakespeare's social vision deepened, so did these ambivalences; and though optimism briefly revived at James's accession, it was quickly replaced first by an intense political scepticism, then by a mature radicalism. In that mood Shakespeare wrote all of the great tragedies except *Hamlet*, which is in more ways than one the transition. And in that mood he wrote, perhaps no more than a year apart, an account of popular power in republican Rome (*Coriolanus)* and a fantasy (*The Tempest)* of class relations reduced to their most elemental form, the Master–Slave dialectic.

In order to tell this story with maximum force and economy, I have selected seven plays that cover the entire span of Shakespeare's career, and that represent all of the major categories into which we have analyzed the plays. I start with one of the earliest English histories, *Henry VI, Part 2*, and with Jack Cade's rebellion, because this is where Shakespeare is thought to have given most ground to the Coleridgean position. The focus then moves to the later 1590s, to comedy, and the predominantly festive *A Midsummer Night's Dream*, a play, however, that intimates underlying troubles – crop failure, Elizabeth's waning magic, artisanal protest in the background, and, in the artisans' play-within-the-play, a model of how the Elizabethan theater was dramatizing class consciousness.

In *Henry V*, written in 1599 and published in 1600, events turned Shakespeare's attention to a specifically political form of populism – the definition of popular leadership and the competition for public loyalty that the queen was forced to wage with the earl of Essex, a situation actually addressed by Shakespeare in the play's fifth Chorus. This national crisis, in which Shakespeare's company was peripherally involved, and to which Shakespeare was connected through his patronage relation with Southampton, had a long destructive half-life in the cultural environment. In Shakespeare's case, it created the ambience of *Hamlet* (as also of *Troilus and Cressida*, source of the greatest speech on maintaining the social hierarchy that Shakespeare ever wrote, placed in the mouth of a legendary liar).

Since *Hamlet* is also, by its first complete printing in 1604, transitional in a sense to the reign of James, I pair it with *King Lear*, arguably the greatest of the Jacobean tragedies, and certainly the only one, excluding *Coriolanus*, in which Shakespeare frontally addressed the situation of popular culture under the new regime. But if *King Lear* is the play that most candidly stages socioeconomic difference and the problem of how that can be made to register in the political consciousness, it also retreats finally into a merely affective and domestic reconciliation. *Coriolanus* (1609) reverses that retreat. By returning to Roman history, more specifically to a founding moment in the Roman republic, Shakespeare countered his sceptical analysis, in *Julius Caesar,* of republicanism in decay with a study of its beginnings. In this play the plebeians themselves (as distinct from their tribunes) are generously represented, and the popular voice, as they themselves speak it, has genuine grievances to express. This was Shakespeare's point of furthest reach in exploring the claims of the many against the few, involving the representation of an alternative political structure; and two of Shakespeare's earliest critics, one favorable, the other reproving, would subsequently, as my epigraphs show, define him as a 'Plebeian', a loaded term in seventeenth-century constitutional theory.

Was it, however, the point of no return? This question implicates the so-called romances, whose felicitous resolutions are difficult to square with the concept of a mature radicalism; especially *The Tempest*, whose plot implies a belief in benevolent monarchism, providential occurrences and happy endings. In this world the 'many-headed Monster' of popular protest has literally been reduced to what the metaphor promised, a single figure, whose subjugation was both possible and morally correct. Yet Shakespeare clearly puts pressure on this plot, this belief, by invoking troubling thoughts – of the ethical status of Prospero's colonialism, the enslavement and manumission of Ariel, the monopoly of power (as magic), the relation of power to education (Prospero's books), Caliban's intelligence, the relation of literary fantasy to utopian thought. The complex effect is to resubmit the *substance* of popular claims, grievances, behaviour and credos in philosophical, even allegorical, disguise.

Who, finally, will read this book? It was Jack Cade's primitivist contention (Shakespeare imagined in the early 1590s) that the spread of literacy had 'traitorously corrupted the youth of the realm' and that by 'erecting a grammar-school,' (4:7:31–2) that is, by making the ability to read requisite to success or even to survival, injustice rather than progress was served. In 1816 Coleridge addressed 'to the higher classes of society' a *Lay Sermon* whose real message was the dangerous spread of literacy among the working classes. 'Not even as a Sermon,' Coleridge wrote, 'would I have addressed the present Discourse to a promiscuous audience':

> and for this reason I likewise announced it in the title-page, as exclusively *ad clerum*...I would that the greater part of our publications could be thus directed, each to its appropriate class of Readers. But this cannot be! For...we have now a READING PUBLIC...our Readers have, in good truth, multiplied exceedingly, and have waxed proud...From a popular philosophy and a philosophic populace, Good Sense deliver us![17]

The separation of cultures that Coleridge desired, in making his appeal exclusively *ad clerum*, is now a fact of life, frequently lamented; and today's clerisy tends to widen the gap by making their philosophy of literature arcane. But between these two extreme positions, between Coleridge and Cade, there may be room for negotiation. This book intentionally mimics its subject. Deliberately written in the most accessible style I can muster; lightly annotated so as not to suggest one must come to such arguments only through a long negotiation with the academic authorities on the subject; and priced, by negotiation with the publisher, within reach of almost anyone who buys paperback books, it aspires, simply, to the largest and most popular audience that can be reached. Whether it deserves that audience is, of course, an entirely different matter.

1

Caviar or the General: Hamlet and the Popular Theater

> *Hamlet* was the Play, or rather Hamlet was the Character, in the intuition and exposition of which I first made my turn for Philosophical criticism.
>
> Hamlet's character is the prevalence of the abstracting and generalising habit over the practical... I may have a smack of Hamlet myself, if I may say so.
>
> Samuel Taylor Coleridge

My first order of business is to situate Shakespeare in his own working conditions. I begin, therefore, with Hamlet's instructions to his players, an aspect of the play that has never been strenuously interrogated, so preoccupied have most of its readers been with Hamlet's delay in pursuing his revenge. Given the need to account for this delay by causes invisible on the surface of the plot, in terms interior to Hamlet, the play has been construed primarily in moral, philosophical, psychological or psychoanalytic terms. Yet Hamlet, though a philosopher and deeply troubled individual, was also a playwright, producer and actor. And although many intellectuals have suspected themselves, with Coleridge, of having a smack of Hamlet in their own disposition, and have constantly rewritten Hamlet in their own image, they have not argued backward from that self-reflexion to imagine that Shakespeare, as playwright, producer and actor, might have seen this play as a commentary on his own professional life.

Hamlet's remarks on theater are, like his motives, elliptical, extraneous to the plot and occasionally imperspicuous to a degree that itself demands attention. More because of these characteristics than despite them, they constitute notes towards a theory of the drama in late Elizabethan and early Jacobean society. While it would be naive to suppose that Hamlet's dramatic theory was identical with Shakespeare's own, this play contains more *information*, simply speaking, on the business of play-production than any other in Shakespeare's canon; and unlike *A Midsummer Night's Dream*, its closest rival on this score, this material is already *theoretical* when it reaches us, already, if incompletely, transformed by Hamlet's critical perspective. It may be the closest we can come, therefore, to Shakespeare's 'own' conceptualization of that unique, short-lived and otherwise extraordinary cultural phenomenon, the Elizabethan popular theater.

Re-collected, Hamlet's comments on the nature and function of drama are paradigmatic of a central question: how do words relate to material practice? This question takes us in the opposite direction from that of a philosophical criticism as Coleridge understood it, as an extension into literature of the 'abstracting and generalising habit'. It will be an odd discovery, however, that Shakespeare, in *Hamlet*, used both 'abstract' and 'general' as terms to denote his own form of material practice, writing for a popular audience, 'the general', and abstracting their experience and his own into safely fictional forms. The playtexts we read as literature, therefore, both invite and resist understanding in terms of other phenomena: the social structuration of the original audiences, and how that might relate to their supposed interpretive competence; the socioeconomic and political conditions in which the Elizabethan and Jacobean theater was required to operate; the relation between various forms of external restraint and the status of dramatic texts as representations of events and issues contemporary to Shakespeare; and, by virtue of the fact that suspected topical allusions are also textual cruces, the complex and circular argument that connects analytical bibliography with other forms of interpretation.

Shakespeare's Audiences

Almost from the beginning, Hamlet's theory of the theater is presented as insecure, full of confusions that Shakespeare himself must already have advanced beyond. Greeting the company of 'tragedians' as old friends, he asks eagerly for a sample of their craft, a reminder of past pleasures. But his choice of play immediately raises the linked problems of what, in Shakespeare's environment, was considered to be 'good' drama, and how far the evaluative process depended on the nature of the audience. To select a play 'that was never acted, or if it was, not above once, for [it] pleased not the million: 'twas caviary to the general' is to make value dependent on the existence of a superior interpretive community, himself and 'others' whose judgement declared it 'an excellent play.' (2:2:431–5).[1] But the Trojan tragedy so introduced, as represented by the fifty-eight lines delineating Pyrrhus's slaughter of Priam, scarcely endorses that judgement. Manifestly an example of how poorly a classical, humanist education translates into successful theatrical experience, the speech provokes even Polonius, not marked for locutionary economy, to complain 'This is too long,' (2:2:494); and Hamlet's emotional commitment to it

('Look where he...has tears in's eyes' 515–16) is the one clear instance that supports Eliot's theory of Hamlet's behavior, that it lacks an 'objective correlative.' Moreover, the educated taste that knows it is supposed to enjoy caviar (as a luxury), when the untrained palates of the 'general' will reject it as fishy, has already betrayed its connections with social elitism.

These linked questions of value, reception and audience competence are, therefore, connected to those that intellectuals have always posed, and that the phenomenon of Elizabethan public theater had undoubtedly foregrounded. To what extent, Hamlet's theory of the audience asks (in more ways than he realizes), can writing for the theater combine the imperatives of intellectualism and success? But beyond this lies the more threatening issue of the theater's and the playwright's social responsibilities. To what extent does intellect require that it should *not*, paradoxically, speak only to the judicious few, whether clustered in the universities, the Inns of Court, or the Court itself, lest it render itself marginal? To what extent should it demand access, and demand of itself concessions, to the tastes and apprehensions of the 'general'?

This inquiry takes a new turn at the very center of the play (3:2), just prior to the staging of 'The Mousetrap,' when Hamlet defines for the actors an appropriate (realist) style of acting, and frames his definition with two comments on audience reception: the first, a complaint about actors whose hamming caters to 'the groundlings, who *for the most part* are capable of nothing but inexplicable dumb-shows and noise' (11–12; italics added), and the second, an insistence that popularity not be their criterion, since though they may make 'the unskilful laugh', it 'cannot but make the judicious grieve, the censure of the which one must in your allowance o'erweigh a whole theater of others' (25–8). Here begins the legend that Shakespeare himself was contemptuous of the groundlings, and hence a debate on the social composition of Shakespeare's audience, which, if these comments were reliable as either theater criticism or sociology, would be largely incapable of understanding them. Yet Hamlet's distinction between the 'unskilful' many and the 'judicious' few is, at the very least, statistically unrealistic, and given his own purposes as director, fatally alienated; the competent audience is here restricted to 'one', presumably himself. More subtly, the qualification that Hamlet himself introduces – 'for the most part' – is, if one considers its potential impact, actually educative; for no one who happened to be standing at the Globe would willingly place herself among the incapable, a category which therefore shrinks proportionately as that of the hopefully judicious expands.

This insight, not available to Hamlet himself, allows us to pass beyond the idea, sometimes derived from his extravagantly polarized comments, that Shakespeare wrote for a double audience, the division between its two components an impermeable barrier of class. Even the word 'audience' is ambiguous, given that *Hamlet* survives in not one but three texts for *readers*, whose relationship to stage productions can only be guessed. Paradoxically, it was the first ('bad') Quarto that claimed on its title-page an academic context, offering its readers a play as 'diverse times' acted 'by his Highnesse servants' and as performed 'also in the two Universities of Cambridge and Oxford', yet exhibiting most of the symptoms of an abridgement produced for the popular theater; while the second Quarto of 1604–5, 'Newly imprinted and enlarged to almost as much againe as it was', which makes no such claims about performance, has the more leisurely, rhetorical and philosophical expansiveness that might well have been intended for the specialized audiences claimed by its textual predecessor. We will probably never know whether (or how corruptly) the first Quarto represents *the* acting version for public theater performance in London; whether the second Quarto represents a more complex play that was actually performed at Oxford and Cambridge, or one that Shakespeare never expected to see produced in entirety; or why only the posthumous 1623 Folio, an ummistakably 'readerly' text, provides a detailed account of something that Shakespeare had personally experienced, the 'war' between the private boys' companies and the adult actors of the public theaters.

The ghostly presence of multiple audiences to which these different texts may witness acquires no more flesh (solid or sullied as the case may be) in the light of the surviving socioeconomic data. Arguing from ticket prices (a penny for general admission, two pence for a new play), as well as from contemporary descriptions of audiences, E. K. Chambers and Alfred Harbage believed that the audience was socially heterogeneous, with the balance in favor of the lower social strata.[2] This belief received a major challenge from Ann Jennalie Cook's thesis of a predominantly 'privileged' audience in the public theaters as well as in the private, privileged in the sense of belonging to an elite, to which they could claim membership (even if very recent) by virtue of birth, wealth, education or other achievements.[3] Cook began her study with a trenchant analysis of the sociopolitical investments that have lurked unacknowledged in the double audience theory: 'The snobbery that presumes courtiers more worthy of Shakespeare is paralleled by the reverse snobbery that presumes commoners more worthy of him', (p. 7). But her solution to the standoff was to revise the commoners statistically out the picture. While her economic revision was well taken, countering overemphasis on the penny admission with reminders of depressed wages (9d. a day for common laborers) and the cost of transportation (3d) across the Thames, her use of statistics about theater attendance has itself been challenged.[4] And while she was also persuasive on the need to correct early hostile witnesses for bias against theater audiences, she equated Hamlet's disparagement of the groundlings with Shakespeare's own (p. 261), ignoring even Hamlet's own qualification, 'for the most part,' and failing to see that her argument about bias might be strengthened by observing that Shakespeare himself had acknowledged (through Hamlet) its presence in his own profession. In fact, while seeming to mediate between two kinds of 'snobbery,' Cook's category of the privileged had its own sociopolitical work to do; admitting her opposition to any account of Shakespeare's audience that assumes class interests and conflict (p. 15), she denied also the social organicism that her predecessors found in the public theater: 'the playhouses neither fostered democracy nor presented a social microcosm', (p. 271).

The idea of the theater as a social heterocosm, however, proved resistant. Recently restated by Walter Cohen, in the hope of maintaining it for the purposes of leftist criticism, the Elizabethan audiences – 'a plurality of artisans and shopkeepers, and a majority consisting of these groups and the ones beneath them – servants, prostitutes, transients, soldiers, and criminals' – invited or demanded a theater that itself thematized populism and nationalism.[5] This concept links 'public' theaters with public *issues*, and posits a moment in English history in which the national culture was capable, in part through drama's mediations, of genuine unity. Cohen was candid in proposing 'a single and simple hypothesis: that the absolutist state, by its inherent dynamism and contradictions, first fostered and then undermined the public theater', (p. 20). 'Elizabethanism' as a privileged moment in English culture was thus redescribed in language that simultaneously castigated and celebrated it, combining Perry Anderson's analyses of how Europe became a cluster of highly centralized monarchies[6] with the Marxist myth of organic communities prior to the development of capitalism (p. 388).

Given these contrary agendas, and the slim chance that the data of theater and economic history will prove capable of forcing a clear decision between them,[7] it is tempting to abandon the question of Shakespeare's audience to the ludic territory of personal preference, to 'As You Like It' and 'What You Will'. There is, however, an alternative model, at least for ordering and understanding the otherwise conflicting testimony of documents, statistics and opinions contemporary to Shakespeare. This model may be found in unlikely territory. I have already invoked Levine's well-documented account of how, in early nineteenth-century America, the theater constituted 'a microcosm of the relations between various socio-economic groups', whose interaction under the same roof initially spoke to democratic ideals, but whose tensions would ultimately lead to their separation.[8] Something similar also emerged in France under Napoleon III. In *The Painting of Modern Life* T. J. Clark brilliantly analyzed the temporary phenomenon in Haussmannized Paris of the cafe-concerts, places where the new 'army of clerks, accountants, cashiers, brokers, petty bureaucrats, insurance agents, bank tellers, salesmen...stenographers, telegraphists, primary-school teachers, and advertising men' gathered to drink and enjoy rowdy. pseudo-popular, live entertainment. As was also true of Shakespeare's theater, the cafe-concerts were scandalous in their apparent jumble of classes, itself a result of new social mobilities; and, more subtly, this very social mélange was itself a form of theater, a two-way impersonation. As Clark put it:

> The cafe-concert *produced* the popular, which is to say that it put on class as an entertainment...There were unmistakably two main types of travesty going on: first the pretence of the bourgeois to be working-class; but second, mixed in with that general slumming...the pretence of a certain kind of worker to be bourgeois, or something quite like it.[9]

These sentences could be rewritten to describe the arts of social falling and climbing in Elizabethan and Jacobean England, their representation on the stage, and the stage's representation of its own role in such social schizophrenia, as, for example, in Fletcher's *Knight of the Burning Pestle*, where the citizen and his wife purchase for themselves the coveted on-stage stools that connote a privileged audience status, or in Shakespeare's own treatment of Christopher Sly in *The Taming of The Shrew*, where the beggar becomes for a night the courtly audience of a private showing. And one could add, thinking especially of Shakespeare and Jonson, that the Elizabethan and Jacobean playwrights assumed on-stage stools in the world of two-way travesty they inhabited, their own socioeconomic aspirations apparent in the records of court patronage, pensions, real-estate deals, their access to the ultimately privileged category of the intellectual unpredictable from their origins as the sons or stepsons of glovemakers and bricklayers.

Restraint and Regulation

If Shakespeare's audience were, as the nineteenth-century analogies suggest, a more complex social phenomenon than envisaged by either Cohen's version of populism or Cook's theory of privilege, it helps to explain the records that have survived of how the Elizabethan and Jacobean theater was regulated by various governmental persons and bodies. What needs explaining is the inconsistent nature of such regulation, the lack of a clear, centralized policy. These vagaries imply that there were conflicting theories of audience composition, as also of what we might call the politics of public recreation. Such official indeterminacy was also found, according to Clark, in the relations between the Parisian 'popular' entertainments and the imperial censorship. Not only did the cafe-concerts 'produce' the popular as entertainment, but the censor who constantly policed it had his own view of which version of the popular was acceptable to the authorities, and which was dangerous. Acceptable popularity, Clark imagined, was 'moral, sentimental, patriotic...a dream world of hard work and high emotion' (p. 227–8). But what the continual presence of the censor's agents at the cafe-concerts demonstrated was the difficulty of maintaining that tone. 'The circuitry of popular art' is delicate, and stands 'in need of fairly constant overhaul if it is not to produce undesirable effects....The material called popular had to be continually renewed and recast, lest its working class users find ways of giving it back its original consistency' (pp. 229–30).

These insights can be modified to reveal in the Elizabethan 'documents of control'[10] the complex and competing interests that sometimes dictated the closing of the theaters, sometimes assured their uninterrupted operation. Questions of audience composition (expressed as fears of disorderly behavior and criminality) interacted with public health concerns (the need to close the theaters during high incidence of plague); economic concerns (when the theaters were closed the watermen were deprived of income, and, as the borough of Finsbury realized with alarm in 1600, they lost the tax on theater revenues that went to support the poor); religious and moral concerns, especially in connection with Sunday performances; and a shifting and elusive imperative to political surveillance, shifting according to the relative stability or instability of the larger political environment. It is here that the question of censorship meets most directly those of audience composition and competence; but it is also here that the delicacies of the social balance need most to be observed in our own criticism.

What the documents reveal most certainly is the difficulty of certain conclusions. The major agents change their position, and the emphases alter from year to year, from month to month. In May 1559, for instance, at the very beginning of Elizabeth's reign, and long before the development of the great secular theater, the queen published a proclamation against the performance of 'common Interludes in the Englishe tongue' outside of 'All Halowtyde,' unless licensed by the local mayor or two justices of the peace. 'As they will aunswere,' her majesty charged her local officers 'that they permyt none to be played wherein either matters of religion or of the governaunce of the estate of the common weale shalbe handled or treated, beyng no meete matters to be wrytten or treated upon, but by menne of aucthoritie, learning and wisedome, nor to be handled before any audience, but of grave and discreete persons.' This was simultaneously a prudential showing by the new regime of firm intentions and, as Virginia Gildersleeve argued intelligently at the beginning of our own century, a 'conciliatory policy' designed to allow the theater a certain toleration precisely by removing it 'from the field of political and religious controversy,'[11] that it had occupied under her predecessors.

Gildersleeve should not have concluded, however, that the 'Elizabethan drama was, indeed, essentially non-controversial,' still less that Shakespeare himself 'obviously in sympathy with the government. . . seems to have looked with some contempt upon the populace and their desire for civic rights' (p. 135). The 1559 proclamation pointed not only to a new era of local (municipal) supervision and jurisdiction over the theaters, but also to a new hermeneutics of the drama, in which playwrights were silently instructed to make plays that could indeed be 'tolerated' (one of the prevailing terms in the lexicon of control), and to develop their own prudential strategies of representation. That they were not always prudent was part of the dynamic. In November 1589 the Privy Council wrote to Archbishop Whitgift requesting his appointment of a reputable churchman to work with Edmund Tilney, the new Master of the Revels, to 'reform' the plays of the public theaters, which had evidently been dealing in forbidden topics, matters of church and state (Chambers, 4:306). Matters had become too complicated for more than one official mind to deal with.

But the relationship *between* church and state authorities was not always simply collaborative. Particularly, of course, the reform or Puritan wing of the church was hostile to theater on moral and iconoclastic grounds. In 1564 Edmund Grindal, bishop of London, using the pretext of plague (indistinguishable in his thought from moral contagion) wrote to request intervention by William Cecil, lord Burghley:

> By searche I doo perceive, that ther is no one thinge off late is more lyke to have renewed this contagion, then the practise off an idle sorte off people, which have ben infamouse in all goode common weales: I meane these Histriones, common playours; who now daylye, but speciallye on holydayes, sett up bylles, wherunto the youthe resorteth excessively, & ther taketh infection: besydes that goddes worde by theyr impure mowthes is prophaned, and turned into scoffes; for remedie wheroff in my iugement ye shulde do verie well to be a meane, that a proclamation wer sette further to inhibitte all playes for one whole year (and iff itt wer for ever, it wer nott amisse) within the Cittie, or 3. myles compasse.[12]

This hostility had originally been focused on the popular religious drama of the medieval cycles. It was Grindal who, notoriously, took possession of the single copy of the York Paternoster play in 1572, 'ostensibly to bowdlerize the text' as Collinson reported,[13] 'but in fact to impound it,' so that it was never played again. Once extended to secular theater, however, iconoclasm acquires an anti-populist flavor. There is a telling conflict in Grindal's vocabulary between the positive and negative connotations of 'common', 'goode common weales' being incompatible, in Grindal's thinking, with 'common playours'.

As the reign advanced and the secular theater grew in national importance, the London City Council increasingly sounded like Grindal, whereas the

Privy Council, no doubt on authority from the queen, sometimes preferred a more liberal policy. On 11 April 1582, five members of the Privy Council wrote to the mayor of London, Sir Thomas Blank, 'to revoke your late inhibition against their playeng on the said hollydaies...onely forbearing the Sabothe daie', and provided, of course, that 'care be had that their comodies and enterludes be looked into, and that those which do containe mater that may bread corruption of maners and conversacion among the people...be forbidden' (Chambers, 4:288). At Midsummer 1592, the Council hastily closed the theaters because, as we shall see in the next chapter, they were thought to be implicated in an uprising of feltmakers in Southwark; yet in 3 November 1594, the current mayor, Sir John Spencer, was forced to complain to Burghley against the allowance of a new theater to be erected by Francis Langley on Bankside, arguing that it would be preferable 'rather to suppresse all such places built for that kynd of exercise, then to erect any more of the same sort'. In 1600, a year when even the Privy Council recognized that the city had gone theater-mad, their order of 22 June 'to restrain the excessive number of Plaie howses & the imoderate use of Stage plaies' still allowed that 'the use and exercise of suche plaies, not beinge evill in yt self, may with a good order and moderacion be suffered in a well governed estate' (4:330).

How are we to account for this unstable policy? Its most frequently stated motive, that the queen enjoyed a good play and that therefore the players needed to rehearse, was totally inadequate to the scale on which the theaters were tolerated, indeed encouraged. The pretext of rehearsals was, therefore, itself part of a continuous drama enacted between court and city, their mutual communications often primarily ritual. But Mayor Spencer's letter to Burghley adds a significant clue as to how these scenes may be read:

> I am not ignorant...what is alleadged by soom for defence of these playes, that the people must have soom kynd of recreation, & that policie requireth to divert idle heads & other ill disposed from other woorse practize by this kynd of exercize.

The Mayor's response to this 'politic' argument was to stigmatize the audience as 'beeing of the base & refuse sort of people or such yoong gentlemen as have small regard of credit or conscience' (pp. 316–17). He thereby implied that the politic argument for diversion will not work when the audience is incapable of profiting from social therapy. Yet the very structure of his argument (which Cook would locate in the territory of bias) implies its converse, that there *was* a theory of acceptable popular theater that equated the audience with 'the people', or society at large, not with society's refuse, and that saw it as having a social function of which the central government, if not the municipal authorities, could afford to be tolerant.

Who were the 'soom' (besides Burghley and presumably his employer) who argued for a liberal public policy with respect to theatrical entertainment? And was it merely a 'bread-and-circuses' policy that assumed (with Hamlet) that the popular audience was 'capable of nothing but inexplicable dumb shows and noise'?[14] Or was it, rather, a policy that assumed a theater audience so expressive of the new social mobility that it required a more complex entertainment, one that might mediate social difference and even make it a source of social cohesion? One such argument, at least, was available in a culturally respectable form. Spencer's and Grindal's position on the theater is the converse of that expressed in one of Montaigne's *Essais*, first published in 1580. We know that Shakespeare, who shared with John Florio the patronage of Southampton,[15] made use of Florio's translation of Montaigne, entered in the Stationers' Register on 4 June 1600. Concluding his thoughts to Lady Diana of Foix on the education of children, Montaigne had advanced a defence not only of private humanist drama, but of public theater, whose vocabulary, as rendered by Florio, bears careful comparison with that of Archbishop Grindal, especially with respect to the polysemantics of *common:* 'I have ever...blamed those of injustice,' wrote Montaigne:

> that refuse good and honest Comedians, or (as we call them) Players, to enter our good townes, and grudge the common people such publike sports. Politike and wel ordered common-wealths endevor rather carefully to unite and assemble their Citizens together; as in serious offices of devotion, so in honest exercises of recreation. Common societie and loving friendship is thereby cherished and increased. And besides, they cannot have more formall and regular pastimes allowed them, than such as are acted and represented in open view of all, and in the presence of the magistrates themselves: And if I might beare sway, I would thinke it reasonable, that Princes should sometimes, at their proper charges, gratifie the common people with them, as an argument of a fatherly affection, and loving goodnesse towards them; and that in populous and frequented cities, there should be Theatres and places appointed for such spectacles; as a diverting of worse inconveniences, and secret actions. (p. 190)[16]

It would have been useful for Walter Cohen, in pursuit of a model of culture that promoted 'common societie and loving friendship', to have discovered Montaigne's sociology of theater; but behind its geniality lies a more sinister notion of public control through the media, belonging to the other side of Cohen's argument, the theory of the Renaissance state as absolutist in structure and behavior towards its citizens. This more cynical proposal was in fact articulated. In its crudest form (though probably ironically) it appears in Thomas Heywood's *Apology for Actors* (1612) as a statement about *playwrights* and their 'ayme...to teach the subjects obedience to their King, to shew the people the untimely ends of such as have moved tumults, commotions, and insurrections, to present them with the flourishing estate of such as live in obedience, exhorting them to allegeance, dehorting them from all trayterous and fellonious stratagems.'[17] And in the mid-seventeenth century it was restated by Sir William Davenant, himself a royalist playwright currently in political exile, but now (like Montaigne) conceiving of drama's function from a governmental perspective. Arguing against the 'receav'd opinion that the People ought to be continu'd in ignorance', on the grounds that public education is the best basis for civil obedience, Davenant reminded his readers in 1650 that the drama had historically contributed to what we would now call 'ideological state apparatuses'. When art serves ideology, Davenant argued, 'then even Tyranny will seem much lighter, when the hand of supreme Power binds up our Load and lays it artfully on us.'[18] And he proceeded to develop against Puritan objections a *political* defence of the stage, of great if appalling sophistication. To those who argue that 'Poesy on our Stage...is prejudicial to a State, as begetting Levity, and giving to the People too great a diversion by pleasure and mirth', Davenant replied that recreation for the masses is necessary to keep them hard at work, and to prevent them from having the time to consider their condition:

> Whoever in Government endeavours to make the People serious and grave, which are attributes that may become the Peoples Representatives but not the People, doth practise a new way to enlarge the State, by making every Subject a Statesman; and he that means to govern so mournfully (as it were, without any Musick in his Dominion) must lay but light burdens on his Subjects, or else he wants the ordinary wisdome of those who to their Beasts that are much loaden whistle all the day to encourage their Travail.

And he reminded his readers that ancient states survived as long as they did by manipulating the theatrical instincts of their people, 'the wise Athenians, dividing into Three parts the publique Revenue, expended one in Plays and Showes, to divert [the same word that appears in Spencer's letter to Burghley] the People from meeting to consult of their Rulers merit and the defects of Government'; and the Romans, Davenant added, would not have 'so long continu'd their Empire but for the same diversions at a vaster charge' (pp. 47–8).

In our own time, a version of this argument has been rediscovered and promoted by critics of Renaissance drama influenced by Michel Foucault. In place of the competing interests and constant negotiations exhibited in the Elizabethan documents of control, Renaissance theater is imagined to have operated in a climate of endless, ubiquitous but impersonal surveillance, which itself had no agents or operators. Behind these moves lies Foucault's statement that modern political analysis 'should not concern itself with power at the level of conscious intention or decision':

> Instead, it is a case of studying power at the point where *its* intention, if it has one, is completely invested in its real and effective practices . . . power is not to be taken to be a phenomenon of one individual's consolidated and homogeneous domination over others, or that of one group or class over others. . . . Power must be analyzed as something which circulates . . . It is never localised here or there, *never in anybody's hands.* (italics added)[19]

In the arena of Renaissance drama criticism, these principles manifest themselves either as a dismissal of Shakespeare as *anybody*, an actual playwright who wrote (by hand) out of his own experience of social relations;[20] or, more subtly, in a theory of the theater's 'containment' by the power system. So Stephen Greenblatt has read Shakespeare's English histories as witnesses to a 'Machiavellian moment' in the culture, to record the 'transformation of subjects into citizens' and the 'subordination of transcendent values to capital values'. But because the moment was transitional from one economic and political system to another, the literature acts as a medium in which the newly dominant culture is tested. As part of the test, subversive doubts are expressed and alien voices are allowed to be momentarily heard; but only so that both may be finally silenced. The result is 'the English form of absolutist theatricality', or the triumphant celebration, after all the doubts, of monarchical power.[21]

Such arguments elide rather than explain the conditions in which Shakespeare's theater was required to operate. The impersonality of the Foucaultian model cannot account for specific cases of intervention and non-intervention by the authorities; nor for the famous instances of textual censorship, such as those affecting the deposition scene in *Richard II*, or Edmund Tilney's instructions concerning *Sir Thomas More* that the company 'leave out the insurrection wholly'; nor for the problematic fabric of the playtexts that we have, which textual scholarship is beginning to reassess as the symptoms of a linked set of contingencies, political, social, economic and personal. And as for the ideological appropriation of the theater by the state, it is clear from the witnesses just cited that it was conceptually thinkable, by writers themselves, in several different, articulate versions. Benignly or otherwise, the ideological containment of society as represented by the theater audiences clearly occurred to Elizabeth and to James I as well as to Burghley and Mayor Spencer, to Montaigne, Heywood and Davenant. Yet the very existence of censorship and its mechanisms testifies to the fact that not all dramatists consented to the role that Heywood (ironically) and Davenant (with manic cynicism) allotted them.

Greenblatt's containment theory implies that Shakespeare's histories were, unbeknownst to himself, serving the Elizabethan and Jacobean state apparatuses, not by explicitly 'dehorting...from all trayterous and fellonious stratagems', (although that was the older view of his history plays that E.M.W. Tillyard and others promoted) but rather by allowing a limited expression of resistance. By this view, Shakespeare becomes not the unquestioning monarchist whose support of the system was ensured by royal patronage; not the manipulative dramatist complicit in a scheme of diversion from 'other woorse practize'; but merely the safety valve its mechanical and unknowing self. Such a theory seems even more condescending to Shakespeare than Hamlet is to the groundlings. We need to return to a less impersonal, less totalitarian account of how Shakespeare's theater probably functioned, in a network not of power in the abstract and in nobody's hands, but rather of local ordinances, unwritten and unstable policies, fads, fashions, pretexts, improvisations, human impulses, and the occasional application of discipline and punishment both to texts and to persons, by other persons whose names and motives are not indecipherable. And with respect to the playwrights, we also need to return to a common-sense view that they were likely to differ from each other in their reactions to both the opportunities and the restrictions that the craze for theater engendered. It may be possible to construct an account of Shakespeare's reactions as themselves unstable, beginning with a hopeful view of the stage's potential for mediating social relations (the theory that Cohen shares with Montaigne), but moving at the turn of the century to a more pessimistic prospect, which did not, however, require him to adopt the position of either Davenant or Foucault.

In such an evolution, *Hamlet* would be pivotal; and *Hamlet* undoubtedly includes in its metatheatrical comments restrained allusions to theatrical restraint and control. Polonius remarks that the players at Elsinore are the 'only men' for 'the law of writ and the liberty' (2:2:397). A purely writerly interpretation which opposes the rules of dramatic construction to the freedom of invention has long been dominant here, governed by Polonius's preceding (and absurd) account of Renaissance genre theory; but Dover Wilson suggested in 1934 that this could refer to the two acting areas of London, the City where the theaters were controlled by Sheriff's writ, and the liberties outside the walls and hence outside such controls.[22] More recently, Steven Mullaney has argued for the cultural importance of the liberties, both as terrain and as metaphor, as a marginal space in which the public theaters played the same ritual role as did the leper-houses established outside the city walls.[23] Yet the writ that is *Hamlet* makes less of its liberties than it does of the problems the players have been facing, which are themselves announced in so taut and obstructive a form (or forms) as simultaneously to suggest the presence of external restraint and to protect the writer against it.

In Act 2, Scene 2, Rosencrantz announces the arrival in Elsinore of the 'tragedians of the city', and Hamlet inquires as to why they have been travelling. The three 'reading' versions of *Hamlet* that have come down to us give three different answers to this seemingly harmless question. In the 1603 Quarto, the answer is brief; Gilderstone states that 'noveltie carries it away / For the principall publicke audience that / Came to them, are turned to private playes / And to the humour of children.'[24] The reference here seems unmistakably to the so-called 'war of the theaters' initiated by the turn-of-the-century revival of the Paul's boys as a theatrical company, with the creative support of Marston, Chapman and Middleton, and the parallel revival of the Children of the Chapel Royal at the Blackfriars. The Folio text of 1623 develops this explanation at greater length, producing, as Philip Edwards observed in his Cambridge edition, 'a bravura on contemporary theatre problems...unique in Shakespeare'.[25] 'There is, sir,' explains Rosencrantz, 'an eyrie of children, little eyases, that cry out on the top of question and are most tyrannically clapped for't. These are now the fashion, and so berattle the common stages – so they call them – that many wearing rapiers are afraid of goose-quills and dare scarce come thither,' (2:2:337–42). And so the conversation continues, somewhat awkwardly, with Rosencrantz revelling apparently in the internecine feud, and Hamlet expressing rather concern for the boys' financial support and for their future when their voices break.

The economic future of such children was raised in 1583 by William Hunnis, master of the Chapel Children, complaining that the queen had made no financial 'allowance...for those children whose voyces be chaunged, whoe onely do depend upon the charge of the sayd Mr. ...unto his no smalle charge'.[26] As Hamlet perceives it, the current competition, however the boys may seem to be winning it, is not in their best interests. 'Will they not say afterwards, if they should grow themselves to *common* players – as it is most like if their means are no better – their writers do them wrong to make them exclaim against their own succession? (italics added). The episode, mysterious in its textual status, stands as a tiny *mise en abyme* of the play's central Oedipal conflict, anticipating a tragedy of failed 'succession'. The very point, too, contested between Cook and Cohen appears to be raised by the Folio's terminology; the threatened theaters are 'common'; 'so they call them,' adds Rosencrantz, in case we had not noticed, recalling Florio / Montaigne's defence of 'Comedians, or (as we call them) Players'; and Hamlet refers not to the men's companies, but to 'common players'. In such a semantic network as we have seen existed in the early sociology of theater, 'common' acquires a force that speaks of social and professional cooperation.

The Hamlet of the supposedly more authoritative second Quarto, however, has no such concerns, since the only explanation he is given as to why the players have been travelling is as follows: 'their inhibition comes by the meanes of the late innovation.'[27] If the Folio text exhibits a failure of communication between Hamlet and Rosencrantz, and between the private and public theaters, the second Quarto here insists that communication fail between playwright and audience, or at least remain incomplete. Does 'innovation' here refer to the fad for the children's companies, as 'noveltie' clearly did in the Quarto of 1603? Or does 'innovation' rather refer to a historical crisis external to the theater's economy? Harold Jenkins, in the New Arden edition, states as linguistic and cultural fact that in Shakespeare's day the strongest meaning of 'innovation' was a 'challenge to the established order...often...the specific sense of an uprising.'[28] He cites Shakespearean analogues from *Othello*, *Sir Thomas More* and *Coriolanus*, the 'Poore Discontents, / Which gape and rub the Elbow at the newes / Of hurlyburly Innovation' in *Henry IV*, *Part 1*. He might have added, also, its appearance in Montaigne's essay on 'Custom', an important contemporary meditation (known to Shakespeare) on the inverse relation between intellectual scepticism and political reformism. 'I am distasted with noveltie,' wrote Montaigne, from the perspective of one appalled by the French wars of religion:

> Those which attempt to shake an Estate, are commonly the first overthrowne by the fall of it...the best pretence of *innovation or noveltie* is most dangerous... it argueth a great selfe-love and presumption, for a man to esteeme his opinions so far, that for to establish them, a man must be faine to subvert a publike peace.[29]

'Innovation' in Montaigne's sense, but with an English topical force, appears also in a letter to Sir Robert Cecil about an uprising that was indeed 'late' when *Hamlet* was first produced, and that has sometimes been adduced as the 'real' content of Rosencrantz's otherwise mysterious remark: the insurrection against Elizabeth's authority in early February 1601, led by Robert Devereux, second earl of Essex.

In chapter 4 the case will be made again for connecting Shakespeare and his company to the Essex rebellion, on the grounds that they could not have been unaffected by the crisis of censorship provoked in 1599 by Sir John Hayward's *History of Henry IV* and its dedication to Essex. Here I want simply to argue that what *Hamlet*'s 'innovation' means must be affected by its semantic proximity to 'inhibition', that concreteness comes by the vibrations between these two Latinate abstractions. In Shakespeare's preFreudian culture, the primary meaning of 'inhibition' was legal or institutional *prohibition*. In that sense it appeared, as a glance backwards will reveal, in Grindal's letter to Cecil requesting that he inhibit theatrical productions in London for a full year, and in that of the Privy Council to Mayor Blank requesting that he release the theaters from inhibition, so long as they observed Sundays and the city officials 'looked into' the playtexts with the proper caution. The documents of control collected by Chambers frequently use this same terminology. The presence of 'inhibition' in the text of the second Quarto, therefore, is more likely to have signified the anxiety of the theatrical world about external restraints, including textual inspections and censorship, than internal economic competition.

History and Its Representation

Not merely the differences between the Folio and Quarto texts, then, but also their semantic peculiarities (when found in positions of what we might call textual stress) may be the formal and elliptical signs of historical referentiality. If so, the theoretical center of Hamlet's instructions to the players must be his statement on the nature of dramatic mimesis. 'Suit the action to the word,' Hamlet demands of his actors

> with this special observance, that you o'er step not the modesty of nature; for anything so o'erdone is from the purpose of playing, whose end both at the first and now, was and is, to hold as 'twere the mirror up to nature; to show virtue her own feature, scorn her own image, and the very age and body of the time his form and pressure.(3:2:20–4)

This passage seems clearly to distinguish between three forms of mimesis, two of which are well documented in Renaissance literary theory, such as it was: the abstractions of idealization ('show virtue her own feature'), and of satirical debasement ('[show] scorn her own image') both presented as female personifications. But in the third category the personal pronoun changes to the masculine, '*his* form and pressure', creating a slight syntactical tremor; while the phrase itself does not seem to satisfy the logical expectation created by the sentence: that we would find between the exaggerations of praise and blame the golden mean of fidelity to life.

Instead we find a phrase that requires glossing from other points in the playtext. For the 'time' to which Hamlet's third type of mimesis directs itself recalls his earlier definition of the players to Polonius: 'Good my lord, will you see the players well bestowed? Do you hear, let them be well used, for they are the abstract and brief chronicles of the time.' And he adds, threateningly, 'After your death you were better have a bad epitaph than their ill report while you live' (2:2:518–22). Taken together, these phrases point to the 'real' time of Elizabethan and Jacobean history as that to which Shakespeare's fictions pointed. But they do not merely point. Hamlet's comment to Polonius indicates that one of the purposes of playing is to 'report' on the behaviour of contemporary statesmen, with strong suggestions of accountability; and, of course, the function of 'The

Mousetrap' will be literally to bring Claudius to account, by producing his guilty identification with its plot.

But the definition of the actors (and presumably their product) as 'the abstract and brief chronicles of the time' also admits that the theater was accountable to others. In its very brevity and abstraction the phrase mimics its own brilliant suggestion, that dramatic fictions reproduce their own historical environment in condensed and densely signifying metaphors. If metaphor is the *form* in which history is represented, the *pressure* that produces abstraction derives from the various constraints, external and internal, under which the theater was compelled to operate.

Academicism

One more intertextual gloss must have been central to Shakespeare's intentions. 'Form and pressure' echoes Hamlet's initial commitment to the Ghost, to erase from the 'table' of his memory 'all trivial fond records, / All saws of books, *all forms, all pressures past*, / That youth and observation copied there' (1:5:100–4). In thus raising the problem of Hamlet's own intentions in terms of bookishness, Shakespeare engaged at least a part of his audience in the question with which I began, 'How do words relate to material practise?' We reach here, in fact, an issue central to the 'form and pressure' of our own historical moment, in which bookishness, or what I shall call academicism, is valued for its own sake and awarded special privileges in society; while literary theory, in league with certain branches of philosophy, has subordinated the signals sent out from the material world in favor of the most abstract conception of the word and the text. Somehow, *Hamlet* anticipates this, representing the danger in that side of Hamlet who, even in the stage directions, is 'reading on a book' (2:2:168). But the Hamlet who saw his mind as a 'book and volume' from which the past might be erased so that only his ghostly father's commandment might exert *its* form and pressure upon him was himself alert to this danger, and constantly berated himself for an undue commitment to words. Even Mallarmé's brilliant symbolic formulation of the problem ('Il se promène pas plus, lisant au livre de lui-même, haut et vivant Signe') presents it as a stage in Hamlet's development that is set aside at last for violent activity. 'He *no longer* walks, reading in the book of himself', but kills indifferently.[30] And Joyce, who as Stephen Dedalus *lectured* on Hamlet in the Dublin National Library, makes the same point more hideous, suggesting that violence delayed by thought is violence exacerbated: 'Nine lives are taken off for his father's one. . . The bloodboltered shambles in act five is a forecast of the concentration camp sung by Mr Swinburne.'[31] Nevertheless, under the influence of deconstruction, this most brutal aspect of *Hamlet's* material world has been made to disappear. It has seemed plausible to describe Hamlet as a 'A Writing Effect,'[32] or to create the ontological tangle of Geoffrey Hartman's 'The Interpreter', where in response to the critic's question, 'Who's there?' mimicking the opening lines of *Hamlet*, 'the book begins to question the questioner, its *qui vive* challenges him to prove he is not a ghost. What is he then?'[33]

Such are the dilemmas of academicism, especially when introspection strikes. Yet not only should the text of *Hamlet*, if closely inspected, have warned against such distortions, it provides its own sociological account of where Hamlet's bookishness came from. As J. M. Nosworthy pointed out in 1965, *Hamlet* is itself a study in academicism: 'five, possibly six, of the play's major characters are university men, and all, save Polonius, are still students.'[34] Hamlet's determination to return to Wittenberg is three times repeated; he charges Polonius, correctly, with once having acted in university theatricals; and the frequent references to scholars, 'fellow student[s]', and to philosophy as that which Hamlet and Horatio studied together create a culture-specific explanation for the 'pale cast of thought' which, in Hamlet's own self-analysis, has weakened his 'native hue of resolution' (3:1:84–5). As André Gide remarked, influenced perhaps by that momentary emphasis on 'native', it was all the fault of Wittenberg:

> Has anyone, in explaining Hamlet's character, made full use of the fact that he has returned from a German university? He brings back to his native country the germs of a foreign philosophy; he has plunged into a metaphysics whose remarkable fruit seems to me 'To be or not to be.' I already perceive all of German subjectivism in the celebrated monologue....On his return from Germany, he has lost his will; he ratiocinates. I hold German metaphysics responsible for his irresolutions. From his masters over there, his spirit has taken the key to the territory of abstract speculation, which imposes itself, so speciously, on the territory of action.[35]

Gide was anachronistic in attributing German subjectivism to sixteenth-century Wittenberg, certainly a name to conjure with, but one more likely, for Shakespeare's audience, to summon up the ghosts of Marlowe's Faustus and Martin Luther, major interventionists both; but Gide was right to focus on abstraction as a university product. And whereas Coleridge, who was the conduit by which German metaphysics entered English literary criticism, celebrated this tendency in Hamlet, and identified with it, Shakespeare makes it clear from almost the outset that 'going back to school in Wittenberg' would have been a form of escapism (1:2:112). Not only Claudius, who for the wrong reasons calls the impulse 'retrograde', but also adult responsibilility require Hamlet's active presence in Denmark, not least because, as rightful heir, he ought to reclaim his patrimony. In the last act, moreover, we learn that Hamlet has been retrograde for at least a decade, since he is now thirty years old.[36] So, while Nosworthy was probably correct in claiming that the academic context, unique in Shakespeare and without basis in any of the known sources, suggests address to a university audience,[37] he erred in supposing that Shakespeare thereby paid it an unqualified compliment, since Hamlet's superannuation in that role undermines its presumed value.

Hamlet's age, too, was probably a sign of Shakespeare's times. In the 1590s, Lawrence Stone has argued, 'the educational revolution . . . turned out men able and anxious to hold high office in numbers far in excess of the capacity of the society to employ them',[38] so that Hamlet's disability might be seen as typical as well as distinctive. This led Thomas Hobbes in mid-century to see the universities as 'the core of rebellion' because they were creating a new, large and disgruntled group of middle-class intellectuals with no clear role to play in the state: 'For it is a hard matter for men, who do all think highly of their own wits, when they have also acquired the learning of the university, to be persuaded that they want any ability requisite for the government of a commonwealth.'[39] Without endorsing Hobbes's politically-motivated anti-intellectualism, which had much the same underlying principles as Coleridge's 'abstracting and generalizing habit', we can see that *Hamlet* might constitute a warning to the university audiences as the turn at the century. *Not* that the play pointed to the ill consequences of higher education as such; but that, as in the Essex rebellion, which was plentifully supported by intellectuals, an overly-theorized approach to sociopolitical intervention could produce, paradoxically, rash and self-destructive behavior. In chapter 5 we will return to *Hamlet* to consider, among other matters unmentioned here, its protagonist's alienated, fragmentary and guilty adoption of a popular voice – another symptom of troubled intellectualism that might, in different circumstances, have led him towards organized resistance to Claudius, but which Hamlet, caught in the trap of his rank and training, is forced to abandon.

In our own time, it seems fair to suggest, the problem of academicism, viewing itself in the mirror of the text, is often reversed. In Hartman's rewriting of the Ghost scene we can see revealed what the 'form and pressure of the time' has done to the Hamlets of our profession today. Inside the university, it may sometimes appear that there are no more dreadful challenges than those of the text to the interpreter. But there are ways of relearning the conditions in which Shakespeare produced *Hamlet*, in the aftermath of a failed rebellion (for whose leader he had once thought to intercede), on the threshhold of a new regime (whose character was not yet imaginable), for a theater perceived at the time as powerful social practise, that might possibly be salutary for our own.

2

The Peasant's Toe: Popular Culture and Popular Pressure

> The toe of the peasant comes so near the heel of the courtier, he galls his kibe.
>
> *Hamlet*, 5:1:136–8

> O what a rogue and peasant slave am I!
>
> *Hamlet*, 2:2:544

'Peasant', in these complaints by Hamlet and in everything that follows here, is a symbolic term not specific to agricultural labor, still less (unlike 'serf') in precise relationship to feudal agriculture. By Shakespeare's time it had already, as Hamlet witnesses, come to stand as shorthand for that huge group of persons below the condition of gentleman and yeoman whose interests were unrepresented in the emergent nation state. As Sir Thomas Smith's *De Republica Anglorum* had defined the system in 1583, at its bottom was a 'fourth sort of men' which 'have no voice nor authoritie in our common wealth, and no account is made of them but onelie to be ruled'. This group included, as well as 'day labourers', 'copiholders' and 'poore husbandmen', that is, the Elizabethan equivalent of the feudal peasantry, the urban underclasses: 'marchantes or retailers which have no free lande . . . and all artificers, as Taylers, Shoomakers, Carpenters, Brickemakers, Bricklayers, Masons, &c.'[1] And in Hamlet's application of the term to himself, we can discern a more philosophical notion. In a society from which villeinage has technically vanished, 'peasant' and 'slave' have become pejoratives, implying degradation.

This chapter explains how the popular voice was in fact represented in Elizabethan and Jacobean England, despite or because of its political silencing, as a cultural tradition of protest. To call it a cultural tradition begs central questions about popular culture in early modern Europe, whose most recent archaeologists have developed rather different paradigms. Peter Burke, for instance, has deliberately blurred the older distinction between elite and popular culture, as also between folk culture, spontaneously created from below, and mass culture – culture for the masses – imposed from above, and argued that we need a more subtle model of interaction or interpenetration between the two. Modifying Robert Redfield's anthropological model, which distinguished between the 'great' tradition of the educated and the 'little' tradition of the folk, Burke remarked that cultural interpenetration was not symmetrical: 'The elite participated in the little tradition, but the common people did not participate in the great tradition', because they were excluded from the institutions – grammar schools and universities – by which it was transmitted. 'The little tradition, on the other hand, was transmitted informally. It was open to all, like the church, the tavern and the market-place.'[2] In another essay, specifically focused on England in the seventeenth century, Burke also proposed a more flexible model for determining the communicative function of texts and artefacts:

> Whether one is considering songs or stories, images or rituals, it may be useful to ask: 'who is saying what, to whom, for what purpose and with what effect'? However, in asking this question we must not let ourselves assume that the message transmitted was necessarily the message received.[3]

These new questions have considerable heuristic value; but they cannot possibly be answered if the 'little' culture continues to be defined as the cultural residue that remains when the 'great' tradition is accounted for: 'folksongs and folktales; devotional images and decorated marriage-chests; mystery plays and farces; broadsides and chapbooks; and, above all, festivals.'[4] It is hard to ask new questions about fragments of a culture that has already been defined as primarily recreational. But *was* the 'little' culture (paradoxically that of the vast majority) primarily recreational, or at most at the convergence of recreation and religion? We know that pedlars distributed printed ballads in rural communities. Shakespeare's Autolycus usually carried them in his pack; to him they have equal value with bracelets and pomander balls, and appeal to the same instincts. But how often were ballads taken more seriously? And if we ask whether popular culture was self-consciously protected or even developed by the voiceless classes, as distinct from being merely habitual, we run up against the phenomenon of the printing revolution, which, by creating a new readership or acculturation to print, obscures as much as it clarifies.[5] Inevitably, the record is distorted by our necessary dependence on texts *selected* for wide dissemination, whether printed ballads, almanacs or chapbooks, or on the references to festival morris dances, May games, etc., that can be painstakingly collated from other texts, usually in the dominant culture.

There was, certainly, a form of popular culture which, though not entirely separable from festive practices, had manifestly non-recreational functions; and it also demonstrates (although some would deny this) the purposive development of a 'popular voice', a self-conscious speaking from below. Burke follows his description of the London civic pageants, which appealed, like the public theaters, to very mixed audiences, with a brief reminder of 'happenings which, if not entirely unplanned, were rather more spontaneous and rather less carefully scripted than the Lord Mayor's Shows: ...riots and ...organized non-violent happenings which it is convenient, if technically anachronistic, to call "demonstrations".'[6] He thereby invoked an extensive debate as to whether such 'happenings' were (as 'spontaneous' implies) natural outbursts, or whether (as 'organized' suggests) they exhibited a popular political consciousness.

It has now become evident that the period in which Shakespeare began his work for the London stage was far from the scene of national unity and social harmony presupposed by many, and the most influential, accounts of Elizabethan literature. Historians, of course, have always been less sanguine than literary critics about the managerial problems the queen and her ministers faced when aristocratic ambitions and religious controversy threatened the premise, necessarily unstable, of a single monarchical authority. But with the emphasis now on social history, the source of the problems she faced has been redescribed. As Brian Manning puts it with statistical firmness:

> No part of England was troubled by popular protest to such a degree as London. Between 1581 and 1602, the city was disturbed by no fewer than 35 outbreaks of disorder. Since there were at least 96 insurrections, riots and unlawful assemblies in London between 1517 and 1640, this means that more than one-third of the instances of popular disorder during that century-and-a-quarter were concentrated within a 20–year period.[7]

For Manning, this concentration of disorder in the last two decades of Elizabeth's reign was primarily a crisis of urbanization. 'It was not the harvest failures of the 1590s that precipitated outbreaks of disorder in London so much as the effects of war and the extraordinarily rapid population growth' (p. 187). Of those thirty-five outbreaks of disorder between 1581 and 1602, he argues that 'at the very most' twelve could be attributed to economic distress, twelve were protests against the administration of justice, and four each were directed against alien workers, or against gentlemen and lawyers.

One should not assume that statistics are neutral. Here their rhetorical function is revealed partly by that phrase, 'at the very most', discounting economic distress as the primary factor. There is obviously an economic, protectionist motive for attacks on alien craftsmen, and those on prisons have always been symbolic of a group sense of injustice whose roots are some personal experience of hardship. But while one might dispute Manning's categories, his summary certainly shows how unstable the social framework must have appeared to Shakespeare, beginning his analysis of Elizabethan history and culture in the early 1590s, and how intimately the theater was connected to official fears that disorder was becoming endemic. Shakespeare would certainly have known of the two midsummer disturbances in the city, the small but highly dramatic rebellion of the crazed prophet William Hackett in July 1591, and the confrontation, in June 1592, between a group of Southwark feltmakers and the guards of the Marshalsea Prison. In the second instance, the relation between theater and disorder was explicitly invoked in the records of the case. It was claimed that the 'principall actors' in the riot had 'assembled by occasion of a play', as 'pretense', that is, using the theater as a pretext for unlawful assembly; and the Privy Council promptly ordered that the real theaters be closed, a ban imposed on 23 June and temporarily rescinded on 13 August.

The Privy Council's language is worth recalling in some detail. It defines the offenders as 'certaine apprentyces and other idle people theire adherentes' and announces its intelligence that this group 'have a further purpose and meaninge on Midsommer evening or Midsommer night or about that tyme to renewe theire lewd assemblye togeather by cullour of the tyme for some bad and mischeivous intencion.' The authorities are therefore charged 'that there maye be a stronge and substancyall watche kept bothe on Midsommer eveninge, Midsommer night and Sondaye at nighte' by all householders and masters of apprentices, who are to keep their servants and apprentices temporarily confined. Householders are to be armed, a street curfew established, curfew breakers imprisoned. 'Moreover for avoidinge of theis unlawfull assemblies' they are instructed to 'take order that there be noe playes used in any place neere thereaboutes, as the theator, curtayne, or other usuall places . . . nor no other sorte of unlawfull or forbidden pastymes that drawe togeather the baser sorte of people.'[8] The Council assumed a connection between seditious intention, theater and other 'forbidden pastymes', and the Midsummer season, which provides 'by cullour of the tyme', the excuse for 'unlawfull assemblies'.

The happening outside the Marshalsea Prison is a vivid instance, also, of the problems facing a historicist criticism. Those who have excavated it from the records disagree, not only in their interpretation, but even as to the facts. For Richard Wilson the feltmakers' demonstration, though sparked by an arrest of one of their colleagues, *was* a summer solstice festival, only by the accidents of custom staged near the Marshalsea prison, and *misread* by the prison governor, whose guards stormed out and killed 'several innocent persons'.[9] Manning, using the same sources, accepted the intentionalist, official account, by which 'under pretext of attending the theatre, a large group of feltmakers *made plans* to break into the Marshalsea Prison and rescue [their colleague].'[10]

Wilson and Manning, in other words, represent two opposed views, not only of what actually happened between the feltmakers and the authorities, but of popular protest in general. For Wilson, the cloth-workers were merely engaging in traditional, recreational, popular rituals, (almost) innocent of political intent. For Manning, they were clearly engaged in planned extra-legal activity, which continued, only momentarily 'deterred', after the violence in which several of them were killed. Both of them agreed, however, that the theater was somehow implicated in the event, at least as consequence and possibly as cause; and Wilson, whose sympathies were evidently with the feltmakers,[11] made a third connection. Convinced of the majority view that Shakespeare was always a law-and-order playwright, Wilson furiously attacked the account of Jack Cade's uprising in *Henry VI, Part 2*, which he assumed to have been an immediate response to the Southwark happening, a 'travesty' of historical fact, and 'an instance of the brazen manipulation of records practiced to buttress the regime' (p. 167). This argument depends on a redating of the play between March and August 1592,[12] but more likely, Wilson argued, subsequent to 23 June, when the ban on theater would have released Shakespeare from acting and given him time to write. Wilson even went so far as to argue that Shakespeare and his company hoped, by producing at short order a play hostile to popular protest, to earn 'exemption from their ban' (p. 176) which, he claimed, was delayed in their case by several days.

It appears that Burke's question to popular culture, 'Who is saying what, to whom, for what purpose and with what effect?' could equally be posed to today's commentators. The message transmitted by contemporary scholarship, also, may not necessarily be the message received. Wilson's conviction that there *was* an economic crisis in London in the 1590s,[13] and that 'London's middle class theatre sided' (p. 175) against its victims, would have been better served, perhaps, by admitting into his account of the Southwark tragedy some of the evidence that points to political consciousness among the feltmakers, that a focus on the prison was a way of appealing, symbolically, against injustice conceived on a broader scale. Moreover, his assertions about the London theater's social alignments and attitudes are more the product of bias than evidence. Theater people were certainly capable of thinking of themselves as victims of governmental or city regulation. In 1597, Thomas Nashe wrote to William Cotton that he was out of employment because 'the players...ar piteously persecuted by the L. Maior & the aldermen, & however in there old Lords tyme they thought there state setled, it is now so uncertayne that they cannot build upon it.'[14] Significantly, Nashe found an analogy in Jack Cade's rebellion, and the terminal effect it had ('they hanged up the L. cheife justice') on the practice of law. Reversing the official relationship between the theaters and the authorities, Nashe imagined the actor a persecuted lawyer, and the city officials the rebels. As Lear in his madness was later to say, 'Change places, and, handy-dandy, which is the justice, which is the thief?' (4:6:156). Evidently, the question of alignment needs more patient interrogation.

But the connection Wilson proposed between the Southwark riot and *Henry VI, Part 2* may well exist, independent of the conclusions he drew from it. If the play was indeed written after the theatrical ban of 23 June, 1592, it was almost certainly generated by current events in London. And even if it was written and produced before *Part 1*, and hence, perhaps, in late 1591,[15] it would still have been conceived in the light of one popular uprising, Hackett's, and might even have contributed to the other. It was not only the theater's role as a pretext for unlawful assembly that bothered the authorities, but the clear possibility that plays, by raising public consciousness, could organize popular feeling. If so, it would help to explain the 23 June ban on the Rose theater, where we know that one unit of the trilogy was produced on 3 March 1592. In that scenario, Wilson's argument about Shakespeare's motives would have to be diametrically reversed.

We also need to put further pressure on the disagreement between Wilson and Manning with respect to the feltmakers' intentions in 1592; for this is the most disputed issue in the theory of popular protest. The motives of social groups who do not record their own opinions is, as I have said, in dispute across the disciplines today. Among the most important contributors to this debate, indeed, one of its pioneers, is E. P. Thompson, who dedicated himself to countering the condescension with which historians had, in the main, treated the underclasses. In what Thompson named 'the spasmodic view of popular history', these groups were usually regarded by social historians as entirely incapable of political thinking. Their group 'happenings', whether denoted a riot, an uprising, or a rebellion, were assumed to be compulsive responses to economic stimuli, usually hunger, rather than self-conscious acts, still less strategic acts in a larger program. Conversely, Thompson showed that in the eighteenth century the so-called food riot was actually 'a highly-complex form of direct popular action, disciplined and with clear objectives', those objectives being to retain an older, more moral, economy that forbade overpricing, hoarding and adulteration.[16]

Thompson's position represented a middle ground, like most compromises beset on both sides by apparently stronger, more extreme positions. On the one side is a strain in Marxist thought, the belief that only in a fully capitalist environment can real class consciousness develop. So Perry Anderson attacked Thompson for failing to remember 'the great distance' between the 'relatively blind' popular protests of the 'immemorial past' and the 'conversion of them into conscious contests in the 19th and 20th centuries'.[17] On the other side, ironically, there rapidly evolved a school of social history expanding Thompson's claim – that food 'rioters' invoked a juster, less voracious economy in the past – in a way that he could not have countenanced: that is to say, into a new orthodoxy that popular unrest was always essentially conservative. So the demonstrable fact that food riots were often the last phase in a series of petitions to the authorities, and conceivable as an appeal to ideals of regulation, becomes the conviction that 'society emerged from the crisis intact, with its values and structure of authority reinforced, for dearth highlighted the former and enhanced the latter's legitimacy.'[18] Or the written demands of Robert Kett's rebels in 1549 (inarguably a sign of political consciousness) are read as the wish 'to recapture an imaginary past in which society had consisted of watertight compartments' and as 'heavy with disapproval of social mobility in any direction'.[19]

An alternative argument focused not on the supposed conservativism of popular protest, but on whether or not it was *continuous*, in the sense that later protests looked back for their inspiration to earlier ones. Was there a tradition, of intelligent, historically conscious, reformism carried within popular culture itself? At the heart of this question is the vexed significance of the Peasants' Revolt of 1381. And whereas thinkers on the left from William Morris to Christopher Hill have always looked back to 1381, it is harder to establish that those who preceded them in the sixteenth and seventeenth centuries did so, or if they did, how those memories were transmitted. E. B. Dobson, for example, denied that they *were* transmitted:

> Many civil rebellions in late medieval, Tudor and Stuart England certainly reflected several of the aspirations and grievances previously expressed in 1381; but these sometimes striking similarities were ones of which it seems certain that the later rebels were themselves largely unaware. When, as late as the summer of 1549, Robert Kett's Norfolk rebels demanded 'thatt all bonde men may be ffre for god made all ffre with his precious blode sheddyng,' they presumably had no conception that they were re-echoing the sentiments of John Ball's sermon. Post-medieval England experienced an important, and unjustly neglected, history of revolutionary movements, but not – as far as we can tell – an articulate revolutionary tradition.[20]

I propose to develop Thompson's argument for the period in which Shakespeare was working, beginning with the counter-claim that there *was* a cultural tradition of popular protest, a tradition in the sense of something handed down from the past, cultural in the sense that what was transmitted were symbolic forms and signifying practices, a history from below encoded in names and occasions, a memorial vocabulary and even a formal rhetoric. For a start, it is now a commonplace that Shakespeare appropriated the chronicle accounts of the Peasants' Revolt to thicken his description of Jack Cade's rebellion in *Henry VI, Part 2*. In so doing, he was clearly participating in an Elizabethan cultural practice, that of collating the popular protests of the past, both with each other and with the issues of the day. In particular, Jack Straw of 1381, Jack Cade of 1450, and Robert Kett's Norfolk rebellion of 1549, were linked together in an ideological chain, extended when necessary to include the Martin Marprelate reformists of the 1580s, poor prophetic Hackett in 1591, the earl of Essex in 1601 and the parliamentarians of the 1640s.

Usually, of course, such linkages are found in the dominant culture, their authors being government spokesmen or leading members of the clergy.[21] Two of the most interesting are Richard Bancroft, archbishop, and George Puttenham, literary critic. In Puttenham's *Arte of English Poesie* (1589), among the rhetorical figures discussed is *amphibologia*, or the ambiguous, an aspect of style of which Puttenham strongly disapproves; and, thanks to ambiguity, we are told:

> many insurrections and rebellions have bene stirred up in this Realme, as that of Jacke Straw, & Jacke Cade in Richard the seconds time, and in our time by a seditious fellow in Norffolke calling himself Captaine Ket. . . lead altogether by certaine propheticall rymes, which might be constred two or three wayes as well as to that one whereunto the rebelles applied it.[22]

In Bancroft's *Survey of the Pretended Holy Discipline*, published in 1593 as anti-Puritan propaganda, the dissenters are compared to the insurrectionists of 1381:

> We live in a worlde (you know) that crieth out: *the first institution, the first institution:* everything must be brought to the *first institution*. The wordes be good, if they be well applied. But something was amisse in the Priestes application of his text, being such a like saying amongest a multitude of rebelles, viz: *When Adam digged and Eve spanne, who was then the Gentleman.*[23]

Both Bancroft and Puttenham, notably, conflate history more than they quite intended, Puttenham placing Jack Cade 'in Richard the second's time' and Bancroft repeating the mistake in a marginal note against 'When Adam digged': 'John Wall, or Ball in the time of Jacke Cades rebellion, in Rich. 2 daies'. And this conflation of notorious rebels (and of reigns) has been compared with Shakespeare's use of the records of 1381 to describe the events of 1450.[24]

But there is more here than potential comparison or contrast. Both Puttenham, writing just before the *Henry VI* plays, and Bancroft, writing immediately after them, speak to the existence of a popular *culture* of protest; that is to say, to the power of certain formulae carried in the oral tradition to act as an incentive, an organizational credo, a symbol of radical claims that are themselves broadly defined. The 'certain propheticall rymes' in Puttenham's complaint, and the 'like saying amongst a multitude' in Bancroft's are, in effect, the grudging tributes paid by the dominant culture to the power of the popular voice gainsaying. The famous Edenic motto introduced into radical culture in 1381, 'When Adam delved and Eve span', appealed, as Bancroft's worried repetitions attest, to the 'first institution', to inborn principles of natural justice and equality always recuperable by radical Christianity, and that in Wat Tyler's demands, as recorded by the early chroniclers, were also expressed in terms of political liberty.[25]

The source of Puttenham's disapproval was surely the militant if ambiguous prophecy associated with Kett's rebellion, and recorded by Alexander Neville, secretary to Matthew Parker, the first Elizabethan archbishop of Canterbury, whose Latin history of the rising, commissioned by Parker, was twice reissued during Shakespeare's lifetime, and twice translated in the early seventeenth century:

> The Country Gnoffs, Hob, Dick, and Hick,
> With clubs and clouted Shoon,
> Shall fill the Vale
> Of Duffin's Dale
> With slaughter'd Bodies soon.[27]

Like Puttenham, Neville and his translators were concerned by the power, however in the event rebarbative, of the 'certain Prophecies and superstitious Rhymes that they had among them, which were rung in their Ears every Hour.' But the significance of this verse lies also in its self-conscious acceptance, by the rebels themselves, of a 'peasant' ideology of the primitive, expressed both in the crude generic names, Hob, Dick and Hick (the last retaining exactly that force in our own parlance), and also in those symbolic attributes of an ill-shod peasantry, the 'clouted shoon'.[27] It is no accident that Shakespeare's Cade makes this his distinguishing mark of class:

> And you that love the commons, follow me.
> Now show yourselves men; 'tis for liberty.
> We will not leave one lord, one gentleman:
> Spare none but such as go in clouted shoon.
>
> (4:3:175–8)

But we can add to this category of radical ideologemes. To it belonged also the 'syxe old Proverbs' of the anti-enclosure tract *Certayne Causes*, published in the year before Kett's uprising[28] as well as the 'just complaint made by the poore people of England against the covetousnes of gredy fermours' at the time of the Midlands Rising of 1607, self-defined as 'an old ballad prynted by Yarath James'.[29] Both of these, as printed texts, are intermediate between the internal communications of popular protest movements and the external messages that the popular voice sends out to the authorities in the form of written or published petitions. And both of them, evidently, deployed the 'old' as a way of validating their messages. This was a crucial aspect of the 'peasant ideology' circulating in 1381, an appeal to the past as the source of 'ancient rights', some of which were actually imagined as embedded in charters;[30] but it was still to be found as a *strategy* from 1610 to the 1640s, when the parliamentarians were developing their case against the king on the grounds of 'ancient liberties' that Stuart absolutism was said to have abrogated.

A return to origins, then, was integral to the popular conception of *how* to protest, as well as providing theoretical grounds for the 'demands', for the transformation of local and individual grievances into a political program. But there was also, apparently, a popular version of the hostile official genealogy of rebellion in England from 1381 onwards, a claim, in effect, that protest was continuous. For a semi-magical value attached to the sites of previous uprisings or demonstrations, to Blackheath, where Jack Cade followed Wat Tyler, or to Cheapside, where Hackett staged his 1591 uprising, and was followed there by the earl of Essex. Evidently, the failure of previous happenings was not only no deterrent, it provided a pathic center. Bartholomew Stere's choice of Enslow Hill for the puny Oxfordshire attempt of 1596 was as fatalistic as his estimate of popular support was deluded: according to local tradition 'there was one a rising at Enslow by the commons, and they were persuaded to [submit] and after were hanged like doggs.'[31]

But the most important evidence, finally, of the popular voice raised in articulate protest has come down to us by way of ventriloquism, in the texts of the dominant culture. This phenomenon has been brilliantly grasped by Pierre Macherey in his study of Balzac's *Les Paysans*, a novel committed to revealing 'the unceasing conspiracy' of the rural working class against the French bourgeois. Balzac's unqualified hostility to the peasant, whom he believed to be undermining the French system of land-ownership, forced him, according to Macherey, into a procedural dilemma:

> In a single movement...the author intends to inform and to disquiet. The ideological proposition is...most apparent; but it is easy to reveal by its side, as the condition of its realisation, the utterance of the fact which contests it.... If one is going to speak against the people, effectively, one must speak of the people: they must be seen, given form, *allowed to speak*.[32]

In sixteenth-century England, this dilemma is actually given rhetorical form, in the trope of reported speech. So in 1589 Bishop Thomas Cooper, in his attack on the Martinists, recalled 'to the People' the people's arguments of 1381: 'At the beginning, *say they*, when God had first made the world, all men were alike; there was not principality, there was no bondage, or villeinage; that grew afterwards by violence and cruelty. Therefore, why should we live in this miserable slavery under these proud lords and crafty lawyers, etc.?'[33] The form of the dilemma, obiously, is that the ventriloquist must himself utter, in order to refute them, ethical and pathetic claims whose force may linger beyond his powers of persuasion.

A more complicated instance occurs in the public accounting for Jack Kett's Norfolk uprising, whose historians claimed the reliability of personal witness. Richard Woods, in 1615, described himself as having seen 'part of these things with his yong Eyes'. Evidently, young ears were also involved; for an extraordinary amount of space is devoted to the rebels' account of their grievances. And although the text makes its law-and-order motives unmistakable,[34] the message transmitted, in the words of Peter Burke, was not necessarily the message received. The common people are described as 'desiring...not only to lay open the common Pastures, inclosed by the injurie of some men, but to powre foorth their ungodly desires against the Commonwealth...to the spoile, and overthrow of all things': that is, their grievances desire structural *expression*. And pour them forth, thanks to the hegemonic historian, they do:

For, *said they*, the pride of great men is now intollerable, but their condition miserable. These abound in delights, and compassed with the fulnesse of all things, and consumed with vaine pleasures, thirst only after gaine, and are inflamed with the burning delights of their desires: but themselves almost killed with labour and watching, doe nothing all their life long but sweate, mourne, hunger and thirst... their miserable condition, is a laughing stocke to most proud and insolent men. Which thing...grieveth them so sore, and inflicteth such a staine of evill report: as nothing is more grievous for them to remember, nor more injust to suffer...The common Pastures left by our Predecessors for the reliefe of us, and our children, are taken away. The lands which in the memory of our fathers, were common, those are ditched and hedged in, and made severall; the Pastures are inclosed and we shut out: whatsoever fowles of the aire, or fishes of the water, and increase of the earth, all these doe they devoure, consume and swallow up; yea, nature doth not suffice to satisfy their lusts, but they seeke out new devices, and as it were, formes of pleasure...while we in the meane time, eate hearbs and roots, and languish with continuall labour, and yet [they] envie that we live, breathe, and injoy common ayre. Shall they, as they have brought hedges about common Pastures, inclose with their intolerable lusts also, al the commodities and pleasure of this life, which Nature, the Parent of us all, would have common, and bringeth foorth every day for us, aswell as for them?...Nature hath provided for us, aswell as for them, hath given us a body, and a soule, and hath not envied us other things. While we have the same forme, and the same condition of birth together with them, why should they have a life so unlike unto ours, and differ so farre from us in calling? We see now that it is come to extremitie, wee will also proove extremitie: rend downe hedges, fill up ditches, make way for everie man into the common pasture... Neither will we suffer ourselves any more to bee pressed with such burthens against our willes, nor endure so great shame, as living out our dayes under such inconveniences, wee should leave the Commonwealth unto our posteritie, mourning, and miserable, and much worse then we received it of our fathers. Wherefore we will trie all meanes; neither will we ever rest, untill wee have brought things to our owne liking. We desire libertie, and an indifferent use of all things. (B1v-B2r)

In this extraordinary document, the historian has, willy nilly, given almost more than we could ask for in terms of attributing rational motives and emotive force to radical agents. The speech shows precisely how a local issue (enclosures) could lead to a meditation on the concept of the 'common', or natural, inheritance; it offers an ethical model of how socioeconomic inequality is perceived as by no means inevitable by the losers, but as caused by the greed of the winners; it includes a striking account of the psychology involved, of the humiliation poverty causes ('nothing is more grievous' than the perception that they have become 'a laughing stocke' to their oppressors); and it ends with a ringing statement of how a change for the worse in their environment (the increase in enclosures) produces a sense of 'extremitie'. Finally, in the peroration, it becomes starkly clear how abstract ideals of justice can emerge from a concrete perception of unfairness: 'We desire liberty, and an indifferent use of all things.' There seems little doubt that such bold thinking was encouraged by the Edwardian Reformation and by Somerset's Protectorship. Protestant services were held by the rebels under an ancient oak known as the 'Tree of Reformation', and although the uprising was largely non-violent, symbolic trials of gentlemen were held there also.[35]

And, as if this richness for our purpose were not enough, Neville/Woods make the same connection as the Privy Council in midsummer 1592, the connection between 'unlawfull assembly' and 'illegal (theatrical) pastimes'. 'Not long after' these grievances were voiced, 'there was a Play at Windham, by an old custome, which lasted two daies, and two nights.' The conspirators took the opportunity, by this gathering of 'a multitude of all degrees', to spread discontent throughout the crowd. 'First therefore were secret meetings... then withdrawing themselves, secret conferences: but at length they all began to deale tumultuously, and to rage openly' (B2v). In 1592 Shakespeare would have been able to speak with men who had been eyewitnesses of these events; and in all probability the official connection between protest and theater in both 1549 and 1592 was common knowledge.

It is helpful to compare this history of Kett's rebellion with contemporary anthropological work on the social dialogue, especially with findings from parts of the world whose development is roughly comparable to England in the sixteenth century. In particular, James C. Scott, in *Weapons of the Weak*, has discovered political self-consciousness in peasant culture in Malaysia in the wake of the 'green revolution', or the coming of agrarian capitalism and mechanization to a single village. Arguing particularly against the theorists of the left whose ideas of 'false consciousness', ideology and hegemony leave no space for rational agency except by intellectuals, Scott takes issue particularly with the claim that structural social change is unthinkable in peasant cultures. 'The fact that serfs, slaves or untouchables have no direct knowledge or experience of other social orders' is no obstacle, he concludes, to their creating 'what would have to qualify as "revolutionary" thought.'[36] In fact, 'subordinate classes – especially the peasantry – are likely to be more radical at the level of ideology than at the level of behavior, where they are more effectively constrained by the daily exercise of power.' This argument is not only deduced from empirical study of Sedakan peasants, from their own social commentary, but by analogy with worldwide rituals of status inversion, as well as from the frequency with which, over historical time and geographical space, we see a recurrence of utopian ideologies of classlessness. Both inversion rituals, however 'contained', and egalitarian fantasies prove that subordinate classes can *imagine* how things might be absolutely different.

The argument that peasant docility implies belief in the inevitability or rightness of their condition is based, Scott argues, on a misunderstanding of the role of individual prudence in a subsistence economy, on mistaking for ideological acceptance a stance of 'pragmatic resignation' (p. 335) when nothing else seems possible; but it is when change occurs for the worse that pragmatic resignation itself becomes imprudent, and radical action necessary. (As Kett's rebels were said to say, 'We see now that it is come to extremitie, wee will also proove extremitie.') For, Scott insists, it is by the dominant classes that economic change is initiated, and capitalism itself has provoked its resistance by undermining 'previous understandings about work, equity, security, obligation, and rights' (p. 346). In Sedaka the larger farmers, seeking to improve their returns, had 'dismissed tenants, raised the rent, switched to leasehold, and called in the machinery. It is they who have steadily abrogated the customs of *zakat*, charity, loans, and large feasts' (p. 345). In England in the sixteenth century, as agrarian historians have equally shown, the enclosure of common ground was merely one of a host of other 'advances' that improved agriculture at the expense of the poor; but as the Neville/Woods account of peasant grievances shows, the idea of the 'common' had much wider ideological force, and stood for customary practices and 'rights' that were clearly perceived as such at the time of, and because of, their rescinding.

And so, Scott concludes, with immediate pertinence here, 'the backward-looking character of much subordinate class ideology and protest' is not incompatible with looking forward.

> It is the revolutionary character of capitalism that casts them in a defensive role. If they defend a version of the older hegemony, it is because those arrangements look good by comparison with the current prospects and because it has a certain legitimacy rooted in early practice. The defense and elaboration of a social contract that has been abrogated by capitalist development is perhaps the most constant ideological theme of the peasant and early capitalist worker.' (pp. 346–7)

We can now turn with sharpened sight (or better hearing) back to the Elizabethan documents. It is important to know that the strategy of ventriloquism was also employed by avowedly populist writers who would not have experienced the Macherey/Balzac dilemma. In the mid-sixteenth century, Robert Crowley built a people's complaint into his *Way to Wealth*, a reformist pamphlet published in the immediate aftermath of Jack Kett's rebellion, and adopting, for form's sake only, an anti-sedition posture. 'If I should demand of the poor man of the country what thing he thinketh to be the cause of sedition,' wrote Crowley, 'I know his answer' (sig.A viiir) Although clearly the poor man's spokesman, Crowley dramatized both voices in the social dialogue. The poor complain: 'They take our houses over our heads, they buy our grounds out of our hands, they raise our rents, they levy great (yea, unreasonable) fines, they enclose our commons' (sig.A iiir). The rich 'cormorants' say: 'We will teach [the poor commons] to know their betters. And because they would have all common, we will leave them nothing. And if they once stir again or do but once cluster together, we will hang them at their own doors.'[37]

Edmund Spenser's *Shepheardes Calender* had originally been sent to the press in 1578 with 'a free passeporte' to go on a mission 'emongste the meaner sorte', a closing message that clarifies Spenser's intentions. It was, significantly, republished in 1591, and so became part of the immediate cultural environment of Shakespeare's *Henry VI*. The most unmistakably populist of its eclogues is *September*, in which Diggon Davie acts as spokesman for popular complaint against a corrupt and avaricious clergy:

> *They sayne* the world is much war then it wont,
> All for her shepheards bene beastly and blont.
> *Others sayne*, but how truely I note,
> All for they holden shame of theyr cote.
> *Some sticke not to say*, (whote cole on her tongue)
> That sike mischiefe graseth hem emong.
>
> *Thus chatten the people* in theyr steads,
> Ylike as a Monster of many heads.[38]

Here the rhetorical sign of ventriloquism, 'they say', is governed evasively by 'how truly I note', where 'note' can be either the archaic 'Ne woot', (I know not) or may indicate the speaker's agreement with the views he reports. So too the reformist premise of change for the worse ('the world is much war then it wont,') and the implications of prophetic speech ('whote cole on her tonge' from Isaiah 6.6) pull in one direction, while the trope of the many-headed monster, a sign of antidemocratic bias, pulls in the other. But because Spenser frames this act of ambiguous reporting in a debate on the possibility of social change, we can guess where its ambiguities come from. The more cautious speaker Hobbinol appeals to precisely that 'pragmatic resignation' defined by Scott: 'Better it were, a little to feyne, / And cleanly cover, that cannot be cured. / Such il, as is forced, mought nedes be endured.' The 'cleanly cover' so invoked is both the prudence that restricts a more open protest, and the ideology of patience which, knowingly, the socially powerless use in order to retain for themselves some modicum of personal dignity.

Clearly, these documents / texts witness to a range of attitudes towards the popular voice, and demand for their scrutiny a more flexible hermeneutics than has hitherto been available. We need to determine in any given instance of ventriloquism whether the author experiences the Macherey / Balzac dilemma, or whether, like Crowley and Spenser, he is engaged, rather, in cautious social reformism. And where the text in question is generically, rather than momentarily, dramatic, any ambiguity is intensified, thanks to the absence of a supervening authorial posture. *The Life and Death of Jack Straw* (1593) is often aligned with Shakespeare's play, and generally assumed to have had a law-and-order agenda; but even Dobson observes that the author 'gives the best lines' to the radical priest John Ball, who thereby recirculates through the London audiences the central ideologemes of 'peasant' ideology – its Edenic egalitarianism, its archaism, its claim that the world has grown worse through greed, its psychological awareness of poverty as humiliation, and its declaration that force is justified by 'extremitie':

> England is growne to such a passe of late,
> The rich men triumph to see the poore beg at their gate.
>
> But when Adam delved, and Eve span,
> Who was then a Gentleman.
> Brethren brethren, it were better to have this communitie,
> Then to have this difference in degrees:
> The landlord his rent, the lawyer his fees.
> So quickly the poore mans substance is spent,
> But merrily with the world it went,
> When men eat berries of the hauthorne tree,
> And thou helpe me, Ile helpe thee.

To see such dealings with extremitie,
The Rich have all, the poore live in miserie:
But follow the counsell of John Ball,
I promise you I love yee all:
And make division equally,
Of each mans goods indifferently,
And rightly may you follow Armes,
To rid you from these civill harmes.[39]

For Dobson, this destabilizing effect in *Jack Straw* was produced 'more by accident than design', a phrase which assumes that we know what the design must have been. This is the assumption with which most readers today will approach *Henry VI, Part 2.* A typical modern introduction to the first tetralogy states that, while 'the principal rebel' is Richard of York, to 'display the horrors of rebellion Shakespeare uses chiefly Jack Cade and his followers', whose uprising is 'the very antithesis of God's plan.'[40] These are the consequences of believing that Shakespeare believed that the goal of a quiet polis had supernatural backing. Surprisingly, when the critic begins with neo-Marxist assumptions, little has changed. For Walter Cohen, *Jack Straw*'s author was so unambiguously monarchical in his views that he could recreate Ball's appeal 'in the serene confidence that it will be contemptuously dismissed'. And while Shakespeare's methods are 'more subtle,...the result is not qualitatively different.'[41] If we gather a different message from these plays, Cohen argues, it is only because of their 'pattern of unconscious revelation', the capacity of their social 'blindness' to 'communicate significant insight' to the later and less-deceived.

It ought to be possible, nevertheless, to start again. And the place to start, in the playtext itself, is not with Cade at all, but rather with the formal act of ventriloquism performed at the play's center, in relation to the murder of Humphrey, duke of Gloucester, and the popular outrage it caused. Gloucester has been carefully established as the Lord Protector who 'would not tax the needy commons' for the French wars (3:1:116).[42] Suffolk, in contrast, has been defined by his mockery of the petitioners who approach him for assistance. Note especially the 'poor petitioner of [a] whole township' who mistakenly appeals to Suffolk, mistaking him for Gloucester, against Suffolk himself, for 'enclosing the commons of Long Melford' (1:3:20–22). Suffolk, in planning Gloucester's assassination, is aware that 'the commons [may] haply rise to save his life' (3:1:240); and indeed, when news of his death becomes public, 'The commons, like an angry hive of bees / That want their leader, scatter up and down, / And care not who they sting in his revenge' (3:2:124–6). The beehive metaphor, unlike the animal fables with which the text is peppered, has, of course, a specifically political force, and its traditionally monarchical associations are both a critique of Henry VI as a failed monarch and a tribute to the genuinely popular leadership of Gloucester, of which the commons are now deprived. In a speech of crucial importance for Shakespeare's conception of popular protest, Salisbury enters as the temporary substitute; that is to say, the people's spokesman:

> Dread lord, the commons sends you word by me,
> Unless false Suffolk straight be done to death,
> Or banished fair England's territories,
> They will by violence tear him from your palace
> And torture him with grievous ling'ring death.
> *They say*, by him the good Duke Humphrey died;
> *They say*, in him they fear your Highness' death;
>
> *They say*, in care of your most royal person,
> That if your Highness should intend to sleep,
> And charge that no man should disturb your rest,
>
> It were but necessary you were wak'd,
> Lest, being suffer'd, in that harmful slumber,
> The mortal worm might make the sleep eternal:
> *And therefore do they cry*, though you forbid,
> That they will guard you, whe'r you will or no, (3:2:241–65)
> From such fell serpents as false Suffolk is.

The rhetorical 'They say' formula identifies Salisbury as ventriloquist, while the dramatic situation ensures his recognition as the people's sincere advocate. Their protest is, therefore, both morally authoritative and, as petitioning from strength, effective. Henry will banish Suffolk; though not before Suffolk has further justified his banishment by revealing his anti-populist bias:

> 'Tis like the commons, rude unpolish'd hinds,
> Could send such message to their sovereign;
>
> But all the honour Salisbury has won
> Is that he was the lord ambassador,
> Sent from a sort of tinkers to the King. (3:2:270–76)[43]

With this conditional approval of the role of popular protest in the play – conditional, that is, on rightful motives, a basic loyalty to the crown, and a proper spokesman – we can now return to the far better known, indeed notorious, scenes of the Cade uprising.

Compared to Salisbury, Cade fails every test for the proper popular spokesman. In Hall's *Chronicle* and in Shakespeare's play he is 'seduc'd' by Richard, duke of York, to create a popular uprising from which

Richard alone will profit. Having been a double agent in Ireland, Cade's function is to reveal 'the commons' mind' to Richard, 'How they affect the house and claim of York' (3:1:374–5). Hall explains the plot to establish Richard as a popular rival to Henry VI, who 'wolde, (if he once ruled in the Realme of England) depose evil counsaillors, correct evil judges, & reforme all matters amisse.'[44] In Shakespeare's play, the order of events is rearranged; this scheme now precedes the episode of the commons' intervention, through Salisbury, in the feudal power struggle. Richard's cynical and exploitative populism therefore casts both Gloucester's and Salisbury's as ideal alternatives; but, by the same token, when Cade finally appears, everything that he says is already suspect. Little is proved, therefore, by demonstrating how inconsistent is Cade in his recapitulation of the ancient tropes of levelling, or how much Shakespeare simplified and darkened the model he found in Hall. If anything, the values inherent in the echoes of 1381, 'All the realm shall be in common', 'Adam was a gardener', and the abstract ideal of 'liberty' (4:2:65, 128, 176) are enhanced by the fact that Cade is also an impostor aristocrat, a traitor to his class, hawking his false claims to the name of Mortimer by way of romantic fiction, the tale of a noble child stolen from its cradle by a beggarwoman, and now returned to claim its inheritance.

Hypocrisy in Cade is not, however, completely impenetrable by the real content of the role he assumes. One of his speeches raises the Macherey/ Balzac dilemma in an especially interesting form. Confronting Lord Say (who in Hall was impeached by his connection with Suffolk), Cade delivers an attack on the new education that in his view is disadvantaging the poor:

> Thou has most traitorously corrupted the youth of the realm in erecting a grammar-school; and whereas, before, our forefathers had no other books but the score and the tally, thou hast caus'd printing to be us'd; and contrary to the King his crown, and dignity, thou has built a paper-mill. It will be prov'd to thy face that thou hast men about thee that usually talk of a noun, and a verb, and such abominable words as no Christian ear can endure to hear. Thou hast appointed justices of the peace, to call poor men before them about matters they were not able to answer. Moreover, thou hast put them in prison; and because they could not read, thou hast hang'd them; when, indeed, only for that cause they have been most worthy to live. (4:7:30–44)

This speech is both intellectually confused and ideologically unstable. A primitivist defence of the old crafts against mechanization is blurred by a negative focus on language skills (grammatical *techne*) as an evil science; but the absurdity of condemning those who 'usually talk of a noun, and a verb' – a line designed for a laugh – quickly gives place to pathos, and, more profoundly, to the connection between educational disparity and unequal access to legal justice. All this was faithfully recorded in the Quarto text of 1594, with two significant differences. The Quarto expands the clerical context by having Cade complain 'thou kepst men in thy house that daily reades of bookes with red letters', that is to say, rubricated editions of the classics or historical lawtexts like Justinian; and it substitutes for the 'poor men... [interrogated] about matters they were not able to answer' 'honest men that steale for their living', a phrase that might be either comic or tragic, depending on delivery.

The attack on literacy was an emphasis Shakespeare derived from the annals of the Peasants' Revolt, where the burning of legal records was apparently motivated by a belief that law is malignant because enscripted.[45] But when Lord Say pleads for his life on the grounds that 'ignorance is the curse of God, / Knowledge the wing wherewith we fly to heaven', the confrontation between Cade and himself acquires larger significance. If Cade represents a doctrinaire inerudition, Say stands for that salaried version of liberal humanism whose appeal to metaphysical values, as in Coleridge's lay sermon to the clerisy, has continually justified its institutional rewards: 'Large gifts have I bestow'd on learned clerks,' Say continues, 'Because my book preferr'd me to the King' (4:7:66–71).

Here, then, is a double ventriloquism: the voice of popular protest speaking through Cade (despite his insincerity) speaking through Shakespeare's playtext. But Shakespeare's own intentions have already been indicated by his dramatizing different styles of populism, by distinguishing between authoritative and specious mediation of popular goals and grievances. And if more evidence were needed, we could go back to the scene on Blackheath when Cade's arrival is expected. 'Well,' cries John Holland, 'I say it was never merry world in England since gentlemen came up.' Not 'they say', but 'I say'. 'O miserable age!' cries Bevis, 'Virtue is not regarded in handicraftsmen', but 'the King's Council are no good workmen.' And Holland replies, 'True; and yet is it said, "Labour in thy vocation"; which is as much to say as, "Let the magistrates be labouring men"; and therefore should we be magistrates' (4:2:10–18). These minor characters are free of the cynicism of Dick the Butcher, and natural in their echoes of the tropes of popular protest. They introduce the criterion of labor as a test of social value, a theme that Shakespeare will return to constantly; and they demonstrate beyond a shadow of a doubt that the real popular consciousness, as distinct from the impostor, is capable of penetrating hegemony's aphorisms, and turning against themselves what Scott, in *Weapons of the Weak*, calls 'official platitudes'.[46]

In this scene, then, Shakespeare identified a 'peasant ideology' which united leather aprons with clouted shoon. If the play records the potential corruption of this ideology by Cade as a paid incendiary, and its internal confusions on the subject of literacy and educational access, these are necessary qualifications, precisely what one expects of a historically informed social analysis. But there is nothing in *Henry VI, Part 2*, read carefully, that can justify its use as the court of last appeal in a claim for Shakespeare's conservativism. By applying the 'official platitudes' of their own doctrines to selected parts of the text only, critics have been deaf to the carefully modulated story it tells.

There is one postscript, appropriately enough from the environment that required Coleridge's defence of Southey for *his* dramatization of the Peasants' Revolt, and hence his remarks on *Henry VI, Part 2*. In 1792, in the first wave of anti-Jacobin censorship, John Larpent's *Richard the Second* was suppressed in its original form, imprudently supportive as it was of the peasants and anti-taxation insurgency. In April 1793, the play reappeared, thoroughly revised to the censor's specifications, and now entitled *The Armorer*. The main plot, concerning the rebellion, disappeared, along with Wat Tyler himself. And as for the protagonist, who in the first version murdered a tax collector and fled from the law to join the rebels, he now stays to face his trial: 'Let come what will,' he announces dutifully, 'the laws of my Country, & the authority of my King, shall neither be evaded, nor opposed by me.'[47] Although the circumstances of 1592 suggest equally strict surveillance of the theater as was demonstrated again exactly two hundred years later, it is a tribute to Shakespeare's independence that not even Cade, on his uppers in Iden's garden, is prepared to sell his 'unconquer'd soul' in this way. Instead of the 'brazen manipulation of records practiced to buttress the regime' of which he has been accused, what Shakespeare provided in 1592 was an opportunity to discriminate: between contrasting attitudes toward the popular voice protesting; and between socially useful or abusive styles of its mediation.

3

Bottom's Up: Festive Theory

> Even though chronology places regularity above permanence, it cannot prevent heterogeneous, conspicuous fragments from remaining within it. To have combined recognition of a quality with the measurement of the quantity was the work of the calender in which the places of recollection are left blank, as it were, in the form of holidays.
>
> Walter Benjamin: *On Some Motifs in Baudelaire*

On 29 September, Michaelmas Day, 1662, Samuel Pepys recorded in his diary a characteristically guilty moment:

> This day my oaths for drinking of wine and going to plays are out, and so I do resolve to take a liberty to-day, and then to fall to them again. To the King's Theatre, where we saw 'Midsummer's Night's Dream,' which I had never seen before, nor shall ever again, for it is the most insipid ridiculous play that ever I saw in my life. I saw, I confess, some good dancing and some handsome women, and which was all my pleasure.[1]

The psychological conflicts for which Pepys's diary is famous have in this instance an ideological quotient – the conflict between the Restoration court's support of the stage and the Puritan principles he had incorporated[2] – a conflict which descends, obviously, from the Elizabethan theater's relation to governmental allowance and control. And lest we should doubt that this conflict, in Pepys, was serious, we should take note of his 'Observations' at the New Year, 1662: 'This I take to be as bad a juncture as ever I observed. The King and his new Queen minding their pleasure at Hampton Court. All people discontented; some that the King do not gratify them enough; and the others, Fanatiques of all sorts, that the King do take away their liberty of conscience' (3:208). The moral embarrassment in which Pepys finds himself is especially signified by the contradictory function of 'liberty' in these two entries, the Nonconformist liberty of conscience threatened by the Act of Uniformity dialectically opposed to the festival liberty that Pepys resolves to allow himself (one of many such suspensions of his private rules) for Michaelmas Day.

Pepys's critical reaction also speaks to the theater history of *A Midsummer Night's Dream*, which already, one can tell from his mention of 'good dancing', had succumbed to operatic or balletic impulses. These impulses dominated all productions from 1692, when it was rewritten as a spectacular opera with music by Henry Purcell, through 1914, when Harley Granville-Barker produced the uncut text 'in a world of poetic and dramatic rather than scenic illusion'.[3] For over two centuries, then, the play that Shakespeare wrote was rendered invisible by conspicuous display; and its most striking metadramatic feature, the concluding amateur theatricals of Bottom the weaver and his colleagues, lost both its structural and social force. In 1692 'Pyramus and Thisbe' was moved to the middle of the performance, and in 1816 the Covent Garden performance had as its grand finale a pageant of 'Triumphs of Theseus'. The result was a performance whose last word, in the year after Waterloo, was the extravagant celebration of monarchical and military power.

The *Dream* has also tempted literary critics to subordinate Bottom and his colleagues, or to neutralize the impact of the play-within-the-play. The temptation is posed by the speech of Theseus that both summarizes the erotic experiences of the young Athenians on midsummer night, and serves as the aristocratic prologue to the artisan's playlet:

> More strange than true. I never may believe
> These antique fables, nor these fairy toys.
> Lovers and madmen have such seething brains,
> Such shaping fantasies, that apprehend
> More than cool reason ever comprehends.
>
> The poet's eye, in a fine frenzy rolling,
> Doth glance from heaven to earth, from earth to heaven,
> And as imagination bodies forth
> The forms of things unknown, the poet's pen
> Turns them to shapes, and gives to airy nothing
> A local habitation and a name.
>
> (5.1.2–17)[4]

Like the stage history, the tradition of privileging this Thesean aesthetic as the locus of Shakespeare's intentions had the effect of making the *Dream* an 'airy nothing', unaccountable to social or political realism, while at the same time giving to Theseus an exegetical authority that his own behavior scarcely justifies. And though this critical tradition has been roundly challenged, most notably by Jan Kott's counter-privileging of Bottom and his fellows[5] (the academic equivalent of Peter Brook's famous 1970 production) it probably retains its dominance in the classroom.

In fact, even as within this speech imaginative process requires the assistance of things known – bodies, names and local habitations – Shakespeare gave the *Dream* a 'local habitation' so historically specific that the play would make no sense (as Pepys discovered) when performed outside its own cultural environment. The evidence occurs in two passages, close neighbours to each other, in the second act, where the story of Oberon's quarrel with Titania over the changeling boy is told from its beginnings and given a new impetus. In planning his revenge on Titania for her refusal to give up the child into his retinue, Oberon describes to Puck where he may find the 'little western flower', that will be the instrument of her enchantment. Quite gratuitously in terms of plot or strategy, he explains the origins of the flower's erotic capacities as an instance of displaced energies:

> That very time I saw (but thou couldst not),
> Flying between the cold moon and the earth,
> Cupid all arm'd. A certain aim he took
> At a fair vestal, throned by the west,
> And loos'd his love-shaft smartly from his bow
> As it should pierce a hundred thousand hearts.
> But I might see young Cupid's fiery shaft
> Quench'd in the chaste beams of the watery moon;
> And the imperial votress passed on, (2:1:155–64)
> In maiden meditation, fancy-free.

Missing its target, the shaft strikes the flower, which is thereby transformed from milk-white to purple, from mere flower to concept, 'love-in-idleness'. The erotic drive is displaced into the territory of the symbolic, producing an excess of textual energy that seems to require special attention. The original audiences would certainly have recognized its galvanic source in the implied presence of Elizabeth herself. As H. H. Furness remarked in 1895,

> That there is an allegory here has been noted from the days of Rowe, but how far it extended and what its limitations and its meanings have since then proved prolific themes. According to Rowe, it amounted to no more than a compliment to Queen Elizabeth, and this is the single point on which all critics since his day are agreed.[6]

Was it, however, so clearly a compliment? Increasingly as she aged, the problems posed by Elizabeth's status as unmarried female ruler were either finessed or exposed to critical scrutiny by the motif of virginity as power. As the moon goddess, Diana, Cynthia or Phoebe, she was celebrated as the Belphoebe of Spenser's *Faerie Queene*, and the Cynthia of Ben Jonson's *Cynthia's Revels* and Ralegh's *The Ocean's Love to Cynthia*, all texts of the 1590s when Elizabeth was approaching or in her sixties.[7] And as *A Midsummer Night's Dream* is in one sense a play about moonshine, the lunar presence invoked in its lines is far from a positive force: 'O, methinks, how slow/This old moon wanes!' cries Theseus, 'She lingers my desires.'

Further, as the title of Spenser's poem indicates, the myths of the classical moon-goddess also merged, for the unique moment of Elizabeth's reign, with fairy legends of Titania and Oberon. Even in Ovid's *Metamorphoses*, Titania was another name for Diana (3:173); during a royal progress of 1591 the 'Fairy Queen' presented Elizabeth with a chaplet that she had received from 'Auberon, the Fairy King';[8] and after her death Thomas Dekker referred to Elizabeth as Titania in his *Whore of Babylon* (1607). This alternative mythology also appears in the *Dream*, and with equally problematic resonance. For Titania, far from remaining chastely aloof, engages in a struggle for domestic power with Oberon that, however we attribute the fault, has had a disastrous effect on the environment.

Titania herself rehearses these natural disasters, in the other passage of topical significance:

> The ox hath therefore stretch'd his yoke in vain,
> The ploughman lost his sweat, and the green corn
> Hath rotted ere his youth attain'd a beard;
> The fold stands empty in the drowned field,
> And crows are fatted with the murrion flock;
> The-nine-men's-morris is fill'd up with mud,
> And the quaint mazes in the wanton green (2:1:93–100)
> For lack of tread are undistinguishable.

And on the basis of this passage, and our knowledge that the one season in Shakespeare's career that was notorious for its bad weather and bad harvests was 1595–6, a consensus has developed for dating the *Dream* at some point in 1596. This dating alone might have generated speculation about the frontal presence of a group of artisans, whose amateur theatricals contribute the play's conclusion, if not its resolution. It was not until 1986, however, that Titania's lament and the artisanal presence were connected, by Theodore Leinwand, to the abortive Oxfordshire rising of November 1596, when Bartholomew Stere, a carpenter, and Richard Bradshawe, a miller, had planned an anti-enclosure riot of distinctly violent proportions.[9] Depositions concerning this event were still being heard in London by the Privy Council during January 1597; it was said that Stere's 'owtward pretense was to...helpe the poore cominaltie that were readie to famish for want of corne, But intended to kill the gentlemen of that countrie...affirming that the Commons, long sithens in Spaine did rise and kill all the gentlemen in Spaine, and sithens that time have lyved merrily there.'[10] The handful of leaders were all artisans; and although the rising literally came to nothing (the leaders could find no followers), the Privy Council took the matter extremely seriously.

To write seriously about comedy can unfortunately give the impression that one has no sense of humor. Yet it is not implausible to see an allusion to a time of hardship not only in Titania's speech, but also in the name of one of Shakespeare's artisan actors, Robin Starveling. Titania's speech, with its invocation of natural rhythms and cosmic distress, invites large and complex notions of drama's relation to festivity and ritual action, traditionally connected with the seasonal cycle and the socialization of fertility; but Starveling's name and artisanal status reminds us that harvest cycles have social and economic correlatives. Their intersection in Shakespeare's play needs to be warily described, not least because certain theorists of popular culture, especially in France, have emphasized how easy it was for festival or carnival events to get out of control and become riots, or, conversely, as in the notorious Carnival at Romans, to serve as the pretext for organized class warfare.[11]

It cannot now be erased from our consciousness that when Shakespeare committed himself to write *A Midsummer Night's Dream* his environment was, if anything, even more disturbed than it had been in 1591–2. Nor do we need to posit his knowledge of the puny Oxfordshire rising, late in 1596. According to Brian Manning, there were at least thirteen disturbances in 1595 alone in London and suburbs, of which twelve took place between 6 and 29 June,[12] that is to say, in that same Midsummer season that the Privy Council had seen as part of the problem in 1592. Of these, on was initiated by a silk-weaver who reproached the mayor for misgovernment, and was rescued from confinement in Bedlam by the intervention of the crowd. Another, on 29 June, involved 1,000 rioters, a mixture of artisans and apprentices (including silk-weavers), took several days to suppress, and concluded, on 24 July, with the execution of five persons.[13] A pamphlet published to explain the severity of the punishment insisted that the insurgents were precisely not to be excused by the concept that carnival behavior had gotten out of hand:

> But it may (by some) be here objected, sedition and rebellion are unfit tearmes to be used in the case I am now to handle: for the Prentises of London had no seditious purpose, no intention of open rebellion. Truely I perswade me, a headlong wilfulnes continued by a custome of abused libertie, gave first fyre to this unadvised flame: but he that shall dout, that a most trecherous resolution, and dangerous purpose followed, shall make question at a most apparent truthe . . .[14]

On 5 November 1595, the Stationers' Register listed *The poor man's Complaint*, and on 23 August 1596, *Sundrye newe and artificiall Remedies against famyne . . .uppon the occasion of this present Dearthe*. Well before November 1596, then, when Stere staged his sequel to these events Shakespeare would have seen the social and cultural signs of unusual, economic distress; and he might even have noticed how frequently weavers were featured in the more public and violent protests. As Buchanan Sharp observed,

> Most of the symptoms of social distress are to be found in the words and actions of artisans in general and clothmakers in particular;...they made the loudest complaints about food prices and unemployment by means of riot, attempted insurrections, and frequent petitions to local justices and to the Privy Council...it was to their complaints above all that the authorities listened and responded in the formulation of policy.'[15]

All this being said, and all the more clearly for its admission, Shakespeare's play evidently staged its own resistance to social pessimism, and especially, perhaps, to the argument that festival liberty leads to violence. Shakespeare did not, however, close his eyes to the social scene. By invoking the dangerous Midsummer season in his title, by featuring a group of artisans as his comic protagonists, by making their leader a weaver, by allowing class consciousness to surface, as we shall see, in their relations with their courtly patrons, and especially in the repeated fears expressed by the artisans that violence is feared from them ('Write me a prologue, and let the prologue seem to say we will do no harm with our swords' (3:1:15–17)), he faced his society squarely; and instead of the slippage from carnival to force, he offered it a genuinely festive proposition. Bartholomew Stere's assertion that rebellion was the only route to 'a meryer world'[16] is countered (whether before or after its utterance) by Shakespeare's promise that 'Robin shall restore amends'. The *Dream*, therefore, seems to have aspired to the role of legitimate mediation that, in *Henry VI, Part 2*, only an aristocratic counsellor was authorized to perform.

Of all the comedies, this one offers the most powerful invitation to explain it by some theory of festive practices. The question is, which branch of festive theory? There are three main branches to which the *Dream* has hitherto been tied, directly or implicitly. All have support from some part of the text, but none by itself can explain the whole. Indeed, they tend partially to contradict each other, or perhaps to repeat a contest that was actually occurring in Shakespeare's day. The first is based on Shakespeare's allusion to Elizabeth's lunar presence in Oberon's speech, which, as in Rowe's theory of compliment, has been used to argue that she must have been present in the original audience: and this assumption, combined with the fact that *within* the play a marriage is celebrated, has produced an 'occasionalist' argument: that the *Dream* was itself written to celebrate an aristocratic wedding.[17] This occasionalist theory relies, primarily, on the *Dream's* opening and closing emphasis on a season of 'merriment' ordered by Theseus, in order to change the tone of his courtship of Hippolyta from conquest to celebration, and on his goodnight speech after the artisans' play is ended:

> ...Sweet friends, to bed,
> A fortnight hold we this solemnity,
> In nightly revels and new jollity.
>
> (5:1:369–72)

Despite the difficulty that critics experience in finding an appropriate marital occasion during 1595–6, and an uneasy recognition that the play seems rather to *problematize* than celebrate marriage, it is somewhat alarming to see how readily this hypothesis has been absorbed as fact into texts designed for students; Sylvan Barnet, in the Signet edition, for example, states categorically that the *Dream* 'was undoubtedly intended as a dramatic epithalamium to celebrate the marriage of some aristocrat' (xxv). And the occasionalist premise also associates the reader with the courtly circle around Theseus, and therefore with the Thesean aesthetic. Yet this framing festive plot actually represents a strategy by which popular drama was increasingly brought, involuntarily, under court control. By identifying Philostrate (in the list of Dramatis Personae) as 'Master of the Revels' to Theseus, the Folio text of the *Dream* alludes to an office created by Elizabeth in 1581 as an instrument for ensuring high quality in her own entertainment, for initiating the recentralization of the theater under court patronage, and for keeping it under surveillance.[18] Although the office did not become as influential under Elizabeth as later under James, and the theater in the 1590s continued to be alternatively tolerated and regulated by local authorities, with the Privy Council and the Lord Chamberlain intervening as little or as much as court policy dictated, its very title designates a much smaller, more tightly supervised and essentially courtly concept of dramatic entertainment than Shakespeare's theater generally assumes. Rather, Shakespeare's own situation as a member of the Chamberlain's company would situate him somewhere *between* the court and amateur popular theatricals, with the occasional 'command performance' bringing him closer to Bottom and his colleagues than to those, frequently themselves aristocrats, who created the royal entertainments. The artisanal hope of being 'made men', with 'sixpence a day' for life, is a parodic version of that discontinuous patronage relation; but the play speaks more to its uneasiness than to its rewards, as well as to Shakespeare's self-consciousness about how the popular theatrical impulse was in danger of being appropriated to hegemonic ends.

The second branch of festive theory refers not to courtly revels but to popular rituals, and assumes that the play was motivated less by the social needs of the Elizabethan court than by instincts and behavior usually interrogated by anthropologists. When C. L. Barber published his groundbreaking *Shakespeare's Festive Comedy* in 1959,[19] he connected Shakespeare with a large and today still expanding intellectual movement that includes the work of Durkheim, Van Gennep and Victor Turner. Barber's innovation was to set Shakespeare's early comedies in the socio-historical context of English popular games, entertainments and the rituals accompanying Easter, May, Whitsun, Midsummer, or Christmas holidays, or the harvest home. Some of these festive occasions, like the annual excursions from rural parishes to bring in the May, which Robert Herrick's gorgeous *Corinna's Going a Maying* and Phillip Stubbes' virulent *Anatomie of Abuses* both, though from opposite points of view, represent as an excuse for feminine defloration, were vestiges of ancient pagan fertility rites. In the *Dream*, Theseus assumes that the four young lovers whom he has found asleep in the forest 'rose up early to observe / The rite of May' (4:1:135–6). Others, like the lord of Misrule festivities primarily associated with the twelve days of Christmas, were secularized versions of the religious Feast of Fools, which enacted the Christian inversions of exalting the low and humbling the proud. In *Twelfth Night*, this temporary misrule is epitomized in the name of Olivia's 'allowed fool', Feste, and in Feste's antithesis to Malvolio the puritan, who would unduly narrow the space permitted to fooling in a courtly household and so becomes its victim. But misrule was also adapted to and merged with the country feasts and improvized in taverns, a social fact that Shakespeare explores in *Henry IV*. Morris dances, too, like May Day rituals with their phallic Maypoles, were genetically connected to fertility rites, as well as to the legends of Robin Hood with their theme of social outlawry. The morris, as a mixture of sexual energy and political subversion, was extremely interesting not only to Puritan writers like Stubbes but also to Elizabethan and Jacobean dramatists. While Titania's reference to the 'nine men's morris. . . filled up with mud' is a pun (within a lament for infertility) that overrides an alternative etymology,[20] Shakespeare alludes to the transgressive aspects of the morris in *Henry VI, Part 2*, where Jack Cade is described by Richard of York, who plans to exploit his energies, as capering 'like a wild Morisco, Shaking the bloody darts as he his bells' (3:1:346–66). In *Henry V* the Dauphin, assuming that Henry is still in his tavern phase, mocks the English preparations for war as a 'Whitsun morris dance' (2:4:25); and Hamlet compares his dead father to the morris-dancer's hobby-horse, 'whose epitaph is 'For O, for O, the hobby-horse is forgot' (3:2:140–1); his mother's disloyalty and the failure to commemorate his father participates in the broader betrayal of drama's roots and his country's ancient customs.[21] These instances carry important valences, national, cultural and political, which seem to privilege the past and the primitive even as they are registered as such.

In Barber's view, however, all of these festive or folk elements in Shakespeare's plays were part of a cultural migration in which the archaic and amateur forms of dramatic representation and ritual were absorbed by the mature national theater. Claiming that saturnalian impulse, 'when directly expressed, ran head on into official prohibition', Barber concluded that the transfer of festive impulses to the theater was an enforced 'shift from symbolic *action* towards *symbolic* action' (p. 57).

> Shakespeare's theater was taking over on a professional and everyday basis functions which until his time had largely been performed by amateurs on holiday. And he wrote at a moment when the educated part of society was modifying a ceremonial, ritualistic conception of human life to create a historical, psychological conception. His drama, indeed, was an important agency in this transformation:... In making drama out of rituals of state, Shakespeare makes clear their meaning as social and psychological conflict, as history. So too with the rituals of pleasure, of misrule, as against rule: his comedy presents holiday magic as imagination, games as expressive gestures. (p. 15)

This is the move that aestheticizes; that seeks to distinguish between 'art' and 'life', between literary and non-literary texts; and that therefore, in its invocation of the unexaminable (Thesean) term, 'imagination', begs the very questions that cultural historians must attempt to answer. Barber's strongest message was that both the archaic festivals and their Elizabethan echoes functioned to reaffirm, through reconciliatory symbolic action, the hierarchical structure of society.

If Barber represents the idealist version derived from social history, its equivalent in anthropology is found in the work of Victor Turner, himself much influenced, however, by Barber. In a late work, *From Ritual to Theatre*,[22] Turner admitted that his own thinking had been shaped by 'early exposure to theatre', specifically *The Tempest*, which Turner had seen as a child of five. In *The Ritual Process* (1969), Turner developed his theory of *communitas*, or the individual's sense of belonging, voluntarily, to a larger, cohesive and harmonious social group, on the idealist model of ritual action inherited from Durkheim and Van Gennep. Thus Turner argued initially that 'cognitively, nothing underlines regularity so well as absurdity or paradox. Emotionally, nothing satisfies as much as extravagant or temporarily permitted illicit behavior.' This regulatory motive accounts for the fact, he thought, that inversion rituals occur most often 'at fixed points in the annual cycle...for structural regularity is here reflected in temporal order'.[23] However, in the later *Dramas, Fields, and Metaphors*, inversion rituals were seen rather as motivated by some natural disaster or 'public, overt breach or deliberate non-fulfilment of some crucial norm', which requires remedial intervention rather than regulatory confirmation.[24] And communitas was reconceived as running *counter* to the stratified and rule-governed conception of society, in the space that Turner called *liminality*, in which social distinctions are temporarily suspended. In liminal situations, the lower social strata become privileged, and bodily parts and biological referents, conceived as the source of regenerative energy, are revalued; hence the ritual use of animal disguises, masks and gestures. An exchange takes place, Turner argued, between the normative or ideological poles of social meaning, which dictate attitudes to parents, children, elders and rulers, and the physiological poles or facts of life (birth, death, sexuality) which the norms exist to regulate; and in this exchange 'the biological referents are ennobled and the normative referents are charged with emotional significance' (p. 55), which renders them once again acceptable.

By proposing this ritual exchange between rules and energies as demanded by natural disasters or unusual breaches in social relations, Turner's model seems more promising than Barber's for interrogating the most ritual components of the *Dream*, the breach between Oberon and Titania that has resulted in crop failure and disrupted the natural cycle, and the manner in which that breach will be healed. But even in its late form Turner's festive theory remains idealist, in the sense that the purpose of festive rituals is, in the last analysis, reconciliation, getting the social rhythms running smoothly once more.

There is, of course, an alternative possibility: that popular festival forms and inversion rituals were actually subversive in intent and function all along. This position is represented in Shakespeare studies by Robert Weimann, and more generally by Mikhail Bakhtin's study of Rabelais, preceded as it was by a social history of carnival forms. Weimann's magisterial study established the possibility of a class-conscious analysis of popular traditions, and, by extending the inquiry to the tragedies, discovered the levelling implications of Shakespeare's fools, clowns and grave-diggers.[25] Bakhtin, to whom Victor Turner acknowledged a debt, provided our most powerful explanation of carnival's emphasis on the material grotesque, or the 'lower bodily stratum', belly, buttocks and genitals. This movement of festive impulse downwards, or degradation, Bakhtin argued, was intended as social fertilization: 'to bury, to sow, and to kill simultaneously, in order to bring forth something more and better. . . .Grotesque realism knows no other level; it is the fruitful earth and the womb. It is always conceiving.'[26] But he also insisted that fertilization was essentially a social myth of populist self-definition and incorporation:

We repeat: the body and bodily life have here a cosmic and at the same time an all-people's character; this is not the body and its physiology in the modern sense of these words, because it is not individualized. The material bodily principle is contained not in the biological individual, not in the bourgeois ego, but in the people, a people who are continually growing and renewed . . . the collective ancestral body of all the people. (p. 19)

Yet, though both of these influential studies assume a Marxist theory of history, neither finally provided a radical solution to the old polarities that have plagued aesthetic debates since their first beginnings: high versus low culture, mind versus body, consciousness versus material practise. Weimann's book was as deeply influenced by Barber as by Marx, producing in effect a version of the Thesean aesthetic, by which the festive and ritual elements that Shakespeare recorded were seen as the raw material for a new formal synthesis of the natural with the conventional, of primitive with learned humanist materials; and Shakespeare himself, working at a transitional moment when social change made visible the very concept of archaism, appears as the genius at the end of evolutionary trail. Leaning on the modern preference for a disinterested art, Weimann praised 'Shakespeare's universal vision of experience' as 'more comprehensive and more vital . . . in . . . its skepticism and its freedom', than either of the traditions it drew from (p. 251); and even his own insights into the subversiveness of topsy-turveydom were constrained by the conviction that class consciousness was not fully available as a category of thought in Shakespeare's time. The echoes of folk misrule in the plays were, he thought, 'playfully rebellious gestures', and 'the contradictions between the popular tradition and the culture of the ruling classes were to some extent synthesized with the needs and aspirations of the New Monarchy and were overshadowed by an overwhelming sense of national pride and unity' (pp. 24–5).

Bakhtin could equally be charged (and indeed has been) with universalism, for insufficiently specifying the historical vectors of carnival events.[27] For while he situated Rabelais in a 'history of laughter' from the middle ages to the nineteenth century, with occasional references to Marxist historiography, Bakhtin explicitly rejected Veselovsky's nineteenth-century theory of clowning as a populist defence against feudal values: 'No doubt,' wrote Bakhtin, 'laughter was in part an external defensive form of truth':

It was legalized, it enjoyed privileges, it liberated, to a certain extent, from censorship, oppression, and from the stake. But . . . laughter is essentially not an external but an interior form of truth . . . Laughter liberates not only from exterior censorship but first of all from the great interior censor; it liberates from the fear that developed in man during thousands of years; fear of the sacred, of prohibitions, of the past, of power . . . The seriousness of fear and suffering in their religious, social, political, and ideological forms could not but be impressive. The consciousness of freedom, on the other hand, could be only limited and utopian (pp. 94–5)

'It would therefore be a mistake,' Bakhtin concluded, to presume that festive and carnival forms expressed 'a critical and clearly defined opposition' (p. 95).

In what follows, I propose to create a gargantuan mingle-mangle of the strongest and boldest suggestions that these different festive theories proffer, while pushing them beyond their own aesthetic or procedural inhibitions. I rely for conceptual support on Shakespeare himself, who within the text of *A Midsummer Night's Dream* seems to have recognized much of the thinking I have just described and the conflicting interests it represents (then and now); and, by making the different versions of festive theory modify and correct each other, produced in the end a more capacious proposal. Within the aristocratic premise of 'revels', for instance, certain surprises are introduced. Theseus's selection of the 'tragical mirth' of the artisans' play is carefully articulated as a rejection of learned, humanist entertainments:

> 'The battle of the Centaurs, to be sung
> By an Athenian eunuch to the harp.'
> We'll none of that;
> 'The riot of the tipsy Bacchanals,
> Tearing the Thracian singer in their rage.'
> That is an old device
> 'The thrice three Muses mourning for the death
> Of Learning, late deceas'd in beggary'?
> That is some satire, keen and critical,
> Not sorting with a nuptial ceremony.
>
> (5:1:44–55)

What does sort with a nuptial ceremony, apparently, includes the ribald: the by-play on Wall's 'stones' (a vulgarism for testicles) 'chink' and 'hole', through which Pyramus and Thisbe try to make physical contact. 'My cherry lips,' complains Thisbe to Wall, who is of course a man, 'have often kiss'd thy stones, / Thy stones with lime and hair knit up in thee' (5:1:190–1). It is noteworthy that neither the Quarto nor the Folio text authorizes the stage direction 'Wall holds up his fingers', a bowdlerizing intervention added by Edward Capell in 1767 and now a standard feature of modern editions, running counter to the text's bawdry, and discouraging a producer from having Pyramus and Thisbe bend to reach each other through the open legs of Snout the tinker.[28] Yet this interpretation, and the kind of laughter it would provoke, would have 'sorted' well with the sexual ambience of Renaissance wedding festivities, as well as with their archaic precedents in bedding rituals; 'in which,' remarked George Puttenham in his *Arte of English Poesie* (1589), 'if there were any wanton or lascivious matter more then ordinarie which they called *Ficenina licentia* it was borne withal for that time because of the matter no lesse requiring.'[29] Even the main festive plot, therefore, requires the *Dream's* audience, then and now, to consider the relationship between broad sexual humor and the social construction of the audience; for by making his courtiers enjoy this 'palpable gross' entertainment Shakespeare precludes the argument that his obscenity was really beneath him, designed only for those convenient receptacles of critical discards, the 'groundlings'. In Bakhtin's terms, the boundary between courtly and popular entertainment is broached by the material grotesque, by the laughter that drives the festive imagination downwards to the lower bodily stratum.

On the other hand, the festive plot that most attracted Barber's attention, the May game that takes the four young lovers into the forest, cannot be explained merely in Barber's terms, as one of those archaic fertility rituals absorbed and contained by the transforming imagination; not, at any rate, unless that imagination is as defined by Theseus. It is, after all, only Theseus who, finding them asleep after the confusions of identity and erotic attraction are resolved, assumes 'they rose up early to observe / The rite of May' (4:1:131–2), whereas in fact the motive for the transgressive excursion was escape from parental and patriarchal oppression. Barber's account of the magical doings in the forest underestimates the severity not of the 'sharp Athenian law' (1:1:162) by which marital arrangements were based on dynastic as opposed to erotic imperatives, but of Shakespeare's treatment of it; a law administered by Theseus, and manifestly intended to be felt by the audience as unjust, while reminding them of its correlative in Elizabethan England. At the very least, then, we need for this part of the *Dream* a festive theory that, like Victor Turner's, admits the political or ideological dimension of festive actions, some sense of the norms of 'respect for elders' and 'obedience to political authorities' that ritual will again render acceptable. But if we look to Turner for a model for the way this plot is handled we shall still be disappointed. There is no exchange between rules and energies in this tale of adolescent silliness, underlined by the very ease with which the young people's emotions are rearranged. Even Shakespeare's calendrical vagueness (is it May or Midsummer?) which evidently worried Barber,[30] is naughtily incompatible with Turner's original theory that the festival calendar mimics and hence reinforces social order. The callowness of the young escapees, moreover, remains when the parental and societal inhibitions have been finessed away, not by a genuine reconciliation, but by magical legerdemain. It expresses itself in their mockery of the very play that speaks to what their own predicament was, and what its ending might have been. When Bottom leaps up to 'assure' his courtly audience that 'the wall is down that parted their fathers', and that burials are therefore unnecessary (5:1:337–8), he marks, as they themselves are incapable of doing, the sociological seriousness that their own festive plot implied. Once again, the courtly and the popular seem to change places; and it only adds to the complexity of the exchange that the artisans do *not* present an entertainment with its roots in folk tradition; rather, they struggle to give the courtiers what they might be supposed to admire, an Ovidian legend in the high rhetorical and hence self-parodying mode.

But more transgressive still is the third festive plot – Titania's quarrel with Oberon over the changeling boy, which results in disastrous weather and crop failure, and which can only be resolved by the most extreme example of status inversion and misrule that Shakespeare's canon contains, the infatuation of the Queen of Fairies with a common artisan who is also, temporarily, an ass. This is the plot, also, that Louis Montrose has marvellously related to psychoanalytic conceptions of gender and power in Elizabeth's reign, and, under the aegis of Theseus's phrase for imaginative work, 'Shaping Fantasies', suggested that within the fantasy of Titania's liaison with Bottom lies 'a discourse of anxious misogyny' precipitated by the myth of the Virgin Queen and the pressures it exerted on male sensibilities.[31] Montrose put vital pressure on aspects of the play that Barber's benign thesis overlooked – the dark pre-history of Theseus as betrayer of women, the repressed myth of Amazonian independence that Hippolyta represents, the harshness of Theseus's treatment of Hermia (even during his own festive season), Titania's elegiac account of her friendship with the changeling boy's mother, who died in childbirth, even the subjects of the rejected entertainments, with their allusions to eunuchs and Centaurs, rape and dismemberment.

While Montrose's approach is true to the *Dream*'s mixture of light and dark, and subtle in its handling of the Elizabethan semiotics of gender, his psychoanalytic reading does not give Shakespeare his due. It implies that these darker resonances in the play rose up from its author's and the national (male) unconscious, as distinct from being part of a conscious analytic project. Assuming that the *Dream* in its conclusion both 'reaffirms essential elements of a patriarchal ideology', and 'calls that reaffirmation in question', Montrose determines that those contradictory projects occur 'irrespective of authorial intention' (p. 74). And Montrose's psychoanalytic theory also distracts attention from the socioeconomic component in the episode that he reads as the male's revenge – the amazing suggestion not only that a queen could be made by magic to mate with a male from the bottom stratum of society – as well as from the fact that its results are positive. For thanks to Bottom the weaver, the crisis in the natural cycle and the agricultural economy is resolved, albeit by restoring male authority. In Montrose's essay, Titania's liaison with Bottom is related not to festive inversions, but rather to the dream of Simon Forman, professional physician and amateur drama critic, who fantasized that the queen had made herself sexually available to him; and it is only a detail, over which Montrose does not pause, that his dream rival for the queen's affections is 'a weaver, a tall man with a reddish beard, distract of his wits' (p. 62). In *both* dreams, fortuitously, Forman's and Shakespeare's, there is staged a contest for significance, for exegetical control, between critic and weaver, high and low culture. But in Shakespeare's *Dream*, the weaver (who is also a dreamer) wins.

Let us now return to Turner's proposal that rituals of status inversion or revitalization frequently make use of animal masks, and imagine with new eyes what the Elizabethan audience might have seen when Bottom appears on the stage with an ass's head replacing his own. Weimann had noted 'the surprising consistency of the ass' head motif from the *mimus* down to *A Midsummer Night's Dream*,' (p. 50); but he assumed that it, like the calf's hide which the Elizabethan fool still wore in the Mummer's Play, the coxcomb, antlers, horns, and foxtail, was merely 'the survival of some kind of mimetic magic, which, after having lost its ritual function, became alienated from its original purpose and hence misunderstood as a comic attribute' (p. 31). But in the *Dream*, the ass's head distinguishes itself from comic props and animal masks in general, and becomes part of a complex structural pun, by which the ritual exchange between rules and energies does after all take place, and the lower bodily parts are, as in Turner's theory, ennobled. Bottom is not only the bottom of the social hierarchy as the play represents it, but also the 'bottom' of the body when seated, literally the social ass or arse. It is typical of the Oxford English Dictionary's conservativism that it does not sanction this meaning of the word in Shakespeare's day, with the result that generations of editors have been satisfied with 'bottom' as a technical term for the bobbin in weaving. Yet as Frankie Rubinstein observes in her dictionary of Shakespeare's sexual puns, Shakespeare and his contemporaries took for granted that *ass*, as the vulgar, dialectical spelling of *arse*, was the meeting point of a powerful set of linked concepts: 'Shakespeare...used "ass" to pun on the ass that gets beaten with a stick and the arse that gets thumped sexually, the ass that gets beaten with a stick and the arse that gets thumped sexually, the ass that bears a burden and the arse that bears or carries in intercourse.'[32] And she cites in analogy the Fool's rebuke to Lear that speaks to a male humiliation by the female, paternal by filial: 'When thy clovest thy crown i' th' middle, and gav'st away both parts, thou bor'st [barest] thine ass on thy back o'er the dirt: thou hadst little wit in thy bald crown when thou gav'st thy golden one away...thou gav'st them the rod, and putt'st down thine own breeches's (1:4:167–71, 180–1). Here exposed bodily parts, top and bottom, crown and arse, unite in a political allegory of status inversion and corporal punishment. And in the 1640s, John Milton mode the same set of meanings converge in a metaphorical beating of one of his opponents: 'I may chance not fail to endorse him on the backside of posterity, not a golden, but a brazen Asse';[33] thereby including in the multiple pun, for good measure, *The Golden Ass* of Longinus.

In the *Dream*, the structural pun on *ass* is anticipated by Puck's gratuitous 'bottom' humor, his account of pretending to be a stool that removes itself from under the buttocks of 'the wisest aunt telling the saddest tale' being an early warning signal of popular fundamentalism:

> Then slip I from her bum, down topples she,
> And 'tailor' cries...
>
> (2:1:51–4)

Here the play on *tale/tail(er)* is one of the puns that Howard Bloch, himself influenced by Bakhtin, explored in his rule-breaking study of the French medieval fabliaux.[34] Bloch argued that these jokes are ultimately metacritical and serve to theorize the jongleur's profession. The Old French homophony between *con* (cunt) and *conte* (tale) 'or, in English, the tail and the tale...signifies the closeness of physical and linguistic longings'; postmodernist theory fuses 'the desire so often expressed in sexual terms on the level of theme and the desire for the story itself' (p. 109). But because Bottom is also an ass, the structural pun in the *Dream* has a still more complex resonance, one that requires precisely those social categories from which Bloch's deconstructive work, regrettably, would liberate popular obscenity.

In the great medieval encylopaedia of Bartholomaeus Anglicus, translated in 1582 by Stephen Batman as *Batman upon Bartholome*, the ass is defined as a creature in whom coalesce the meaning-systems implied by Shakespeare's puns: 'The Asse is called Asinus, and hath that name of Sedendo, as it were a beast to sit upon....and is a simple beast and a slow, and therefore soone overcome & subject to mannes service' (XIX:419). The theme of servitude symbolized by the ass was, of course, rendered fully allegorical by Apuleius, whose episode of Lucius's period of slavery in the bakery has been recognized as 'the only passage in the whole of ancient literature which realistically...examines the conditions of slave-exploitation on which the culture of the ancient world rested.'[35] And Bakhtin, who claimed that the ass is 'one of the most ancient and lasting symbols of the material bodily lower stratum, which at the same time degrades and regenerates', connected *The Golden Ass* with the 'feast of the ass' which commemorates the Flight to Egypt, and also with the legends of St Francis of Assisi.[36]

As visual pun and emblem, therefore, Bottom stands at the fulcrum of Shakespeare's analysis of the festive impulse in human social structures. Is he merely a comic figure, the appropriate butt of Thesean critical mockery, and his liaison with Titania the worst humiliation an upstart queen could suffer? Or does his (im)proper name, in symbolic alliance with his ass's head, invoke rather an enquiry into the way in which the lower social orders, as well as the 'lower bodily stratum', function, and suggest that the service they perform and the energies they contain, are usually undervalued? Hinting as to how this question might be answered, Shakespeare included a brilliant gloss on the multiple pun that is Bottom, keying his festive theory into the most impeccable source of ideology available to him. At the moment of his transformation back into manhood, Bottom implicates his own ritual naming in the central act of interpretation that the *Dream* demands:

> Man is but an ass if he go about to expound this dream. Methought I was – there is no man can tell what. Methought I was – and methought I had – but man is but a patched fool if he will offer to say what methought I had. The eye of man hath not heard, the ear of man hath not seen, man's hand is not able to taste, his tongue to conceive, nor his heart to report, what my dream was. I will get Peter Quince to write a ballad of this dream: It shall be called 'Bottom's Dream,' because it hath no bottom. (4:1:205–15)

It has long been recognized that this passage contains an allusion to I Corinthians 2:9 ('Eye hath not seen, nor ear heard, neither have entered into the heart of man, the things which God hath prepared for them that love him'). But so quick have most commentators been to denigrate Bottom that they focus only on his jumbling of the biblical text, rather than on its context of profound spiritual levelling. Even Weimann, who connected it to his theme of popular topsy-turveydom (p. 40), does not pursue the biblical context to its logical conclusion, in I Corinthians 12:14–15, where the metaphor of the body is developed more fully in terms of a Christian communitas:

> If the whole body were an eye, where would be the hearing? If the whole body were an ear, where would be the sense of smell? But as it is, God arranged the organs in the body, each one of them, as he chose. If all were a single organ, where would the body be? As it is,. . . the parts of the body which seem to be weaker are indispensable, and those parts of the body we invest with greater honor, and our unpresentable parts are treated with greater modesty, which our more presentable parts do not require. But God has so adjusted the body, giving the greater honor to the inferior part, that there may be no discord in the body, but that the members may have the same care for one another.

In the *Dream* which has no bottom because Bottom dreamed it, the 'unpresentable parts' of the social body are invested with greater honor by their momentary affinity with a utopian vision that Bottom wisely decides he is incapable of putting into words, at least into words in their normal order. Shakespeare's warning to the audience is unmistakable; prudent readers, especially those who are themselves unprivileged, will resist the pressure to interpret the vision. Yet its inarticulate message remains: a revaluation of those 'unpresentable' members of society, normally mocked as fools and burdened like asses, whose energies the social system relies on.

But how far did this social criticism intend to go? How much are we really to make of the artisans' fears of frightening the ladies, and the constant need to break the dramatic illusion lest the courtly audience think that their mimic swords are drawn in earnest? What is to be made of the prologue actually written for the playlet, that 'tangled chain [of being]; nothing impaired, but all disordered' (5:1:124–5) which, as Leinwand observed, 'teeters back and forth between deference and offensiveness',[37] creating in its *double entendres* the very sociopolitical apprehensions that the artisans most wished to avoid? And what was the London theatrical ambience in 1595–6? In September 1595 the Mayor wrote to the Privy Council 'Toutching the putting doune of the plaies at the Theater & Bankside which is a great cause of disorder in the Citie', and specifically proposed a connection between this and the 'late stirr & mutinous attempt of those few apprentices and other servantes, who wee doubt not driew their infection from these & like places'.[38] This record connects with the Privy Council's embargo in 1592, as also with the memory of that 'Play at Windham' that had actually, if the historians of Kett's uprising were to be believed, served as the occasion for a major social upheaval. Yet in 1595–6, if *A Midsummer Night's Dream* is to be believed, Shakespeare was willing to argue, with Montaigne, that there could be 'honest exercises of recreation', that plays acted 'in the presence of the magistrates themselves' might actually promote 'common societie and loving friendship'. The *Dream* imagines a festive spirit deeper and more generous than the courtly revels that seemed, in the 1590s, to be appropriating plays and actors; an idea of social play that could cross class boundaries without obscuring them, and by those crossings imagine the social body whole again; and a transgressive, carnival spirit daring enough to register social criticism, while holding off the phantom of 'the Play at Windham', the dramatic scene of violent social protest. It would not be until after *King Lear* (Shakespeare's darkest experiment in role-reversal and carnival exposure), and not until after the Midlands Rising (the country's gravest social crisis since 1549) that Shakespeare was forced to admit that the popular voice had grievances that the popular theater could no longer express comedically. In 1595–6, it only 'rehearse[d] most obscenely and courageously' (1:2:100–1) for that later, more demanding project.

There is, however, one qualification to this otherwise genial thesis. In 1549, we remember, the worst of the grievances listed by the ventriloquist was the rebels' sense that their case was the subject of mockery: 'their miserable condition, is *a laughing stocke to most proud and insolent men. Which thing...grieveth them so sore, and inflicteth such a staine of evill report: as nothing is more grievous for them to remember, nor more injust to suffer.*'[39] Economic deprivation and physical hardships, in other words, are deemed less oppressive than the mockery that makes of those same sufferings a 'laughing stocke'. In relation to the *Dream*, this part of the story is potent. When Bottom and his fellows are mocked by the aristocratic audience, the audience outside the *Dream* has the opportunity to consider whether or not to laugh themselves, which sort of festive spirit to select for their own enjoyment. If laughter is necessary to mediate social tensions, Shakespeare's festive theory seems to argue, then let it be a laughter as far removed as possible from the red-hot iron of social condescension.

4

Back by Popular Demand: The Two Versions of *Henry V*

For the fifth act in his history of the fifth Henry, Shakespeare suddenly required of his audience a shift in historical perspective. They are invited to imagine Henry's return, victorious from Agincourt, in terms of another anticipated return, presumably closer to their own immediate interest:

> now behold
> In the quick Forge and working-house of Thought,
> How London doth powre out her Citizens,
> The Maior and all his Brethren in best sort,
> Like to the Senatours of th'antique Rome,
> With the Plebeians swarming at their heeles,
> Goe forth and fetch their Conqu'ring Caesar in:
> As by a lower, but by loving likelyhood,
> Were now the Generall of our gracious Empresse,
> As in good time he may, from Ireland comming,
> Bringing Rebellion broached on his Sword,
> How many would the peacefull Citie quit,
> To welcome him?
>
> (*Folio*, TLN 2872–85)[1]

This Chorus, with its startling analogy between Elizabeth's most famous predecessor and her most notorious subject, Robert Devereux, second earl of Essex, currently in charge of the Irish campaign, demands that we juggle at least two meanings of 'history' as a category of thought: the fifteenth-century history that Shakespeare took over from Holinshed and others and rewrote to his own specifications, and the events in which he and his theater were environmentally situated in the late 1590s, and to some extent embroiled; while its *content* – the nature of popular leadership and the numerical signs of popularity ('How *many* would the peacefull Citie quit/to welcome him?') – requires a still more athletic intellectual response. Or rather, in Shakespeare's own terminology, the required activity is not so much athletic as artisanal, 'the quick Forge and working-house of Thought' associating the right imagination not with society's leaders but rather with that plebeian citizenry whose very breach of their normal workaday behavior is the sign of the extraordinary. And the fact that this Chorus did *not* appear in the only text of the play published in Shakespeare's lifetime raises still another issue – the relationship between 'history', 'popularity' and bibliography, or the story of how Shakespeare's playtexts were circulated in their own time and survived into ours. In the case of *Henry V* the story of the text is inseparable from the political history that is both its content and its context, as also from the thematics of the popular, here defined not as protest or festival but as the relationship of the many to the charismatic leader.

More than almost any other play of Shakespeare's, and certainly more than any other 'history', *Henry V* has generated accounts of itself that agree, broadly speaking, on the play's thematics – popular monarchy, national unity, militarist expansionism – but fall simply, even crudely, on either side of the line that divides belief from scepticism, idealism from cynicism, or, in contemporary parlance, legitimation from subversion. The most extreme example of the idealizing view, the film directed by Sir Laurence Olivier, was premiered in November 1944, in the context of the invasion of Normandy, and dedicated to the Commandos and Airborne Troops of Great Britian, 'the spirit of whose ancestors it has been humbly attempted to recapture'.[2] In the same year appeared E. M. W. Tillyard's influential study of the history plays, closely followed, in 1974, by Lily B. Campbell's, which to different degrees represented *Henry V* as the climax (successful or unsuccessful) of Shakespeare's own version of the Tudor myth, with Henry himself as Elizabeth's prototype.[3] As the nationalism of these projects was implicit, compared at least to Olivier's production, so their power to suggest an orthodoxy was greater.[4] Conversely, the age of nuclear deterrence and of ethically ambiguous geopolitical alliances has produced a criticism, both in England and in the United States, that looks rather at the tensions and contradictions in the Elizabethan ideology of ideal ruler, unified state, and providential history.[5]

The critical record, then, highlights the problem of intentionality, which will not be made to disappear by our focusing instead on the intentions of Shakespeare's readers; and any attempt to recuperate Shakespeare's own intentions must today grapple with the status of the texts that are all we have to work with. As it happens, the two surviving texts of *Henry V* point in different interpretive directions; the Folio can possibly sustain the hypothesis of ideological confusion or deliberate ambiguity; whereas the theses of Campbell and Tillyard could be better supported by *The Cronicle History of Henry the fifth*, the first Quarto version, which has long been ruled out of interpretive account by Shakespearean bibliographers, and placed in the evaluative category of the 'Bad Quartos', that is to say, beyond interpretive reach.[6] Though less textually unstable than *Hamlet* or *King Lear*, where the Quarto texts have strong claims to authorial cachet, *Henry V* therefore presents a unique challenge to the new textual studies, since its publication history is ineluctably connected to the major critical disagreements over the play's meaning and cultural function.

For the first Quarto version is not only shorter than the Folio but tonally different from it. Among the most striking absences in the Quarto are all five Choruses and the final Epilogue; hence, in the fifth Chorus, the non-appearance of the allusion to Essex's anticipated return from Ireland, which Gary Taylor has called 'the only explicit, extra-dramatic, incontestable reference to a contemporary *event* anywhere in the canon';[7] and with no epilogue, there is no final let-down, no admission that the legendary victory at Agincourt accomplished nothing, since in the following reign the regents for Henry VI 'lost France, and made his England bleed' (TLN 3379). These last lines, which subsume the heroic moment in the recursive patterns of history, were also excised from the Olivier production, which otherwise retained most of the Choruses;[8] and even in 1623 the Folio arrangement of the English histories by chronology of reign rather than of composition submerges the sceptical effect and makes Henry the center of the historical sweep through the fifteenth century rather than the last, inconclusive statement of the second tetralogy.

Also missing from the Quarto is Act 1, Scene 1, where the bishops cynically discuss how they are to motivate the war and distract the House of Commons from their plan to reclaim ecclesiastical property; the Hostess's claim in 2:1 that Falstaff is dying because 'The King has killed his heart'; almost all of the Harfleur episode, including the famous 'Once more unto the breach' speech by Henry, and most of his threats of violence upon the besieged citizens; much of the material in the scene before the battle of Agincourt, especially Henry's closing soliloquy on the hardships of kingship; several scenes in the French camp; all of Burgundy's speech on the damages suffered by France in the war; and much of the wooing scene between Kate and Henry. There is, however, nothing in the stage-historical records to refute the Quarto's claim that it represents the play as it was 'sundry times' acted by the Chamberlain's Company.[9] We simply do not know, in fact, what the performative version of *Henry V* was like; the Quarto may very well be closer than the Folio to what the London audiences actually saw on the stage at the absolute turn of the century.

The interest of the 1600 text has long been obscured by the theory of the Bad Quartos, a conception that took its authority from the piracy theory first circulated by the editors of the 1623 Folio, who referred to 'stolne, and surreptitious copies, maimed, and deformed by the frauds and stealthes of injurious impostors that exposed them' (A3r). And the piracy theory was in turn supported by that of memorial reconstruction, or dictation from memory by one or more actors complicit with a piratical printer.[10] These theories, rich in moral opprobium, easily merged with subjective accounts of the *quality* of the differences observed, with the Folio versions of the plays being designated as 'artistically' superior. But this entire hypothesis is now in question. A more sceptical view is emerging of the claims made by John Heminge and Henry Condell in promoting their own edition; the theory of memorial reconstruction is under attack; and Peter Blayney, in rejecting the notion of piracy, draws our attention to Humphrey Moseley's own advertisement for the Beaumont and Fletcher Folio of 1647, where, in the course of explaining why he has taken the trouble to acquire authorial manuscripts, Moseley witnesses to an entirely reputable method of transmitting abridged playtexts to potential publishers:

> When these Comedies and Tragedies were presented on the Stage, the Actours omitted some Scenes and Passages (with the Author's consent) as occasion led them; and when private friends desir'd a Copy, they then (and justly too) transcribed what they Acted.[11]

The parentheses here, 'with the author's consent' and 'justly too', speak to a theatrical practice of communal ownership of acting versions, and the open, legitimate exchange, commercial or otherwise, of transcriptions made by the actors of those versions.[12]

Memorial reconstruction may still be needed to explain those parts of a Quarto text (fewer than has been claimed) which are patently so garbled as to resist explanation by this new sociology of the theater. But we can now understand a feature of Quarto texts that memorial reconstruction could not account for – the omission of whole scenes or large blocks of material. In the case of *Henry V*, the omitted materials are so bulky and so crucial that other hypotheses have gradually emerged. The Arden edition admits at least three, each implying intention – the aesthetic ('cut for compression'), the political ('cut...possibly for censorship') and the socioeconomic ('cut...for a reduced cast on tour in the provinces.')[13] These suggestions, if not incompatible, derive from quite different critical assumptions and agendas; and poised uncertainly between them is the inference that the style of the Quarto version is more popular, in the sense of being lower and more *common* than the Folio. As John Walter put it for the Arden edition, 'Generally there is a lowering of pitch, a substitution of cliché and common currency of daily speech for the more heightened style of the Folio.'

A. H. 1942

This notion was first proposed by Alfred Hart in 1942, in support of his own version of the Bad Quarto theory. For him the Quartos were memorial reconstructions of previous abridgements of the plays prepared by

Shakespeare's own company in accordance with theatrical experience. The excisions, Hart thought, were often theatrically intelligent but linguistically impoverished. The professional abridger 'knew his audience loved an interesting story, packed with plenty of action and told in simple language, and rid the play of similes, amplificatory passages, platitudes, philosophic reflections, repetition, classical commonplaces, and literary ornament.'[14] But even the best of the Bad Quartos (and *Henry V* is one of the best) reveal reportorial incompetence incompatible with the work of 'an educated man':

> Most of the [divergent] passages share certain characteristics in common – little elevation of thought, a certain coarseness verging on vulgarity, almost complete lack of fancy or imagination, dull, pedestrian and irregular verse, poor and overworked vocabulary, frequent errors in grammar and syntax, and a primitive type of sentence-construction. King, queen, cardinal, duchess, peer, soldier, lover, courtier, artisan, peasant, servant and child all speak alike... Essentially each of these and many other speeches exhibit all the marks of garrulous illiteracy... (p. 104).

From the newly self-conscious posture that a critic in the 1980s is privileged to adopt, one can see how deeply Hart's view of the Bad Quartos has collated the moralism of his predecessors in the field of bibliography with a class consciousness that distinguishes the 'educated' text (one that endorses social hierarchies) from the 'illiterate' reproduction that blurs them.

Hart's theory of the text was split – not only between contradictory notions of good theater and good writing, but also between his wished-for separation of Shakespeare from Badness and the knowledge that within the theatrical practice of the Chamberlain's Men such separation was unlikely. Hart actually imagined a scene in which Shakespeare, having previously, 'on fire with passion and emotions...filled *Hamlet* with 1,600 lines of long speeches', later heard them read aloud. He would then, Hart felt, 'have shaken his head in critical disapproval and accepted the decision of his fellows to declaim less than a half of these speeches on the stage' (p. 168). In this scenario, Shakespeare collaborates in the act of abridgment at least to the point of authorizing major cuts; and the notion of Shakespeare's 'critical disapproval' of his own longer first draft runs counter to Hart's own critical disapproval of the Bad Quartos in general.

Hart's confusions mark the transition from a Romantic aesthetics of genius to a modern sociology of the theater. The notion that censorship was one motive for the Quarto's reductions has different origins. In 1928, Evelyn May Albright argued that the Folio 'represents the text of a play intended for use on a special occasion at the Globe before an audience of statesmen and courtiers at the critical moment preceding the return of Essex from Ireland in the autumn of 1599.'[15] She saw the Folio as being broadly supportive of Essex and his policies, whereas the Quarto, intended for publication, was 'shorn of the most significant personal and political references,' (p. 753). She thus keyed the play not into the history of printing, but into political history, specifically the history of Essex's rebellion, whose connection to Shakespeare's company has long been established. I refer to the special production on 5 February, 1601, the eve of the earl of Essex's rebellion, of 'the play. . . of Kyng Harry the iiijth, and of the kylling of Kyng Richard the second played by the L. Chamberlen's players'.[16] And while Albright's thesis of *another* special performance (of *Henry V* itself) is incapable of proof, that notorious production of *Richard II* is certainly part of the story of why and how the later play came into existence.

But before following up this lead, there is another theory that must first be described and then, to some extent, contested. For Hart's conclusions were eventually recruited by Gary Taylor to the services of the new textual criticism of Shakespeare, which in the 1970s sought to demonstrate that at least some of the Bad Quartos represent alternative *versions* of their plays, with the divergences explicable as authorial revision. Inspired, perhaps, by Hart's passing observation that the Quarto *Henry V* had 'heavier reductions of the cast' (p. 429) than any other, amounting to the disappearance of thirteen speaking characters (an observation which Hart subsumed under the category of blunder) Taylor developed a strenuous argument that abridgement was required not by the attention span of the London audiences but by the economic constraints on a company travelling (like the tragedians in *Hamlet*), in the less remunerative provincial towns.[17]

Taylor claimed that, once casting exigencies ruled, the Chorus could not be played by any of the other parts, who all appear in too close proximity for him to change costumes. Yet it is hard to believe that this distinctive, indeed, extraordinary feature of the Folio version, so essential in offering an epic view of the action, would simply be disposed of for practical reasons.[18] More importantly, Taylor himself admits that casting difficulties cannot explain the omission of the opening scene, which throws such a cynical light on the motives for the war against France (p. 80); of the Jamy and McMorris episode, which was either 'omitted to shorten the play or censored, because of King James's recently expressed irritation at dramatic ridicule of the Scots' (p. 85); that certain character substitutions were made for aesthetic reasons; and that some of the omissions in the Harfleur scene are evidence of 'deliberate and coherent' theatrical cutting 'in the interests of simplifying the play into patriotism' (p. 130).

This last suggestion could well be developed. For by this standard we might also comprehend the Quarto's omission of the cynical first scene with the bishops that undermines their case for the 'just war' against France; Burgundy's missing lament for the despoliation of the French countryside, for which Holinshed provides no mandate; and especially the radical alterations in the scene most crucial to Henry's characterization, the disguised visit to the common soldiers in the night before Agincourt. As Taylor himself observes, the Folio creates a striking contrast between the 'populist morale-building walk' *described* by the Chorus and what we actually see. Rather than building morale, Henry picks a fight with Pistol, enters the conversation with Bates and Williams disingenuously, putting them at a serious disadvantage in the discussion of the limits of military loyalty and the rectitude of the cause for which they fight, and then, after their departure, delivers a soliloquy on the hardship of his *own* condition, excruciating in its self-regard and completely lacking the egalitarian sympathies of his public military rhetoric (p. 88). In the Quarto text, bereft of the contrast between the idealized choric view of the occasion and its actual representation, the king's disguise loses some of its disingenuity, and without the closing soliloquy the scene concludes with 'good-natured Henry joking with his men, as they walk away'. 'What,' Taylor asks, 'was the impetus behind the series of alterations?' (p. 90). Given his own thesis, he is forced to propose that they were triggered by the prior decision to omit the Chorus for reasons of casting economy. We might rather feel in the Quarto a more coherent intention – to omit some of the most disturbing implications about Henry's character and motives.

As Taylor's struggles with the evidence reveal,[19] bibliographical arguments, when isolated from historical or cultural criticism, will tend, when the going gets tough, to fall back on subjective standards of value. The resistance of the textual evidence to bibliographical solution suggests that we need to consider other, more intentionalist explanations. Once one accepts the thesis that the Quarto text represents a theatrical abridgement, which has suffered some textual garbling in its passage from promptbook to printed text, it may fairly be asked what motivated *this* abridgement, these particular omissions. The notion of a *different*, more crudely patriotic Quarto is not, on its merits, implausible; and neither need it be seen as totally unShakespearean. Shakespeare's status as a working playwright is scarcely endangered if we posit abridgement as a tactical retreat from one kind of play to another, from a complex historiography that might have been misunderstood to a symbolic enactment of nationalistic fervor.

We need to resituate both Quarto and Folio in their larger, mutual relationship to persons, events and cultural practices; and among those practices were the writing and rewriting of history, and the surveillance of those who attempted it. Historiography, in the sixteenth and early seventeenth century, was no academic discipline but a matter of public interest, both in the sense that the material of English history was popular material for the emergent national theater, and because (for a set of reasons which included this same popular appeal) the government regarded English historical materials as subject to its own control. Witnesses to this attitude are:

1 The mid-sixteenth century *Mirror for Magistrates*, a collection of lugubrious tales of prominent figures during the Wars of the Roses. When the *Mirror* appeared in 1559, at the opening of Elizabeth's reign, its preface observed that 'The wurke was begun, & part of it printed iiii yeare agoe, but hyndred by the lord Chauncellor that then was.'[20]
2 The censorship of the 1587 edition of Holinshed's *Chronicle*, especially in those sections which dealt with Scottish history and reflected the semi-republican influence of George Buchanan.[21]
3 The inspection by Sir Edmund Tilney, Master of the Revels, of the manuscript of *Sir Thomas More*, and his marginal instructions to the company, whichever it was, to 'Leave out ye insurrection wholy & ye cause theroff.'[22]
4 The publication of Shakespeare's *Richard II*, first and second Quartos, in 1597 and 1598, with the deposition scene removed.
5 The scandal over Sir John Hayward's *History of Henry IV*, which was published in February 1599, with a dedication to the earl of Essex. Three weeks later the Archbishop of Canterbury ordered the dedication to Essex cut out. At Easter Hayward published a second edition with an 'Epistle apologetical', which at Whitsun was called in and burned, while Hayward was confined to the Tower.[23]
6 The Bishops' Order of 1 June, 1599, which included, along with its prohibition of satire, the injunction that 'noe English historyes be printed excepte they bee allowed by some of her maiesties privie Counsell.'[24]

This pattern of official surveillance continued into James's reign. When Fulke Greville wished to write a history of Elizabeth's reign, he was prevented by Cecil from getting access to the necessary documents, on the grounds that he might 'deliver many things done in that time, which might perchance be construed to the prejudice of this.'[25] Sir Walter Ralegh's *History of the World*, which had been begun under Prince Henry's patronage, was published in 1614 after the prince's death while Ralegh was in the Tower on a charge of treason, and promptly called in by James.[26] As Leonard Tennenhouse has demonstrated, the *History* suffered both from the vagaries of patronage and the overdetermined hermeneutics that particularly affected historians.[27] For underlying the official scrutiny of historiography, which included, of course, the possibility of commissioning histories or inducing historians to serve the agendas of particular monarchs, was the concern that the public appetite for knowledge of the past should be satisfied only by such *versions* of history, official history, that the government could itself regard with complacence.

But Shakespeare could have seen from the beginning of his career how difficult it was to maintain the uplifting tone that official history demanded. True, in 1548 the title page of Hall's *Chronicle* had been able to read the wars of the Roses as an essay on 'union', and the dynastic struggles between different stems of Edward III's family tree as culminating naturally in Henry VIII, 'the indubitable flower and very heir of the said lineage.'[28] In 1580, Stow's *Chronicles,* dedicated to the earl of Leicester, offered history to the 'gentle Reader' as a 'discouragement of unnaturall subjects from wicked treasons, pernitious rebellions, and damnable doctrines'.[29] In accordance with this program, pre-Tudor history was interpreted on Stow's ornamental frontispiece as a design in which Elizabeth replaced Henry as dynastic flower, placed symmetrically above the stem of Richard II, the stem that went nowhere. We are beginning to see that such designs were deliberately imposed on more complex and intractable materials.[30] And when Shakespeare turned (for all plays subsequent to *Henry VI, Part 2*) to the 1587 Holinshed, the most obvious lesson offered by the English chronicles was that they continually invoked their own incapacity for closure. History did not stop where one would like it to; worse, it would continue when the Tudor dynasty, for want of a lineal descendant from Elizabeth, would itself be cut off like the stem descending from Richard.

This fact alone is sharply registered by Shakespeare in the Folio epilogue to *Henry V*, where the choric effort to delineate the reign an epic success succumbs to history's incompleteness:

> *Thus farre*, with rough, and all-unable pen,
> Our bending Author hath pursu'd the story...
>
> (TLN 3368–69)

But it was not only in its lost capacity for closure that English history exuded anxiety. The 1587 edition of Holinshed, which continued the story through Elizabeth's reign to the end of 1586, is a calendar of woes. It foregrounds natural disasters, local crimes and their punishment, instances of treason and their punishment, leading for their climax to the Babington Plot and the hideous execution of the conspirators, whose complicity with Mary Queen of Scots leads to *her* trial and condemnation. The supplement thus reveals a design, if not a desire, for a downbeat ending, a dying fall. In support of law and order the chronicler supplies an organicist description of the English state, stressing the 'natural' principle of community and collaboration in the animal kingdom, where all creatures can be observed 'seeking after fellowship of like with like to live together', though each of the animal species cited, including, of course, the bee, has its own natural king. Yet he *also* supplies, as 'A prettie apolog allusorie to the present case of malcontents', a dramatically extended version of the Aesopian fable of the *Frogs desiring a King*. Its overt message is, not surprisingly, 'to be content when we are well, and to make much of good queene Elizabeth, by whom we enjoie life and libertie.' Its uncontrollable content, as the frogs are devoured by the stork, was something entirely different: '(Will they, nill they) the herne should rule over them.'[31] And if even an official (and already censored) history could admit contradiction between orderly 'natural' polities and those raw emblems of power and powerlessness that the fable tradition provided, we should be especially wary of assuming the presence of unproblematical hegemony in *Henry V*, where Archbishop Chichele's beehive metaphor has sometimes been taken, quite out of context, as social hierarchy's endorsement.

Elizabethan historians, then, might have certain difficulties in controlling their material. But there was one phase of pre-Tudor history that, as Sir John Hayward discovered, was a particularly dangerous one for the historian to explore, especially if, as Hayward also discovered, he keyed his version of it into current affairs. By dedicating his *History of Henry IV* to the earl of Essex, Hayward indicated, intentionally or unintentionally, a connection between the popular local hero that Essex had become and the Lancastrian usurper who made himself king at the expense of Richard II. There seems little doubt that Hayward's difficulties were caused by widespread acceptance of this analogy, and exacerbated two years later when, on the eve of Essex's rebellion, his steward Gilly Merrick arranged for that special performance of 'the play...of Kyng Harry the iiijth'. Whether or not that play was *written* by Shakespeare, a question that now seems undecidable, the most important point for our purposes is that the performance was *connected* by contemporaries to Hayward's *History*, and the two were assumed to have had similar subversive motives. William Camden, himself a historian of repute, wrote in his *Annals*:

> Merrick was accused...that he had...procured an old out-worne play of the tragicall deposing of King Richard the second, to be acted upon the public stage before the Conspirators; which the lawyers interpreted to be done by him, as if they would now behold that acted upon the stage, which was the next day to be acted in deposing the Queene. And *the like censure given upon a Booke of the same argument*, set forth a little before by Hayward a learned man, and dedicated to the Earle of Essex, as if it had beene written as an example and incitement to the deposing of the Queene; an unfortunate thing to the author, who was punished by long imprisonment for his untimely setting forth therof, and for these words in his preface to the Earle: *Great thou art in hope, greater in the expectation of future time*. (italics added)[32]

In Camden's view, it is far from always or certainly the case that history, as Stow had claimed in 1580, serves to discourage 'unnaturall subjects from wicked treasons, pernitious rebellions, and damnable doctrines'. Sometimes it encouraged them.

The Quarto text of *Henry V* came out between 4 and 14 August, 1600. It therefore fell smack into the middle of the Hayward/Essex crisis, to which Shakespeare's own company was connected, at least on the night of 7 February, 1601. We might argue indefinitely whether they acted in ignorance of the play's topical significance (an unlikely possibility); their release after questioning by the Privy Council probably reflected the government's wish for as few martyrs as possible. But a decision to print the Quarto, or to let it be printed, could not possibly have been unwary, given the Bishops' Order in June 1599, restating the restrictions on historical publication, and probably in part an official response to Hayward's indiscretion. The Quarto was, moreover, registered less than a month after Hayward's imprisonment in July 1600, which in turn followed closely upon the preliminary examination of Essex at York House in June 1600. But the *Cronicle History* that made it to the Stationer (past the temporary 'stay') was, in fact, a Lancastrian history that would pass the closest inspection. It had nothing to do with deposition, and very little with rebellion. Rather it presented an *almost* unproblematic view of a highly popular monarch whose most obvious modern analogy was Elizabeth herself.

In a benign political semantics, 'popularity' replaces 'obedience'. Elizabeth had had great success in working the cultural signs of popularity, through the myth of the Virgin queen, the progresses, the Accession Day celebrations, and the symbolic icons. But as even Roy Strong's chronology of these icons reveals,[33] the older she grew, and the greater grew the public anxiety about the succession, the more welcome to her were symbolic portraits and emblems of unqualified power and vitality. Yet the eyes and ears on her mantle in the 'Rainbow' portrait (dated 1602 by Strong, in the aftermath of the Essex rebellion) were a none-too-subtle reminder that the myth needed the support of public surveillance, that the cultural forms of late Elizabethanism took the form they did because the queen and her ministers were watching. And if the Quarto *Henry V* could be read as presenting an idealized, figurative, historically displaced portrait of her, and one that was, by regendering, consistent with her own heroic rhetoric at Tilbury, it could only improve the credit of the Chamberlain's Men, who, the Quarto asserted, had 'sundry times' been loyally staging this story.

The Folio text, however, was a very different matter, since it spoke directly, at least in the fifth Chorus, to Elizabeth's last and most dangerous challenge by a rival allure. Precisely at the moment of *Henry V*'s composition, in fact, she was locked into a competition for public visibility and popular sympathy with Essex, who had the charismatic advantages of youth, personal attractiveness, great physical height, a list of military successes at Rouen, Cadiz, and the Azores, and above all his masculinity. Already in Thomas Heywood's *Fair Maid of the West* the stage had recognized in Essex a symbolic focus for national self-esteem. The play opens with this popular perception:

> The Fleet's bound for the Islands.
> Nay, 'tis like
> The great success at Cales, under the conduct
> Of such a noble General hath put heart
> Into the English: they are all on fire....
>
> How Plymouth swells with gallants; how the streets
> Glister with gold! You cannot meet a man
> But trick'd in scarf and feather, that it seems
> As if the pride of England's gallantry
> Were harbour'd here.
>
> (1:1:3–15)

As Richard McCoy discovered, these high spirits were also transferred to the Irish campaign as soon as Essex's commission was made known. An engraved portrait was prepared by Thomas Cockson for public sale in the spring of 1599, showing Essex on horseback (the imperial posture), against a background of the campaigns at Rouen, Cadiz and the Islands, with Ireland emblematically on the horizon.[34]

But the tensions that underlay the commission, and the struggle for power that preceded it, were also common knowledge. In July 1598 Essex had quarrelled with the queen in the Privy Council over who should command the Irish campaign, and she had given him a box on the ear, precipitating his retirement to Wanstead. Camden, the only contemporary to record this incident,[35] used the Latin term *alapa* for 'box,' which carried symbolic meaning; since it was a customary ritual for a master to box the ears of his slave at the moment of his manumission. Perhaps this inference is retained in the imprudent letter that Essex subsequently wrote to Lord Keeper Egerton, full of anger and insurrectionary language:

> No storme is more outragious then the indignation of an impotent Prince. The Queenes heart is indurate, what I owe as a subject I know, and what as an Earle, and Marshall of England: To serve as a servant and a slave I know not...Cannot Princes erre? Can they not wrong their subjects? Is any earthly power infinite?[36]

In February 1599 Essex, having made a temporary submission and returned to court, was himself given the Irish commission that he had sought, with at least mixed motives, for Sir George Carey; but everyone knew that this was a dangerous commission for him to accept, a final test of his usefulness to the regime and of Elizabeth's abilities to harness both his militarism and his popularity to her service. On 15 February Chamberlain had written to Carleton that

> our provisions for Ireland go forward with leaden feet, and the erle of Essex commission is no neerer signing (in shew) then when I wrote last; the jarres continue as they did, yf not worse, by dayly renewing, and our musicke runs so much upon discords, that I feare what harmonie they will make of yt in the end. Many things passe which may not be written, but in conclusion, *Iliacos intro muros peccatur et extra*: there is fault on all sides, and *quicquid delirant reges plectuntur Achivi*, whosoever offends the common wealth is punished.'[37]

The Folio version of *Henry V* shares with Cockson's portrait and Chamberlain's letter an extreme form of topicality, a moment of historical expectation that can be dated with precision, and whose very poise, optimistic or pessimistic, on the edge of the unknown is central to the meaning and function of the artefact. On 28 September 1599, with the campaign a shambles, Essex made his unauthorized return to England, and in forty-eight hours was committed to custody. By late November he was facing charges of misgovernment of the Irish campaign. 'Libels' in his support were circulated in London.[38] On 29 December preachers at Paul's Cross prayed for Essex by name, and attacked the government. On 2 February 1600, as McCoy pointed out, Thomas Cockson's heroic engraving of Essex was circulating, 'with all his titles of honor, all his services, and two verses underneath that gave hym exceeding praise for wisdom, honor, worth';[39] and by the end of August the Privy Council had moved to suppress not only this 'picture' but also any other 'pictures of noblemenn and other persons...sett forth oftentimes with verses and other circumstances not fytte to be used.'

> Because this custome doth growe common and indeed is not meete such publique setting forth *of anie pictures but of her most excellent Majesty* should be permytted yf the same be well done...[the Archbishop of Canterbury] will give direccion that hereafter no personage of any noblemann or other person shalbe ingraven and printed to be putt to sale publiquely, and those prints that are already made to be called in. (italics added)[40]

'Pictures' thus joined the list of cultural forms identified in the Bishops' Order of 1 June, 1599 as under special restriction.

This evidence, taken together with the furor over Hayward's *History*, indicates that from February 1599 to February 1601 England witnessed a struggle not only for the popular imagination but also, obviously, for control of the media by which that imagination was stimulated. And during the summer of 1599, while Essex was in Ireland with the results of his campaign as yet unknown, Shakespeare, we know, was at work on a version of *Henry V* that included the Choruses. If the earlier Choruses are written in the mood of chivalric celebration and enthusiasm (being 'on fire') that *The Fair Maid of the West* associated with Essex's earlier campaigns:

> Now all the Youth of England are on fire,
> And silken Dalliance in the Wardrobe lyes:
> Now thrive the Armorers, and Honors thought
> Reignes solely in the breast of every man.
> They sell the Pasture now, to buy the Horse;
>
> For now sits Expectation in the Ayre,
>
> (TLN 463–70)

the fifth Chorus pinpoints the Elizabethan moment of 'Expectation' more exactly, and explicitly connects it to the theme of popularity that the *Henry IV* plays had inaugurated. By a strenuous act of the visual imagination which must substitute for the deficiencies of dramatic representation, the reader/audience is invited to 'behold' the analogy with which we began:

> How London doth powre out her Citizens,
> The Maior and all his Brethren in best sort,
> Like to the Senatours of th'antique Rome,
> With the Plebeians swarming at their heeles,
> Goe forth and fetch their Conqu'ring Caesar in:
> As by a lower, but by loving likelyhood,
> Were now the Generall of our gracious Empresse,
> As in good time he may, from Ireland comming,
> Bringing Rebellion broached on his Sword,
> How many would the peacefull Citie quit,
> To welcome him? much more, and much more cause,
> Did they this Harry.
>
> (TLN 2872–85)

Almost every term in this extraordinary passage bristles with innuendo and intellectual challenge. In the leisure provided by the 'Forge and working-house of Thought', however quick, as distinct from the instant reception that staged drama imposes, these ambiguities can be unfolded. Not the least of them is Shakespeare's invocation of an artisanal metaphor for thought itself; but the governing peculiarity is that he should have chosen to insert so tendentious a passage into a play already, by virtue of its historical subject, generically suspect. Nor was it only that he had chosen to make a connection with Elizabeth's intransigent favorite only weeks after Hayward's *History* had been called in for doing the same thing. In thematizing the *popular* and its role in earlier historical events (both Roman and English) Shakespeare made visible what the story of Hayward's *History* only reveals if one follows its details, that much of the anxiety it generated in official circles was connected to *its* popularity, its unusually wide circulation and distribution. Hayward, as much as Essex, had courted the public and succeeded. In the examination of Wolfe, the printer of Hayward's *History*, it was part of his defense that he yielded to popular demand for a second edition:

> The people calling for it exceedingly... 1,500 of these books being almost finished in the Whitsun holidays of 1599, were taken by the wardens of the stationers, and delivered to the Bishop of London... The people having divers times since called to procure the continuation of the history by the same author... Since the last edition was suppressed, a great number have been for it.[41]

The same inference is drawn from the records of Essex's trial, where one of the accusations is that, when Hayward originally sent him a copy of the *History*, Essex had waited to see how many copies would sell, and then sent it to Archbishop Whitgift to have it suppressed, in order that the market might thereby improve still further. The *Directions for Preachers* published on 14 February 160l, warning the clergy not to express support for Essex from the pulpit, claimed that 'the Earl, knowing hundreds of them to be dispersed, would needs seem the first that disliked it.'[42] And Bacon's speech at the trial claimed that he wrote 'only a cold formal letter to the Archbishop to call in the book... knowing, that forbidden things are most sought after.'[43] These official concerns with numbers, invaluable for establishing the degree to which the entire crisis was a matter of informed public concern, and for providing statistical content to the then-still-living metaphor of publication, contribute a powerful gloss on Shakespeare's own emphasis on 'how *many*' would have flocked to welcome Essex back from Ireland, an emphasis, however, that the Folio text is prepared to leave, by means of a question mark, indeterminate.[44]

Note also the care with which this passage establishes its own protocols as metaphor, and the posture in which the metaphor is offered. The analogy between Henry's return from France and Essex's return from Ireland is 'a lower, but... loving likelyhood'; lower, in that Essex is *not* the victorious monarch, but only the 'Generall of our gracious Empresse"; loving, in that the playwright offers the analogy not as the kind of challenge suspected in Cockson's engraving, and unmistakable in Essex's letter to Egerton, but as an expression of loyalty and a recognition of structural differences. The syntax, too, is distinctively conditional, positing not only the moment of 'Expectation', but a cautious optimism ('As in good time he may').

Yet even within these self-imposed controls, the language is provocative. The city may be peaceful, but the welcoming crowd 'quits' that stable environment for the liminal territory of Blackheath. The analogy between Essex and Henry is preceded, moreover, by that between fifteenth-century England and 'antique Rome', an analogy that points to a major structural difference between them, since 'conquering Caesar,' by definition Julius, was still the military agent of a republic (however pushing at those limits), as distinct from the imperial model established by Octavian and repeated by 'our gracious Empresse.' The very presence of the plebeians, 'swarming' at the heels of the senators, reminds that empress of the popular 'many' to whom she herself had deliberately appealed and on whose labor, as in the beehive metaphor invoked by Henry's Archbishop, the welfare of the hive depends. But the barely invoked beehive metaphor here has a more alarming connotation. Swarming, bees notoriously desert the hive under the leadership of another monarch.[45] And along with Chichele's speech, the intertextual relation here is with *Henry VI, Part 2*, at the moment of popular protest for the loss of Humphrey, duke of Gloucester: 'The commons, like an angry hive of bees/That want their leader, scatter up and down,/And care not who they sting in their revenge.' (3:2;124–26).

This fact alone makes sense of the representational instability that Shakespeare has introduced into *Henry V*, not merely by praising Essex at a time when a dedication to him could result in imprisonment, but by allowing the analogy between Essex and Henry to confuse the more 'natural' analogy between Henry and Elizabeth. As Jonathan Dollimore and Alan Sinfield have argued, the legend of Henry's reign was 'a powerful Elizabethan fantasy simply because it represented a single source of power in the state,' the fusion of monarch and military hero in a single popular archetype.[46] The allusion to Essex destabilizes that fantasy, along with that other Elizabethan myth propagated at Tilbury, that the queen herself could play both roles. The Archbishop's metaphor of the beehive accomplished the same feat; but the suppressed metaphor of the swarm works rather to distinguish general and empress, by signifying their competition for popular support and approval.

The quick-thinking imaginative forger who wrote this Chorus would also have known, surely, that 'bringing Rebellion broached on his Sword,' was ambiguous not only in the semantics of 'broached', but also in its chronology. For if 'broached', usually glossed by the commentators on this passage as spitted, could also be, as Albright has shown, a verb of mischievous political intention, then the rebellion that Essex is anticipated as bringing on his sword is not past but future, not behind him in Ireland but before him at home. This prophecy, unrecognizable as such when the Folio text was written, would have risen to the surface of the text in February 1601. Indeed, it would be confirmed in the same language; Lord Henry Howard, in a letter reporting the Essex conspiracy, complained that 'all the partisans of the last tragedy resorted to Southampton without impeachment...and new practises were set on broach.'[48]

But even in 1600, the fifth Chorus was so ambiguous that Shakespeare's company, warned by the fate of Hayward's *History*, could not have risked giving it the publicity of print, where its textual instabilities would be fully open to inspection. It brought down with it, I suspect, the rest of the Choruses, including those whose message might well have enhanced the simpler patriotism of the Quarto text as a whole. What Shakespeare intended by creating this dangerous instability in the first place is another question altogether. For what audience was this complex strategy designed, super-imposing two historical eras (or three, if we include the gesture towards antique Rome) and two structures of analogy which contradict each other? Had he imagined a warning to Elizabeth, which would imply that the warning was capable of reaching her? Very unlikely. Or rather, in some version of the Albright hypothesis, had he planned an encoded incitement to Essex, intended for private performance before some audience of 'malcontents'? Even more unlikely, given that we know which play was actually performed on the eve of the rebellion. Or was the Folio version a well meant but ill-advised attempt at mediation, with the public stage conceived as the liminal territory where the playwright and actors took no sides, creating 'loving likelihoods' in the national interest? The representational slipperiness, then, by which Henry could configure *both* Elizabeth and Essex, at the end of a play whose protagonist was, if peerless, certainly not flawless, would not be a sign of Shakespeare's disinterestedness. Rather, it would contribute to an argument for a pragmatic reconciliation between general and empress, pragmatic in the sense that 'history', by refusing to settle their rivalry, provided no basis for decisively altering the current allocations of power and lines of authority. And it would carry the flavor both of Chamberlain's discretion ('many things passe which may not be written') and of his Horatian cynicism ('quicquid delirant reges plectuntur Achivi') which knows that when the leaders are crazed it is the ordinary folk who pay the penalty.

This third alternative has other advantages. 'Mediation' of a local, contemporary crisis gives substance to an important concept in contemporary literary theory – literature mediates material experience to us rather than reflecting it directly – by reinstating within it a common-sense relation between events and human agents. Yet we also know from what happened (the deletion of the Choruses, the rebellion itself) that such a mediation was never effected. That failure must also be incorporated into our theoretical model of how one text became another. I assume that the sense of increased surveillance would have been peculiarly stimulating of self-consciousness, encouraging a dramatist to assess, but not necessarily accurately, the conditions of constraint that defined his medium, the degree of his freedom to operate within those constraints.

In the Folio text of *Henry V*, which still registered, before its abridgement, a hopeful view of that freedom, a vision of national unity is posited, not, as in such comedies as *A Midsummer Night's Dream*, as a festive community, but tenable only within a sober historical perspective. As Henry himself is observed by the French Constable to have advanced beyond the 'Whitsun morris dance' which was the Dauphin's metaphor for his tavern phase (2:4:25), the Folio version of his story produces at the level of consciousness what the earlier plays in both tetralogies merely produced – an image of the nation state as an ideal that survives the continuous struggle for power of competing aristocrats. What the Folio text does *not* produce, however, is the idealized model of national unity that some of Shakespeare's later readers have thought they found there. Where that model is actually found is in Archbishop Chichele's beehive speech, in the Folio firmly qualified by our prior recognition that the Archbishop is cynical, self-serving, and elitist.[49]

In contrast to organicist political theory that was manifestly coated with rhetorical honey, the subdued voice of 'our bending author' offers, penultimately, only the sexual and dynastic version of union, granting a festive and erotic color to France's and Katherine's capitulation, providing we take the story 'thus far' and no further. And while the image of 'antique Rome' with its crowds of swarming plebeians anticipates *Coriolanus*, the play in which Shakespeare would a decade later re-examine the political structure through the lens of classical republicanism, in *Henry V* this inquiry is sporadic. The Folio text remains committed, though not without moments of distaste, to the system of government endorsed by centuries of English, rather than Roman history, and willing to entertain, though not without framing it as extreme imaginative effort ('Work, work, your thoughts'), a commitment to ideas of national greatness and agreement. What happened after the turn of the century was, and produced, another kind of story.

One last problem demands our attention: the role in the Folio version of Michael Williams, common soldier, commonly referred to in the speech prefixes as 'Will'. If 'Will', as the testimony of the sonnets would suggest, is Shakespeare's own signature,[50] his appearance as the voice of the common man in the crucial scene before Agincourt still further complicates the reception of this scene and its direction of reader sympathy. And the fact that speech prefixes are, of course, never spoken, and that Williams, for that matter, is never named in the dialogue, implies that this allusion, if it is one, is the most private gesture of independence that a playwright writing for the stage could conceive.

As Anne Barton has argued, the scene in which Henry confronts his soldiers and attempts to defend the justice of his cause is evidently a critique of the motif of the king-in-disguise, which in the popular theater and the popular imagination was an archaic, utopian gesture, a reminder of the 'wish-dream of a [medieval] peasantry harried and perplexed by a new class of officials' that they could deal directly with the king himself:

> In the ballads, king and unsuspecting subject meet time after time and discover unanimity of opinion and mutual respect. Richard Coeur de Lion banquets in Sherwood Forest on stolen venison, forgives Robin Hood and his men, and confounds the sheriff of Nottingham. Henry II so enjoys the rough but generous hospitality of the miller of Mansfield that he makes him a knight and gives him a royal license to keep the forest of Sherwood. Other ballads describe the meeting of Edward I and the reeve, King Alfred and the shepherd, Edward IV and the tanner, Henry VIII and the cobbler, James I and the tinker, William III and the forester, and many similar encounters.[51]

One could supplement Barton's insight by noting that Puttenham, whose *Arte of English Poesie* was published a decade before *Henry V*, includes two such episodes to illustrate linguistic indecorum, which in Puttenham's courtly aesthetic is also social and political indecorum. So in defining *acyron*, or 'the uncouth', he recalled the meeting of the Tanner of Tamworth with the disguised Edward IV: 'the Tanner having a great while mistaken him, and used very broad talke with him, at length perceiving by his traine that it was the king, was afraid he should be punished for it.' While Puttenham regarded this incident as evidence of the way the common folk 'mistake' their betters and their manners simultaneously, and connected both forms of indecorum to archaism, he had to report that Edward himself had 'laughed a good, not only to see the Tanners vaine fear, but also to heare his ill shapen terme, and gave him for recompence of his good sport, the inheritance of Plumton parke.'[52] This same geniality (and Puttenham's disapproval of it) continued into the earlier part of Elizabeth's reign. Puttenham records the episode when Elizabeth was on progress, precisely in order to solicit popular affection, and her coachman was accosted by one Sergeant Benlowes as follows: 'Stay thy cart good fellow, stay thy cart, that I may speake to the Queene.' For Puttenham, this use of 'cart' for 'coach' was a blatant case of *tapinosis*, or 'the Abaser'; but the queen 'laughed as she had bene tickled . . . although very graciously (as her manner is) she gave him great thankes and her hand to kisse.' (p. 217).

Barton concluded that Shakespeare invented the scene before Agincourt 'in order to question, not to celebrate, a folk convention . . . he used Henry's disguise to summon up the memory of a wistful, naive attitude toward history and the relationship of subject and king which this play rejects as attractive but untrue,' (p. 99). Situated as it is within an implicit teleology of drama, a progress from archaic naivete to sophistication, from comical history to historiographical realism, Barton's own thesis is attractive but not quite true enough. In *Henry V* the fantasy is offered to the audience, as a bait, by the fourth Chorus, in its promise of 'a little touch of Harry in the night'; but not only does the following scene mock that promise, but the bearer of the fantasy is revealed to be not the common man but the king himself, whose self-deluding populism Williams appropriately rebuffs, as a betrayal of the rules that govern both effective rule and decorous subjection:

> Your Majestie came not like your selfe: you appear'd to me but as a common man; witnesse the Night, your Garments, your Lowlinesse; and what your Highnesse suffer'd under that shape, I beseech you take it for your owne fault, and not mine. (TLN 2766–71)

As Barton observed, the congeniality structured into the folk-motif of the disguised king is completely absent: 'The two men do not sit down at table together to any common feast, in the manner of Dekker's Henry V or Heywood's Edward IV' (p. 101), and the glove full of crowns is a weak vestige of the legendary royal generosity, a venal payoff to silence discontent; but the more striking sign of the hostility between them (as mere men) is the box on the ear that 'Harry in the night' had contracted for but that as Henry V he refuses to accept, displacing it onto Fluellen.

And although it is important that Henry fails to answer the question at the heart of their encounter, the question of the justice of the war, the deeper proof that Williams's reproach is legitimate emerges rather in the private soliloquy that the Quarto text erased completely, when Henry reveals the rhetorical shallowness of his populism. In contrast both to the fourth Chorus' egalitarianism:

> For forth he goes, and visits all his Hoast,
> Bids them good morrow with a modest smyle,
> And calls them Brothers, Friends, and Countreymen.
>
> (TLN 1821–23)

and Henry's own hortatory rhetoric on the battle field:

> We few, we happy few, we band of brothers:
> For he to-day that sheds his blood with me,

> Shall be my brother: be he ne'er so vile,
> This day shall gentle his Condition.
>
> (TLN 2302–05)

the soliloquy operates rather at the deep structural level of social prejudice imperspicuous even to this most self-knowing and canny of Shakespeare's kings. What begins as a meditation on the awesome responsibility of political leadership ends as a self-justifying complaint that the common people are mindlessly irresponsible; and the common people are now conveniently redefined not as the soldiers whose lives are at stake but the peasants at home:

> the wretched Slave:
> Who, with a body fill'd, and vacant mind,
> Gets him to rest, cram'd with distressfull bread,
>
> The Slave, a Member of the Countreyes peace,
> Enjoyes it; but in grosse braine little wots
> What watch the King keepes, to maintaine the peace,
> Whose howres, the Pesant best advantages.
>
> (TLN 2118–20, 2131–04)

Is Williams, then, another repository of the popular voice, a common man whose relation to Shakespeare is uncommonly close, and who therefore competes for exegetical control with both the Chorus and 'our bending author'? If so, two opposed (though symmetrically related) conceptions of the popular are here, in this scene of ideological density, set in fully articulate contest with each other: the national leader whose populist style has established the mandate (if not the justice) of his cause, and the un(common) critic of that cause whose intelligence prohibits a simple submission of his will to the idea of popular leadership, merely because it is in the national interest. And within the political context of 1600, Williams' reproaches must have been equally applicable to both the rivals for national leadership: to Elizabeth, as it became apparent that the signs and symbols of popularity were merely signs, not a genuine mandate; and to Essex, who at his arraignment, as Chamberlain reported bitterly in February 1601, delivered his defence 'with such bravery and so many wordes, that a man might easilie perceve that as he had ever lived *popularly*, so his cheife care was to leave a good opinion in the peoples mindes now at parting.'[53] And if Will. is indeed, as in the sonnets, Shakespeare's signature, his rejection of *tapinosis* does not make him a Puttenham, a courtly maker whose sense of decorum, allied with his sense of class, will necessarily prefer *ragione di stato* to the work of the 'gross brain'. Rather, this confrontation anticipates that between Hamlet and the gravedigger, and in the aftermath of the Essex rebellion, the more strenuous socio-political analysis Shakespeare would begin to work on.

Mervyn James, whose provocative analysis of the Essex rebellion was also developed in 'cultural' terms,[54] presented it as the last stand of a culture based on honour, a nobles' revolt against parvenus, and conducted in the old chivalric terms of militarism and pride of ancestry. It collapsed, James argued, because of its own procedural inconsistencies, Essex being unable to choose until too late between an army revolt, a court *coup d'état*, and a London city rising; but after his death his cult of popularity was revived and continued, first by Southampton and then by Essex's son and heir, the third earl. Significantly, in this phase, 'popularity' came to mean 'no longer the charismatic contact between the hero and the London crowd', but rather a working relationship with parliament, and the creation of political pressure through the use of parliamentary privilege, impeachment, and the Lords Committee of Petitions (pp. 462–5). This was the phase into which Shakespeare, too, moved, as James's accession brought with it a new political environment, new definitions of the nation and the nature of monarchy – in short, a whole set of new paradigms for the national theater to contemplate.

5

'What matter who's speaking?': Hamlet *and* King Lear

Hamlet, the beginning of my story, is also its center. If the play is, as I argued in chapter 1, a threshold in Shakespeare's theory of the theater as a site of professional rivalries, social constraints and national political contests, it is also the play that marks Shakespeare's transition from late Elizabethanism to the new dynamics of the reign of James I. That transition is literally marked in its publication history, since the Stationers' Register for 26 July 1602 entered an Elizabethan revenge play 'as yt was latelie Acted by the Lord Chamberlayne his servants', while the first ('Bad') Quarto advertised a playtext acted 'by his Highnesse servants', by which we know it appeared after 19 May 1603, when Shakespeare's company became the King's Men. And when in 1604 a new edition appeared, 'Newly imprinted and enlarged to almost as much againe as it was', it is possible to argue that *Hamlet* had become not only a 'Tragical History' but a Jacobean play for readers; that is, if one assumes that the exceptional length of this version would have prohibited its performance, at least on the London popular stage.[1]

I do not mean to suggest, however, that *Hamlet* was reconceived in terms of the new reign, or that the textual problematic it presents to the modern reader is a consequence of a changed strategy. The textual problematic includes not only the extreme difference in length (and many would say in quality also) between 'Good' and 'Bad' Quartos, but the far more troubling fact that the lines on the War between the Theaters are missing from the otherwise reliable 1604 Quarto, while the presumably definitive Folio omits more than a modern editor is willing to part with, including one of Hamlet's soliloquies. These problems do not, however, affect the tone of *Hamlet*, which remains much the same whichever early text one interrogates. That tone is recognizably a *fin de siècle* malaise, which in England at the turn of the sixteenth century was exacerbated by two related events from which no one could avert his eyes: the Essex rebellion and the imminent death of Elizabeth. It is a play that marks the end, not the beginning, of an era.

In the hundred and seventh of his sonnets, Shakespeare writes in a different tone of the moment *after* that ending:

> Not mine own feares, nor the prophetick soule,
> Of the wide world, dreaming on things to come,
> Can yet the lease of my true love controule
> Supposde as forfeit to a confine'd doome.
> The mortall Moone hath her eclipse endur'de,
> And the sad Augurs mock their own presage,
> Incertenties now crowne them-selves assur'de,
> And peace proclaims Olives of endlesse age.
> Now with the drops of this most balmie time,
> My love lookes fresh, and death to me subscribes,
> Since spight of him Ile live in this poore rime,
> While he insults ore dull and speachlesse tribes.
> And thou in this shalt finde thy monument,
> When tyrants crests and tombs of brasse are spent.[2]

This sonnet tells a political story, though it tells it with such deliberate obscurity that, as Stephen Booth has recorded, there are almost as many theories of its plot as the sonnet has lines.[3] But one does not need to conclude, with Booth, that all the theories are inconsequential. Sonnet 107 is itself one of those 'abstract and brief chronicles' mentioned by Hamlet, its abstractions advertising the latent presence of real persons and events. The 'mortall Moone' is not merely a 'not unreasonable' allusion to Elizabeth, as Booth grudgingly admits, but one that Shakespeare had himself explored in *A Midsummer's Night's Dream*, and one even more accessible to the sonnet's assumed readership. Her total eclipse is precisely a function of her mortality, and is as precisely followed by a new cultural environment, that of James, who in March 1604 had already proclaimed, in his inaugural speech to parliament, his characteristic foreign policy, 'outward peace... peace abroad...public peace.'[4] The invocation of tyranny as the power that love will conquer makes no harsher farewell to Elizabeth than was common in the Jacobean political honeymoon, when certain members of parliament described to James the national hope that 'some moderate ease shoud be given us of those burdens and oppressions under which the whole land did groan', not the least of which had been the 'Incertenties' over the succession that Elizabeth had insisted on maintaining.[5] And the love 'supposde as forfeit to a confin'd doome' is surely Henry Wriothesly, earl of Southampton, Shakespeare's patron since 1593–4, co-conspirator with Essex and released from imprisonment in the Tower by James, whose signing of the release order while he was still in Scotland was his first significant political act.[6] The poem evidently mocks the sad augurs of crisis, the *fin de siècle* pessimists among whose number Shakespeare had enrolled at the time of writing *Hamlet*; and its discarded fears, 'dreaming on things to come' meet Hamlet at the point of his most famous soliloquy, where the fear of 'what dreams may come/When we have shuffled off this mortal coil' is the self's last defence against self-destruction.[7]

In writing *Hamlet*, Shakespeare's response to the waning of the lunar powers was similar to Samuel Daniel's, who had included in the 1595 and 1599 editions of his *Civil Wars* (a project directly parallel to Shakespeare's history cycle) a tribute to Essex that was erased from the edition of 1601. The 1601 edition added to this gradually accreting poem, yet insisted, in its concluding stanza, that its Muse baulks at the sad task of retelling the Wars of the Roses, that the project is 'but little past halfe her long way,' and that its poet, 'Weary with these embroylements' 'Knowes not as yet... Whether to leave-off here, or else go on.'[8] This is, of course, the predicament of Hamlet the character; and in *Hamlet* Shakespeare paused in the midst of his own project, the representation of English culture, and wrote in 1601 a critique of dramatic mimesis, of action, and of intellection. Yet even in this most introspective of his plays, Shakespeare continued in a minor key his inquiry into ideas of popular leadership and the messages sent by the popular voice to those responsible for leadership. In Sonnet 107 the speaker contrasts himself with the 'dull and speachlesse tribes' who cannot perpetuate their love by writing; in *Hamlet*, the prince himself, in his estrangement from what is rotten in the state of Denmark, speaks in language learned from the politically voiceless, who can still be heard elliptically in proverbs, snatches of popular songs, and the upside-down speech that belongs to Bottom and his fellows. By the standards of his court, this means that Hamlet is mad. And conversely, when Hamlet finally comes face to face in the graveyard with a rival spokesman for popular protest, he backs away in alarm from the competition. Discarding alienation, he rejoins the culture of the court, to grapple at the bottom of the grave with Laertes, to end his critique of corruption in an aristocratic duel.

This chapter's title repeats Michel Foucault's ironic and unanswered question, 'What matter who's speaking?' at the end of his essay 'What is an Author?' itself an unanswered question.[9] Citation does not, however, mean agreement. Foucault's question, which he himself declared a 'murmur of indifference', completed his interrogation of the common-sense idea of authorship, whereby a text is attributed, by way of a name, to a self-determining subject; and this interrogation in turn was part of Foucault's larger and often salutary appeal against outmoded or undesirable categories of literary understanding: Romantic conceptions of subjectivity and the *oeuvre*, the banalities of a merely biographical criticism, the arrogant hermeticism of any analysis that presumes itself inaccessible to ordinary readers. To replace this older analysis which (he might have said) existed as a conspiracy of a few for control of cultural history, Foucault posited an omnivorous archeology of past discourses that would register without evaluative distinctions all the traces of a particular cultural formation and that would substitute for individual authorship the impersonal voice, the 'on dit', or it-is-said'.

The analysis of statements operates therefore without reference to a cogito. It does not pose the question of the speaking subject, who reveals or who conceals himself in what he says, who, in speaking, exercises his sovereign freedom, or who, without realizing it, subjects himself to constraints of which he is only dimly aware. In fact, it is situated at the level of the 'it is said' – and we must not understand by this a sort of communal opinion, a collective representation that is imposed on every individual; we must not understand by it a great, anonymous voice that must, of necessity, speak through the discourses of everyone.[10]

My quarrel with Foucault is not, in this chapter, in defence of the common-sense view of authorship (without which this book is impossible) but with the 'on dit' itself. Certain unacknowledged prejudices and dangers lurk in the postmodern preference for the impersonal, the abstract and the general, the last used here in the opposite sense from the way it functioned in my first chapter, as a name for the popular theatrical audience. Foucault's preference for an impersonal archive was partly a consequence of blending the influences of Marx with those of Freud, or Freud's interpreters. In particular, when Foucault concluded 'What is an Author?' by asking 'What matter who's speaking?' he echoed Jacques Lacan's notorious question in 'The Freudian Thing': 'mais qui parle?' Lacan answered his own question by 'repeat[ing] after Freud the word of his discovery: *it speaks*',[11] thus effacing the human subject of analysis. This move was entirely consistent with Lacan's lifelong attack on the Cartesian cogito, first formulated in 1949 in 'The Mirror Stage'. And 'The Mirror Stage' concludes with a statement that psychoanalysts like himself 'place no trust in altruistic feeling, we who lay bare the aggressivity that underlies the activity of the philanthropist, the idealist, the pedagogue and the reformer.'[12] Years later Lacan revealed that his contempt for the humanist idea of an autonomous ego, and the essentially tragic view of the psyche that contempt produces, were linked to a Gallic distaste for American ego-psychology, with its goals of the patient's recovery, via a successful adaptation to society.[13]

Lacan himself has written on *Hamlet*, in an essay (to which we shall return) that shows the extreme consequences of a theory of socialization – the brutal entry into the Symbolic, or language – in which the individual is utterly unfree. Lacan's belief in that failure of autonomy is expressed in bizarre and horrifying terms at the end, where Hamlet's failure to kill Claudius is equated with the fact that nobody during the years of Nazi control of Europe managed to assassinate Adolf Hitler. In the terms of this analogy, those who failed were caught in the Oedipal trap of respect for power, for phallic 'potency,' and the phallus, according to Lacan, in a telling locution, 'always slips through your fingers,'[14]

If Lacan's neo-Freudian 'qui parle' denies to the subject the oldest humanist privilege – speech as a sign of rational self-determination – and Foucault's quotation of it extends that denial to history, transforming it into archeology, a still more sinister version of the question and its consequences appears in the work of Louis Althusser. In a crucial section of *For Marx* Althusser described the theoretical foundations of his newly scientific political economy. This science would, eschewing empirical inquiry, proceed from the general to the general. It would start with Generality I (the present state of Marxist political philosophy); this would be subjected to a negative critique in terms of contradictions between its 'facts' and its 'theory', or Generality II; and it would proceed from thence to the extraction of new 'knowledge', or Generality III, which Althusser claimed would no longer be abstract, but concrete. This process Althusser called work: though he introduced a significant disclaimer:

> Mais qui travaille? Qu'entendre par cette expression: la science travaille?. . . .Si dans ces moyens de production nous faisons provisoirement abstraction des hommes, c'est ce que nous appellerons la *Generalité II*.

> But *who* or *what* is it that works? What should we understand by the expression: the science works?. . .If we abstract from men in these means of production for the time being, it is what I shall call the *Generality II*.[15]

'Mais qui travaille?' Another rhetorical question that desires no answer because there are no agents. Recognized by the English translator as a scandal, which he attempts to defuse by offering instead '*who* or *what* is it that works?', the question in fact supports the proposal that one could abstract, even provisionally, from Marx's theory of labor as the means of production the men who provide it.[16] The lexical abstraction of Althusser's work (a major cause of its inaccessibility to the ordinary reader) is therefore revealed to be part of his system also, supported by his belief that economies (and economic theories) can exist in abstraction from the human beings who produced them.

This chapter will argue that it does indeed matter – that it mattered to Shakespeare – who works and who speaks, and that the plays after the turn of the century are obsessed with the related questions of voice (or political representation) and agency (or political responsibility). In *Hamlet*, where the project was at least in part self-analytical, the problem is stated in highly individualistic terms: how far does responsible agency depend on a secure sense of personal identity?

This is a challenge that cannot be deflected back into purely intellectual concerns. Geoffrey Hartman attempts such a deflection, by rewriting the sentries' opening challenges as if reverberating between play and reader:

Interpreter: Who's there?
Book: Nay, answer me: stand and unfold yourself.

Things get crossed up in this jittery situation. It should be the interpreter who unfolds the text. But the book begins to question the questioner, its *qui vive* challenges him to prove he is not a ghost. What is he then?[17] But this move back into academicism is precisely that which *Hamlet*, and even Hamlet, was designed to warn against. Hamlet manifests suspicion of the power and privilege that literacy, language, philosophy give him while they incapacitate him; and to protect himself against that guilt he enters into a fantasy relation with another, less privileged language: mocking, dynamic, subversive, popular, 'general'.

It is easy to overlook the fact that Hamlet, like Henry V, could himself have become a popular king. This is the fear that Claudius shares with Laertes: 'the great love the *general gender* bear him . . . Would . . . Convert his gyves to graces,' (4:7:18, 21). But while Henry's populism is a strategy, Hamlet's is a sign of vocational anxiety. One can see the point quickly by comparing Henry's (Folio) soliloquy before Agincourt, with its contempt for 'the wretched Slave' and 'Pesant' whose 'grosse braine' is unknowing of the king's efforts in defence of the realm (TLN 2131–04) with the startling terms of Hamlet's self-reproach: 'O, what a rogue and peasant slave am I!' (2:2:544) And again, much later, 'Examples gross as earth exhort me' (4:4:46). In the first he compares himself unfavorably to the professional actor, who, working within the effective and affective terms of his profession, can 'cleave the general ear with horrid speech' (2:2:557). In the second, still more damningly, to the 'twenty thousand' ordinary soldiers led by Fortinbras 'That for a fantasy and trick of fame / Go to their graves like beds' (4:4:61–62). But the echoes reproach Henry even more than Hamlet, who until the last act of his tragedy crosses and recrosses in distress the class barriers that Henry, as Hal, had only transgressed disingenuously.

Confronting the actor's working language, Hamlet, the prince without a profession to structure his expression, 'Must, like a whore, unpack [his] heart with words / And fall a-cursing like a very drab' (2:2:581–82), that is, the lowest representative of the servant class, a kitchen maid or scullion.

So too Hamlet's famous and elliptical statement, 'I know a hawk from a handsaw' (2:2:375), draws, as Robert Weimann noted, 'not only from the aristocratic background of falconry...but also from the background of the common worker', with handsaw/hernshaw poised by textual and social indeterminacy on the same boundary as the two meanings of 'hawk', bird of prey and plasterer's tool.[18]

A still more complex sense of vocational stress is registered almost at the play's end, in Hamlet's explanation to Horatio as to how he outwitted Claudius in the contract killing, and sent his old university companions to their deaths instead. Its interest resides in the way in which writing functions as a sign of class distinctions:

> Being thus benetted round with villainies –
> Or I could make a prologue to my brains,
> They had begun the play – I sat me down,
> Devised a new commission, wrote it fair –
> I once did hold it, as our statists do,
> A baseness to write fair, and labour'd much
> How to forget that learning, but, sir, now
> It did me yeoman's service.
>
> (5:2:29–36).

The simple meaning of this passage is that Hamlet has at last found a use for the penmanship which he had previously believed a demeaning skill for the ruling class; yet the message is made more difficult than it need be by his metaphors of class and craft. Writing merges with playwrighting,[19] and also does him 'yeoman's service', a social category in Shakespeare's England of considerable indeterminacy.

Hamlet, then, is partly and uneasily conscious that uncommon insight and privilege do not necessarily make one superior to the common man, actor, soldier, yeoman, playwright. He partly perceives the paradox of an elitist education, that only those who profit from it have the faculties to question its social justice. And, in the first four acts of the play, the language in which he struggles to express this insight is that of the popular tradition.

Hamlet's populist language has been brilliantly excavated by Robert Weimann in his study of Shakespeare's relation to popular theatrical tradition, and to folk traditions of 'impertinency'; but what was its function in the play, and in Hamlet's personality structure, remained for Weimann something of a mystery. 'Why,' he asks, 'is Shakespeare's greatest representative of humanism so created as to be, not only in favor with the multitude, but in intimate touch with popular speech?[20] The answer can only be given in strongly intentionalist, historicist terms. *Hamlet* is the play in which Shakespeare invested his own conception of the popular theater, and by making Hamlet both playwright and director, made articulate the degree to which Hamlet's introspection resembles his own; Hamlet is the character in whom the dilemmas of the intellectual, seen from the perspective of a theory both of the theater and society, is doomed to divided loyalties. But the division was not so much, perhaps, between caviar and the general, the rewards of court patronage versus those of popular success, as it was between the allure of the judicious few and the claims of the underprivileged many. To speak to both simultaneously was an ambition, the history of Shakespearean criticism makes evident, possible of fulfilment; *Hamlet*, of all the plays, is the clearest *representation* of the wish. The overeducated prince who *himself* speaks in the popular voice knowingly performs the merger that, in *A Midsummer Night's Dream*, Shakespeare had imagined accomplished (magically, sexually, accidentally) in Titania's liaison with Bottom; but since *Hamlet* is also the threshold between a hopeful social theory and a tragic one, the merger fails. And whereas Weimann attributes the attempt to produce the merger to a 1590s mood of national unity (p. 181), a mood which was at best intermittent and at worst a political and politically fostered illusion, *Hamlet*'s disastrous ending is not merely the product of its hero's psychological disturbance but also of its author's turn-of-the-century, post-rebellion, accounting.[21]

Here too, as in festive theory more generally, Weimann's aesthetics inhibited full inspection of Hamlet's transgressive radicalism, as well as of its final betrayal. Believing that art is synonymous with unity and harmony, Weimann must believe also that Shakespeare *reduces* the conflicts between his popular and humanist materials. Thus Hamlet is a 'more poetically unified individuality' than the old Vice (p. 126) and the tensions between low sport and high mimesis are resolved by containing them within Shakespeare's 'larger artistic synthesis' (p. 191). Conversely, I believe that in *Hamlet* Shakespeare *exaggerated* the conflict between these principles, between popular and high culture, by having them fight it out on the site of Hamlet's psyche.

All of these issues come to a head in the scene between Hamlet and the gravedigger, whom Hamlet calls an ass, and who advises his colleague to 'cudgel [his] brains no more...for your dull ass will not mend his pace with beating' (5:1:56–57). This reallocation of the *Dream*'s central symbol for the underclasses is only one of the signs that here, in this confrontation between prince and artisan, Shakespeare produced a less festive account of social difference than was still imaginable in 1595–6.

As Weimann noted, the gravedigger scene has strong intimations of a radical tradition of protest. The first and more intelligent clown locates himself in the long line of 'English and German revolutionary peasant movements' (p. 239); his disrespect for rank, 'There is no ancient gentlemen but gardeners, ditchers, and grave-makers – they hold up Adam's profession' (5:1:29–31) deliberately recalled the Edenic motto 'When Adam delved' that since 1381 had signified resistance to class distinctions and economic injustice, was recirculated on the stage in the early 1590s in *The Life and Death of Jack Straw*, and was echoed in Shakespeare's own definition of Jack Cade's program ('Adam was a gardener'). But especially as a professional Digger,[22] this laborer is symbolically inscribed at the heart of an egalitarianism that equated property with land, and with equal shares in the earth at the beginning and the end.

But there is another echo in the gravedigger's challenge that, though less venerable, has a specifically Elizabethan force. Mockingly testing both his colleague and the audience by asking a riddle, 'Who builds stronger than a mason, a shipwright, or a carpenter?', the clown rejects the first solution – the gallowsmaker – and urges harder thought. 'Ay, tell me that, and unyoke' (5:1:50–2). Malone's edition[23] incorporated Farmer's discovery that here was a trace of a popular song – a workman's song – that appears in the 1587 edition of Holinshed's *Chronicles*:

> My bow is broke, I would unyoke,
> My foot is sore, I can worke no more.

In the *Chronicles*, the song occurs as part of an extended account of the rebuilding of the port of Dover in 1586, an event which the chronicler, probably John Stow,[24] represents as a moment of extreme optimism for the Elizabethan state, one that symmetrically repaired the damage done to the national esteem by the loss of Calais. It is presented also as an instance of high-minded collaboration between classes, of benevolent industrial relations, of technological expertise, and as an instance of natural timekeeping on the job. 'And all this time,' wrote the chronicler, 'there was never anie tumult, fraie, nor falling out, to the disquieting and disturbance of the works, which by that means were the better applied, and with less interruption':

> For they never ceased working the whole daie, saving that at eleven of the clocke before noone, as also at six of the clocke in the evening, there was a flag usuallie held up by the sargent of the towne, in the top of a tower, except the tide or extraordinarie busines forced the officers to prevent the houre, or to make some small delaie and staie thereof. And presentlie upon the signe given, there was a generall shout made by all the workers: and wheresoever anie court (cart) was at that instant either emptie or loden, there was it left, till one of the clocke after noone or six of the clocke in the morning, when they returned to their businesse. But by the space of halfe an houre before the flag of libertie was hanged out, all the court drivers entered into a song, wherof although the dittie was barbarous, and the note rusticall, the matter of no moment, and all but a jest, yet is it not unworthie of some briefe note of remembrance; because the tune or rather the

noise therof was extraordinarie and (being delivered with the continuall voice of such a multitude) was verie strange. In this and some other respect, I will set downe their dittie, the words wherof were these:

> O Harrie hold up thy hat, t'is eleven a clocke,
> and a little, little, little, little past:
> My bow is broke, I would unyoke,
> my foote is sore, I can worke no more.

Here, in effect, is a contemporary record of the popular voice, that is to say, 'a generall shout', or the many singing as one. As the chronicler himself puts it, this phenomenon was both 'extraordinarie' and 'strange'. His report is itself extraordinary among comparable documents in its blend of passive reception ('I will set downe their dittie') which establishes him as oral historian of popular culture in the workplace, and of social prejudice ('the dittie was barbarous, and the note rusticall, the matter of no moment, and all but a jest'). But, like those eye-witnesses who recorded the circumstances of Robert Kett's Norfolk rebellion as a warning to later 'malcontents', or like Shakespeare himself on the subject of Jack Cade's utopian agenda, Stow cannot apparently avoid a seepage into his text of the rational and ethical content of the scene, the beliefs that organize the 'barbarous' practises. The sign that marks the boundaries of the ten-and-a-half hour working day, the display of 'the flag of libertie', inevitably introduces the conflicting idea of bondage. Even to quote the song reveals that the workers fully understood both what their 'libertie' consisted in (the rules of time-keeping) and how often even those rules were infringed by 'some small delaie and staie thereof'; and at the end of his account Stow compares this festival practise of singing oneself into temporary freedom with less admirable habits of the very early Elizabethan theater:

> The song was made and set in Romneie marsh, where their best making is making of wals and dikes, and their best setting is to set a needle or a stake in a hedge: howbeit this is a more civill call than the brutish call at the theater for the comming awaie of the plaiers to the stage.

The civility recognized by Stow in this artisanal culture, however, is not sufficient to redeem it; and the analogy between workplace and theater works finally as a gesture of exclusion, to return the workers to the world of the brute and the barbarous.

This moment of antitheatrical prejudice connects the 1587 *Chronicles* (which Shakespeare certainly read) to the central concerns of *Hamlet*. But it is important to recognize that this slight but telling evocation of the Elizabethan world of work was available only in the readerly text of *Hamlet* of 1604 and was not memorable enough to register in the first Quarto. Its significance lies more in what it can tell us of how Shakespeare understood working-class thought and behavior than in any message capable of transfer to a theater (or even a reading) and audience.

Hamlet and Horatio, however, enter the scene only after the audience has heard those echoes of traditional popular protest, when the clown himself modulates into a different language. As he digs, he sings; and what he sings is emphatically not the snatches of popular song that Hamlet himself associates with social criticism. The verses that begin 'In youth when I did love' are, instead, well-remembered but jumbled fragments from one of the poems published in *Tottel's Miscellany* in 1557, a volume whose associations were as clearly courtly as its editor, Richard Tottel, could make them.[26] Tottel published the volume as 'Songes and Sonettes, written by the ryght honorable Lorde Henry Haward late Earle of Surrey'. Whether or not they knew that the poem was actually by Thomas Vaux, the allusion must have been complicated for Shakespeare and such friends and readers as Southampton by the fact that Surrey had been executed in 1547 by Henry VIII on a trumped-up charge of treason. But from Hamlet's perspective, the song in the gravedigger's mouth means only that a laborer has mistaken his place in the world. The gravedigger echoes the Dover artisans; but Hamlet responds like Stow. Amusement and alarm compete in his comments, but social and aesthetic propriety collaborate. In Hamlet's view, the gravedigger's mind is, like his hands, calloused: 'The hand of little employment hath the daintier sense' (5:1:68–69). And, as he watches him playing the forbidden game of 'loggets'[27] with the bones of his betters, insight into the scene's revolutionary implications makes Hamlet's language prophetic, even linguistically: 'Here's fine revolution, an we had the trick to see't.[28] How absolute the knave is!', he exclaims to Horatio. '. . . By the Lord, Horatio, this three years I have took note of it, the age is grown so picked that the toe of the peasant comes so near the heel of the courtier he galls his kibe' (133–8). We know whose heel is galled, and precisely how; not by the popular tradition with which he had earlier chosen to align himself, at least fragmentarily, but by the social presumption of the worker who, appropriating courtly lyric, has revealed the two-directional process inevitable in social mobility.

The effect is immediate. Radical Hamlet, the Hamlet who spoke the language of popular sports and inversion rituals, when faced with a competing popular consciousness and the *upward* mobility of wit, rejoins the aristocracy. Or rather, he reconstrues the essential competition as that between himself and Laertes, a rivalry now to be redefined in private, affective terms. It has already been established that Laertes is a rival in populist appeal. What Hamlet has failed to do, return in 'a riotous head' to challenge Claudius, Laertes has accomplished:

> The rabble call him lord
> And, as the world were now but to begin,
> Antiquity forgot, custom not known –
> The ratifiers and props of every word –
> They cry, 'Choose we! Laertes shall be king'
> Caps, hands, and tongues applaud it to the clouds.
> (4:5:101–7).

Ironically, Claudius engages, like archbishop Richard Bancroft in 1593, in mocking the appeal to the 'first institution' that underwrote the claims of popular protest, and that Hamlet himself, promoter of radical archaism, ought to have understood. But Laertes' arrival at the grave gives Hamlet the chance he needs to rewrite himself out of politics into erotics, to enter Ophelia's fatal family, taking the route of sexual aggression (always-already the subject of psychoanalysis) to his own grave.

One statement of Hamlet's in the gravedigger scene requires special attention. Between his complaint that the clown is too 'absolute' for comfort, and his fear that the 'peasant's toe' is already hard on the courtier's heel, Hamlet enjoins Horatio and himself, mysteriously: 'We must speak by the card, or equivocation will undo us.' Shakespeare uses 'equivocation' only here and in *Macbeth*, where the Porter develops it into a political hermeneutics that goes beyond the local issue of the Jesuit treason trials to what Steven Mullaney has called a 'rhetoric of rebellion'.[29] Mullaney conflates 'equivocation' with 'amphibologia', and cites George Puttenham's *Arte of English Poesie* (1589), who in illustration of the latter recalled the ambiguous prophecies by which 'many insurrections and rebellions have bene stirred up in this Realme, as that of Jacke Straw, & Jacke Cade in Richard the seconds time, and in our time by a seditious fellow in Norffolke calling himself Captaine Ket.'

In Hamlet's usage, 'equivocation' is genuinely equivocal. We simply cannot determine what it means. Like his earlier 'late innovation', which could refer *either* to the Essex rebellion or to the threat from the children's theaters, like his 'revolution' poised, apparently, between a past and future semantics, 'equivocation' is one of those abstract terms (brief chronicles) whose own hesitation between possibilities – quibbling, double-talk, equal speech or equal vocation – gives it unusual potency at this transitional moment, as Hamlet himself hesitates between his old, quibbling, vocationally undecided, egalitarian self, and the one who decides to speak by the card, or, as an actor, stick to the script.

Jacques Lacan observed as well as anyone the extraordinary force of Hamlet's clowning, his 'punning equivocation', and its relation 'to those characters that are called fools, court jesters whose position allows them to uncover the most hidden motives, the character traits that cannot be discussed frankly without violating the norms of proper conduct.'[30] But for him it belonged to the general Freudian sliding of the signifier; its social import is therefore occluded.[31] And although he believed that the meaning of *Hamlet* can be formulated as the question, 'what takes place in the graveyard?' (p. 35), for Lacan the gravedigger was invisible. Instead, he focused on the phallic rivalry with Laertes, declaring that 'the whole scene is directed toward that furious battle at the bottom of the tomb,' (p. 24). And, finding the word 'mirror' in Hamlet's mockery of Osric ('His semblable is his mirror...his umbrage, nothing more'), Lacan seized an opportunity to reintroduce his mirror-stage in Oedipal development, and to claim, with a sliding of his own, that 'this is Hamlet's attitude to *Laertes* before the duel':

> The playwright situates the basis of aggressivity in this paroxysm of absorption in the imaginary register, formally expressed as a mirror relationship...The one you fight is the one you admire the most. The ego ideal is also, according to Hegel's formula which says that coexistence is impossible, the one you have to kill. (p. 31; italics added)

Dubious exegetical procedures notwithstanding, Lacan had part of the story right. The other half depends on *Hamlet*'s *other* mirror, the one featured in a theory of theatrical representation of the real (3:2:20) that permits the appearance in the text of historical 'form and pressure'. What Lacan failed to see, in laying bare 'the aggressivity that underlies the activity of the philanthropist, the idealist, the pedagogue and the reformer', was precisely the presence of those roles and their social import in Hamlet's confused and divided self. And in fact Hamlet can abandon those roles finally only by denying his own earlier intentions, calling his strategic madness 'poor Hamlet's enemy', and offering as analogy for his previous behavior the domestic accident: 'I have shot my arrow o'er the house/And hurt my brother.'

> If Hamlet from himself be ta'en away,
> And when he's not himself does wrong Laertes,
> Then Hamlet does it not, Hamlet denies it.
> Who does it then?
>
> (5:2:23–33)

The rhetorical question, with its appeal away from self-determination to unanswerability, belongs with Althusser's 'Mais qui travaille?' (the question of agency) and Lacan's 'Mais qui parle?' (the question of subjectivity). Shakespeare has Hamlet answer his own question. 'Who does it then? His madness.' But let us not suppose he intended that answer to satisfy; nor that, in having his own persona abandon responsibility, he thereby abandoned responsibility.

If we use Foucault's version of the question, 'What matter who's speaking', the answer, in the case of *King Lear*, is also, evidently, 'His Madness'. More precisely, his Royal Madness. If *Macbeth* displays to a degree unusual to Shakespeare a set of topics linked by their known pertinence to James I, *King Lear*, which probably shares the same compositional timeframe, comes perilously close to presenting a fictional portrait of the king himself. Ostensibly archaic in its historical location in 844 BC (approximately 800 years before the reign of Macbeth, and 800 after the events represented in *Coriolanus*), the play offered for inspection a disastrous representative of monarchy, and one who shared with the current monarch a striking number of characteristics, so striking, in fact, that it is hard to imagine the resemblance would have gone unnoticed by the censors. The difficulty is compounded by the fact that *King Lear* was, according to the 1608 Quarto, 'Played before the Kings Maiestie at Whitehall upon S. Stephans night in Christmas Hollidayes', an occasion which the Stationers' Register for 26 November 1607 identifies as 'Christmas Last'.

We know, in other words, that on 26 December 1606 King James was regaled by a play whose protagonist was an elderly monarch whose hobby was hunting, whose retinue was distinctive in its foregrounding of a Fool, who during the central acts is evidently insane, and whose authoritarian views ultimately destroyed himself and his entire family. While James himself was only forty in 1606, he prided himself on having ruled Scotland since the age of fifteen, and represented himself to his new subjects as 'an old, experienced king, needing no lessons.'[32] In July 1604 Count Beaumont wrote to Henry IV of France that 'the king is for ever following the chase in order to divert his spirit';[33] and Archie Armstrong, who accompanied James from Scotland, had already established himself as the 'all-licens'd Fool' of Goneril's complaint (1:4:209) who treated the king and men of high rank with astonishing familiarity. With these keys to identity firmly established in the first act, the audience would quickly have realized that the archaic setting was a ruse to permit analysis of a particular style and ideology of monarchy, one that was not only, with James's accession, suddenly topical, but that was also, given the king's preference for publishing his views, a matter already of public record.[34]

The Jacobean audience, also, would probably have not been discouraged from considering the Lear/James analogy by the fact that the pre-Arthurian monarch of the chronicles had a different familial situation from their own. Indeed, the play's very first lines would have momentarily suggested a still closer relationship. When Kent opens by remarking to Gloucester, 'I thought the King had more affected the Duke of Albany than Cornwall', his hearers could immediately have assumed, as Glynne Wickham suggested, some reference to Prince Henry, the current Duke of Cornwall, and his brother Charles, Duke of Albany until November 1605.[35] By contrast, in the old play, *The True Chronicle History of King Leir*, probably in print in the summer of 1605, the two husbands are registered as the Kings of Cornwall and Cambria. When the kingdom is divided between sisters, and the Dukes are re-entered in the playtext as merely the husbands of Goneril and Regan, the audience has been misled. At the very least, this ruse would have encouraged a flexible hermeneutics, a wary approach to the play's exceptionally complex representational structure.

As I have argued elsewhere, the theme of rival sons connected *King Lear* to the contemporary debate, initiated by James himself, on the relationship between England and Scotland, whose Union under himself James had made his reign's inaugural project.[36] On 18 November 1606, a little over a month before the royal performance of *King Lear*, James opened the third session of Parliament with a speech urging decision on the Union issue, and reassuring his subjects that 'he did so equally esteem these Two Kingdoms, betwixt which he was so equally divided, as Two Brothers, and as if they had equal Parts of his Affections...and after him there could never be any so equally and so amply *affected* to them both.'[37] In the light of this speech, Kent's opening words, 'I thought the King had more *affected* the Duke of Albany than Cornwall' and Gloucester's reply that 'in the division of the kingdom, it appears not which of the Dukes he values most', is manifestly misaligned as a key to the story of 844 BC, but rather more intelligible in the context of Christmas 1606, when the discourse of the day was of fathers, sons and divided inheritances.

There seems little doubt that the Union issue was one major form of the topicality in which *King Lear* is saturated, although, given the reversed mirror in which the issue is visible, it is impossible to decide what solution Shakespeare recommended. Evidently, the play includes a critique of the authoritarian, patriarchal and constitutionally absolutist *theories* of James himself, and at the same time reveals the distinction between absolutist theory and its practice, which in *King Lear* is clearly ineffective. The speech in which Lear gives away the 'name, and all th'addition to a king' (1:1:138), lays open to inspection the tautological structure of the Jacobean language of power, a grandiose and inflationary rhetoric that attempted to make the fact of 'rule' seem more than an accident of birth. And, differently again, the play provides echoes of James's other voices, the querulous voice of well-meaning ('I am a man more sinned against than sinning', 3:2:59; 'Your old kind father, whose kind heart gave all', 3:2:19); and even the voice of criticism well-taken, of reforms intended:

> O! I have ta'en
> Too little care of this.
>
> (3:4:32–3)

It is the representation of these voices (in characterological terms, Lear's humanization) that permits the audience to transfer its sympathy back to the king, and to perceive the system that he represents, however flawed, as more capable of amendment than the aggressive, voracious and essentially unstructured alternative of Edmund, Goneril and Regan. At the level, then, of the Union issue whose language and central metaphors the play incarnates, undecidability reigns.

But after the first act the Union issue disappears, though its familial forms remain. What replaces it, extending topicality's range from the narrowly specific to the broadest and deepest of contemporary concerns, is a critique of the socioeconomic system of Jacobean England. Nor can the force of this critique be restricted to Jacobean England, still less to the opening years of James's reign: it was reinvoked, as we shall see, by James Agee as the inaugural premise of *Let Us Now Praise Famous Men*, his extraordinary study of American rural poverty in the Depression. Historicity, then, may itself encourage transhistoricity, even or especially when what is transferred to later cultures is the clash of human with economic values and structures.

It has become something of a commonplace in discussions of *King Lear* that it represents the transition from a feudal economy or culture to a nascent capitalism; or, in a slightly different vocabulary, the decline of a moral in the face of a market economy.[38] But the argument that Lear, Kent, and perhaps Cordelia act out the old feudal values or configure (semi-allegorically) a Moral Economy is deeply unpersuasive. Edmund, Goneril and Regan, the figures who supposedly represent the approach of capitalist values, in no way differ from aristocratic predators anywhere in Shakespeare's canon; while it is Lear himself, by promoting a land transfer tax to be paid in professions of love, who introduces marketability into a simple because arbitrary principle of aristocratic inheritance. As for a Moral Economy, if conceived as an earlier stage of mutual benevolence between a feudal aristocracy and clergy and a grateful, humble and obedient peasantry, such a conception could have been no more plausible to Shakespeare than the specter of a free market regulated only by laws internal to itself, in which no controls could be posited on possessive individualism. Rather, he would have shared in an increasingly articulate body of opinion, articulate in the debates of the Jacobean parliament, that the system combined or should combine elements of morality with economic pragmatism. For the first few years of James's reign saw a distinct change in the fiscal role of parliament, whose previously limited concern with taxation was developed under James (and against his will) into a coherent theory of economic justice.

We will return in the next chapter to parliament's role in regulating the economy, especially as it was brought into sharp focus by the Midlands Rising, producing newly theoretical address to the problems of wealth's distribution. But already in the parliamentary sessions prior to *King Lear*, economics had been made the subject of the day. In the first Jacobean parliament, the Union issue brought immediately to the forefront an old grievance, old in the sense that James had inherited it from his Tudor predecessors, especially Elizabeth: monopolies, or private patents assigned by the monarch for the control of specific products, such as imported wines, salt or starch, to members of their court whom they wished to reward or control. At the end of her reign Elizabeth had acceded to complaints against the procedure, and in her last parliament of 1601, in the aftermath of the Essex rebellion, agreed to issue a proclamation against it. When James succeeded, however, many patents were still extant, and others were distributed in the first rush of liberality (what James called his Christmas) to his Scottish followers. The theme of economic rivalry between English and Scottish, therefore, when it surfaced in the 1604 parliament because James himself provoked it, was merely the hook that drew along with it a group of other fiscal grievances, including wardships, purveyance, the king's personal extravagance, and the hated monopolies, whose connection was made only beneath the debating surface. Loosely grouped under the heading of 'grievances', these issues were posed as the *other* subject of the reign's opening parliament, a subject on which the Commons required satisfaction if the king were ever to accomplish his own darling project, the Union.

Even one of the more conservative historians of this period, J. P. Kenyon, who began with the opinion that the 1604 parliament emitted 'a perpetual rumble' of unfocused discontent which only occasionally 'came to a head on some general issue', came later to the view that economic issues resulted in the formation of a more or less consolidated opposition.[39] Certainly, by the 1610 session, in which Salisbury attempted to resolve the fiscal impasse once and for all by proposing, unsucessfully, the Great Contract, the nature of the parliament's interest in the economy had been greatly clarified. The symptomatic issue was now 'impositions', Salisbury's solution to the royal deficit by arbitrarily placing new taxes on imports. But the real issue was the mutual recognition by both king and parliament that they had entered an arena of contractual relationships, governed by a logic of reciprocal exchange. In a speech of 21 March, which was largely an exercise in unconstrained patriarchal and absolutist rhetoric, the king nevertheless requested the parliament to 'see how great my wants are' and declared both his willingness to deal and his recognition that absolutist theory should not always be put into practice: 'What a king will do upon bargain is one thing and what on his prerogative is another thing.'[40] The opening premise of *King Lear* is likewise the arrival of the deal, of a newly contractual approach to governance, and to the distribution of wealth. In the initial exchange of land for professions of affection, and even in Lear's own sinister and mistaken threat to Cordelia: 'Nothing will come of nothing', Shakespeare might be thought to register a warning against the era of the fiscal bargain.

Yet as soon as the division of the kingdom is completed, the emphasis shifts. Lear learns the contractual relationship between power and responsibility for the powerless, and something about the role of need in establishing economic value. The Fool's gibe about monopolies (1:4:158–9), interestingly omitted from the Folio, is not a casual and hence dispensable topicality, but the opening gambit in an analysis of class and economic difference that the Folio, if anything, intensifies. The Fool assumes that monopolies are the privilege of 'lords and great men'; his remark coordinates with Kent's complaint against Oswald, 'That such a slave as this should wear a sword' (2:2:73), and Gloucester's complaint against Cornwall that putting Kent in the stocks is inappropriate to his earl's rank ('Your purpos'd low correction/Is such as basest and contemned'st wretches/ For pilf'rings and most common trespasses/Are punish'd with' 2:2:142–5). And while Kent's and Gloucester's complaints are against social mobility, upwards and downwards, and therefore conservative, others on the same moral side as they have a more flexible sociology. Edgar's impersonation of a Bedlam beggar, whose models were themselves, in order to 'enforce charity', forced to impersonate the mad (2:3:20),[41] is an example of willed or provisional topsy-turveydom. The transgressive aspect of Edgar's disguise can be better understood in terms of socioeconomic history than (*pace* Stephen Greenblatt) echoes of Samuel Harsnett and the exorcism debate. The Fool's song, 'Come over the bourn, Bess', is found also in the old, black-letter play, *The longer thou livest, the more Foole thou art*, where 'Morus' is introduced 'synging the foote of many songes, as fooles were wont'. And the 'foote' as the sign of transgressive foolishness reappears in *King Lear* in what must be seen as a meta-textual crux, when Goneril, resenting the impediment of her marriage to Albany, complains to Edmund in successively symbolic stages: 'My foote usurps my body' (in the uncorrected first Quarto), 'A foole usurps my bed' (in the corrected Quarto), 'My foote usurps my head', in the second and third Quartos, and finally in the Folio, 'My Fool usurps my body' (4:2:28). Foot, fool and usurpation of a proper space thereby converge in the text's own uncertainty.

But we do not need to rely on the antics of the text for this play's radicalism. As Richard Strier remarks, one of the most politically significant moments occurs at the level of violent physical action, when Cornwall's servant attempts to prevent him from blinding Gloucester, and is stabbed in the back by Regan, 'exclaiming, with the full weight of outraged decorum, 'A peasant stand up thus!' (3:7:79).[42] Not only does this moment, as Strier argues, present the 'most radical possible sociopolitical act in a way that can only be interpreted as calling for his audience's approval', it reintroduces precisely that ancient populism for which the term 'peasant' was now already cultural shorthand, a point reinforced for Shakespeare's audience by the fact that Cornwall insults his servant by calling him 'villain', the stigmatized echo of 'villein'.

And, although Shakespeare's audiences could not have known it, a special value attaches also to the Fool's request to know whether 'a madman be a gentleman or a yeoman', and his own conflation of the choice, 'He's a yeoman that has a gentleman to his son; for he's a mad yeoman that sees his son a gentleman before him' (3:6:9–14). The family predicament speaks obliquely of Shakespeare's own and his father's situation, and for that famous application in 1596, when Shakespeare purchased for John Shakespeare, yeoman, for a gentleman's coat of arms: 'Gold, on a bend sables, a spear of the first steeled argent', with a motto, 'Non Sanz Droit', not without right.[43]

These positions on rank, though presented dialectically, lead inevitably to Lear's great speech of social inversion, which the Folio accentuates by adding the injunction, 'Change places', the heart of a radical theory of economic change and exchange:

> What! art mad? A man may see how this world goes with no eyes. Look with thine ears: see how yond justice rails upon yond simple thief. Hark, in thine ear: [change places, and,] handy dandy, which is the justice, which is the thief? (4:6:151–6)

Social mobility, expressed earlier in the upstart Oswald and the humiliation of Kent, in the yeoman whose ambitious son (unlike Shakespeare) leaves him behind in his climb towards gentrification, implies its own extreme conclusion. If men can change places on the social hierarchy, then those places have no absolute value, and complete inversion becomes, to the seeing ear of madness, utterly thinkable. The echo of Bottom's mingle-mangle of the organs of perception is surely as intentional here as is Lear's recapitulation of Hamlet's 'madness', the scandal of speaking the not immemorial forms of popular protest. But in Lear's case the scandal is the greater, since it is now the king himself, 'the great image of Authority' (4:6:160) who speaks in the popular voice. What matter who's speaking? It matters absolutely.

The central scenes on the heath, then, situate gibes at monopolies or the excessive distribution of knighthoods in a far more radical argument, showing them to be not casual throwaways, but the building blocks of an emergent stuctural analysis of power and class relations. And in the Fool's prophecy, added in the Folio, this analysis is enigmatically performed in terms of the relationship between church, aristocracy, law, finance and the human body:

> When priests are more in word than matter;
> When brewers mar their malt with water;
> When nobles are their tailors' tutors;
> No heretics burn'd, but wenches' suitors;
> When every case in law is right;
> No squire in debt, nor no poor knight;
> When slanders do not live in tongues;
> Nor cut-purses come not to throngs;
> When usurers tell their gold i' th' field;
> And bawds and whores do churches build;
> Then shall the realm of Albion
> Come to great confusion.
>
> (3:2:81–92)

It is not clear whether these distorted relationships are the cause or the consequence of the moral failings of greed, lechery and linguistic corruption; but no one, reading or hearing the last two lines, could avoid the knowledge that Lear's Fool speaks to a national problem, the state of Albion-England both as it is and as it might be if the 'when-then' tensions in the poem, themselves formulae inherited from radical prophecy and medieval social satire, are not resolved in favor of change for the better.[44]

And as in 1604 onwards James I had been responsible for raising those structural relations to the level of consciousness by attempting to theorize them, so in *King Lear* the king himself incorporates that coming to consciousness. Lear begins the analysis out of self-interest, with a critique of Regan's invocation of 'need' as a principle to deny him his retinue. His recognition that if each were to receive only according to his most basic needs he would be reduced to the level of the brute (2:4:265–9) is a first step in his elementary thinking about the ways in which wealth is distributed. It is, of course, vitiated both in moral and practical terms by his current belief (soon to be shattered by contact with Poor Tom) that 'our basest beggars' already have those basic needs satisfied, and that to introduce the principle, 'to each according to his need', would require them to turn in their 'superfluous' goods. Yet this misconception prepares for his later recognition before the hovel on the heath that 'the art of our necessities is strange,/And can make vile things precious' (3:2:70–71), simultaneously an acceptance of need as the source of value (if what we most need is shelter from the elements, the worst kind of shelter will outvalue the most precious clothing) and it leads ironically to his determination to 'shake the superflux', that is, the superfluous wealth that he knows the economy produces, to the 'wretches' whose condition he now experiences. The abstract conception of need, then, previously a mere strategy in his argument with Regan, has been rendered concrete (and its meanness admonished) by empirical evidence.

Following *Hamlet*'s opening challenge, 'Stand and unfold *yourself*', Lear's demand, 'Expose *thyself* to feel what wretches feel', also acquires the status of metacommentary. Self-exposure in *King Lear*, however, is emphatically not a matter of subjective disclosure. Rather, it is the social outreach required for discovering the spirit of the moral economy embedded, always already, in the economic system. For Lear, this outreach is required 'to show the gods more just'. Much later, a secular interpretation revealed more precisely how self-exposure is the point of intersection between humanist values and empirical method. This point was defined by the documentary realism and poetic structure of Agee's *Let Us Now Praise Famous Men*, which offered the American public the most intimate view of the life of Alabama sharecroppers in the late 1930s, a view acquired by Agee's sharing for several weeks their shack and pitiful diet. It was no coincidence that the first words of Agee's project are those of Lear in his madness:

> Poor naked wretches, wheresoe'er you are,
> That bide the pelting of this pitiless storm,
> How shall your houseless heads and unfed sides,
> Your loop'd and window'd raggedness, defend you
> From seasons such as these? O! I have ta'en
> Too little care of this! Take physic, pomp;
> Expose thyself to feel what wretches feel,
> That thou may'st shake the superflux to them,
> And show the heavens more just.[45]

Agee's dilemmas in carrying his project to completion may also illuminate Shakespeare's, as the evolution of Roosevelt's New Deal may retroactively provide a model for the first decade of James's reign, unlikely though the comparison may seem. The book was the chance product of Walker Evans' appointment as 'roving social historian' of the Farm Security Administration and Agee's assignment to write a sociological article for *Fortune* magazine. The material they collected was destined never to be published by *Fortune*, since while they worked in Alabama Henry Luce decided to change the magazine's course, from support of New Deal policies to a more conservative agenda; but even before this occurred, Agee was consumed by guilt about his own procedures, recognizing the aspect of exploitation involved in the assignment. In his 'Preamble' to the book that was eventually published by Houghton Mifflin in 1941, Agee called it 'obscene' that a journal, operating for profit, could propose:

> to pry intimately into the lives of an undefended and appallingly damaged group of human beings, an ignorant and helpless rural family, for the purpose of parading the nakedness, disadvantage and humiliation of these lives before another group of human beings, in the name of science, of 'honest journalism,' (whatever that paradox may mean).

In order to deal with that guilt, Agee and Evans reconceived their role as that of holy spies,[46] witnesses or secret agents of the forces of good, a role that Agee conceived, again in terms of *King Lear*, as that of Edgar in his disguise as Poor Tom. In a poem that he wrote for Evans, subsequently added to the preliminaries of *Let Us Now Praise Famous Men*, Agee proposed that they go on their assignment as:

> Spies, moving delicately among the enemy,
> The younger sons, the fools,
> Set somewhat aside the dialects and the stained skins of feigned madness,
> Ambiguously signal, baffle, the eluded sentinel.

The poem advises Edgar to bring his father to his awakening, but himself to withdraw 'undisclosed'; and it concludes with the statement that it is not yet 'that naked hour when armed, / Disguise flung flat, squarely we challenge the field', for the world is still governed by the ruthless, 'Still captive the old wild king'.

From the beginning, *Let Us Now Praise Famous Men* obeys this poem's prescriptions. Among the most ambiguous of Agee's signals is the placing of Lear's speech on the heath opposite another famous radical text, the Communist Manifesto's call to action: 'Workers of the world, unite and fight. You have nothing to lose but your chains, and a world to win.' And beneath *that* quotation appeared the following disclaimer:

> These words are quoted here to mislead those who will be misled by them. They mean, not what the reader may care to think they mean, but what they say. . . for in the pattern of the work as a whole, they are, in the sonata form, the second theme; the poetry facing them [the quotation from *Lear*] is the first. In view of the average readers' tendency to label, and of topical dangers to which any man, whether honest, intelligent, or subtle, is at present liable, it may be well to make the explicit statement that neither these words nor the authors are the property of any political party, faith or faction.

The reader might well react to this opening like the Porter in *Macbeth*: 'it sets him on and it takes him off; it persuades him and disheartens him; makes him stand to and not stand to; in conclusion, equivocates' (2:2:33–8).

The mention of sonata form, moreover, speaks to the way that *Let Us Now Praise Famous Men* succumbed to the idea of the artefact. The very respect that Agee developed for the sharecroppers, for the simplicity and authenticity of their lives and possessions, was processed as aesthetic appreciation of the worn, the bare, the marginal, or, as Lear put it, 'unaccommodated man'. And in proportion as Agee knew his project was aesthetically and ethically complex,[47] he was completely unable to take his own advice and 'undisclosed, withdraw'. The book is filled with himself, his ruminations on truth, beauty, and the role of the writer in society. He included, as part of this self-examination, his responses to a questionnaire distributed in 1939 by the *Partisan Review* to a number of American writers; and in response to the question, 'Do you think there is any place in our present economic system for literature as a profession?', replied in the negative:

> A good artist is a deadly enemy of society; and the most dangerous thing that can happen to an enemy, no matter how cynical, is to become a beneficiary. No society, no matter how good, could be mature enough to support a real artist without mortal danger to that artist. Only no one need worry: for this same good artist is about the one sort of human being alive who can be trusted to take care of himself (p. 355).

As Agee's reading of *King Lear* is eccentrically acute, the predicament here both lamented and celebrated was one he shared, probably, with Shakespeare. Particularly in his intuition that the artist with a social conscience is the younger son, the fool, the feigned madman, Edgar as Poor Tom, Agee both found a metaphor for his own strategic adoption of the sharecroppers' way of life, and grasped in his own ahistorical manner the radical analysis that Shakespeare performed, in disguise, on the economic structure of his own society. That disguise was, like Edgar's, 'to take the basest and most poorest shape / That ever penury, in contempt of man, / Brought near to beast' (2:3:7–9), that is to say, as a playwright, to take up the case of society's victims, but, by the grace of the dramatic metaphor, to do so 'undisclosed'. Yet Agee's remarks on the 'mortal danger' to the artist of patronage, of becoming society's beneficiary, must also be pertinent to *King Lear*, given that one of the few facts we have of its social existence is the record of that court performance on St Stephen's Night, December 1606, when Shakespeare's play was offered to James I. Leah Marcus may well be correct in reading that emphatic dating as a key to the tone of that one command performance; there is much in *King Lear*, whether or not it was written for this occasion, that fits the festival of St Stephen, whose primary message was charity: 'He that giveth unto the poore, shall not lacke; but he that hideth his eyes from them, shall have many a curse.'[48] And it would certainly be possible to argue that James I was thereby admonished to avoid the fate of Lear, by adopting Lear's hard-learned wisdom.

The fact remains, however, that the play as a whole does not remain faithful to that message, not, at least, at the deep structural level of socioeconomic analysis. For Lear *recovers* from his wisdom-as-madness, and takes nothing from it into his reconciliation with Cordelia that is not a purely domestic intelligence. In fact, in a speech that reveals the source of Agee's concept of holy spying, 'the old wild king' that Agee remembered disappears; or, rather, is domesticated. For when Lear and Cordelia are captured by Edmund's army, Lear responds with political cynicism and privatization:

> We two alone will sing like birds i' th' cage:
> When thou dost ask me blessing, I'll kneel down,
> And ask of thee forgiveness: so we'll live,
> And pray, and sing, and tell old tales, and laugh
> At gilded butterflies, and hear poor rogues
> Talk of court news; and we'll talk with them too,
> Who loses and who wins; who's in, who's out;
> And take upon's the mystery of things,
> As if we were God's spies.
>
> (5:3:9–17)

The temptation to withdraw from the 'general' (in Hamlet's sense) to the particular, from structural analysis to subjective concerns, is as candidly identified here as it was in *Hamlet.*

Is this, then, to be construed as Shakespeare's temptation also, his conclusion that the hope of changing places is, after all, a delusion from which we should recover? I doubt it. Such a conclusion is barely compatible with his most transgressive strategy so far, to make the king his own most powerful social critic. And if the play retreats finally into the domestic and familial, as a shelter from sociopolitical awareness, one of Shakespeare's motives may well have been the need for 'moving delicately among the enemy', and with ambiguous signals, to baffle the eluded sentinel.

Peasant Boots

From the 'clouted shoon' of peasant ideology, through the workers' song at the rebuilding of Dover ('My foot is sore, I can work no more') through

Hamlet's concern about the pressure from behind of the peasant's toe on the courtier's heel, Shakespeare arrived at the usurping foot of *King Lear*'s textual confusion. In *Coriolanus*, when the fable of the body is retold to a group of disordinate citizens, one of them is particularly castigated as the state's big toe, 'one o'th'lowest, basest, poorest' members of the body politic (1:1:156). Slight as they are, these constant references have a story of their own to tell that is still at the heart of our own cultural dynamics. In *Let Us Now Praise Famous Men* Agee included a touching section on 'Shoes':

> They are one of the most ordinary types of working shoe: blucher design, and soft in the prow, lacking the seam across the root of the big toe: covering the ankles: looped straps at the heels: blunt, broad, and rounded at the toe: broad-heeled: made up of most simple roundnesses and squarings and flats, of dark brown raw thick leathers nailed, and sewn coarsely to one another in courses and patterns of doubled and tripled seams, and such throughout that like many other small objects they have great massiveness and repose... They are softened, in the uppers, with use, and the soles are rubbed thin enough... that the ticklish grain of the ground can be felt through at the center of the forward sole... The shoes are worn for work. At home, resting, men always go barefooted (p. 270).

In accordance with their joint program of finding the humblest objects beautiful, ('The art of our necessities is strange, / And can make vile things precious', *King Lear*, 3:2:70–1) Walker Evans included among his photographs the image of a pair of peasant boots, whose placement, empty, on the earth, their laces trailing, was evidently designed as an allusion to the painting by Van Gogh which honors the cover of my own book.[49] This painting has subsequently become significant in literary theory by virtue of its discussion (seriatim) by three eminent theorists: by Martin Heidegger, in his essay on 'The Origin of the Work of Art', given as a lecture in 1935–6, but first published in 1968;[50] by Meyer Schapiro, in 'The Still Life as a Personal Object: A Note on Heidegger and Van Gogh', published in the same volume as Heidegger's piece; and Jacques Derrida's 'Restitutions of the truth in pointing', published in 1987, as a defence of Heidegger against Schapiro in the light of a postmodern philosophy of art.[51] The entire debate highlights one of the premises undergirding this book – that all art (Shakespeare's plays, Agee and Walker's philosophical documentary, Van Gogh's painting) along with its subsequent commentary, is forced to consider how art's images relate to material things. In the case of these peasant boots, as Derrida realized, the object chosen for representation was symbolic of the human point of contact with material necessity, as distinct from what is meant and achieved by the head: 'a certain necessity... of walking, namely, closest to the ground, the lowest degree, the most subjective or underlying level of what's called culture or the institution, the shoe' (p. 264).

In contest between Heidegger and Schapiro was precisely the real origin of the boots in Van Gogh's picture. For Heidegger, they were simply those of a peasant (man or woman), for Schapiro they were the boots of Van Gogh himself, who after 1887 had become a Parisian. But, as Derrida brilliantly observed, beneath this seemingly trivial disagreement lurked fundamental differences. Heidegger's conviction that the boots were those of a peasant was rich with 'the pathos of the "call of the earth", of the *Feldweg* or the *Holzwege*', which in 1935–6, when the lectures on art were delivered, was contaminated by Nazi propaganda. Conversely, Schapiro's conviction that Van Gogh's boots were his own arose out of his loyalty to Kurt Goldstein, who, having fled from Nazi Germany in 1933 and arrived in New York, was the first to observe the political significance of Heidegger's interpretation. At stake, then, was the valence of 'peasant ideology' in Europe and America six centuries after its formation as a cultural structure of resistance against economic repression. And, as Derrida also cogently noted, Schapiro's own resistance to Heidegger's appropriation of the boots was 'dangerously complicated' by the fact that Van Gogh himself, wherever he painted, 'never stopped uttering the discourse of rural, artisanal, and peasant ideology' (p. 273) on his canvases.

But beyond this absolute disagreement there lay an agreement still more absolute, in which Derrida, as the third party, joined. When Heidegger proposed to go back behind the early modern opposition between artist and artisan, and implicitly to draw an analogy, on the basis of ideas of work and production, between artist and peasant, he was in his own way (as Derrida observed) facing the same problematic as Schapiro when he wrote:

> Yet Van Gogh is in many ways like the peasant; as an artist he works, he is stubbornly occupied in a persistent task that is for him his inescapable calling, his life.

And when Heidegger summons up the call of the earth, Schapiro writes of the boots that they function as a self-portrait of the artist 'as an old thing' (Derrida, p. 370), 'that part of the costume with which we tread the earth and in which we locate the strains of movement, fatigue, pressure, heaviness – the burden of the erect body in its contact with the ground. They mark our inescapable position on the earth' (p. 371). As Lear said, 'Thou art the thing itself' (3:4:109). The boots, then, become the face, the foot usurps the head, and performs the philosophical function that the head has been unable to perform: to restore the ground, the trust in material reality, that philosophical speculation had excavated away. As Derrida puts it, the 'reliability' of the peasant boots as an image makes possible not only 'the "profoundest" going-back behind the philosophemes of matter-form, of usefulness, of production, of subjectivity, of objectivity, of symbol and law', but also 'the most naively archaic regression into the element of ingenuous trust', of submission, after all the knowingness, to the primary trap, the 'lure constituted by the mirror play of the world' (p. 355). Van Gogh wrote to his brother: 'Truth is so dear to me, and so is the seeking to make true, that indeed I believe, I believe I would still rather be a cobbler than a musician with colors' (Derrida, p. 368), a brilliant pun that establishes the making of boots at the center of his endeavour. And, it appears, the 'Restitutions' that were Derrida's endeavour here are not only to Heidegger and Van Gogh, but also to that vast and painful territory of realism, expressed as political and social experience, that his earlier philosophy had occluded.

It is, then, the 'ticklish grain of the ground' – the problem of thinking reality – that unites *King Lear* with modern and postmodern metaphysics. In the next chapter, and in what was probably Shakespeare's last attempt at tragic realism, *Coriolanus*, the essentialist humanism of *King Lear* is replaced by that most extreme admission of contingent and historically specific circumstances – the analysis of one political system – and the humanist problematic is shown to be determined by whether we consider the claims of the many or the one.

6

'Speak, speak!' The Popular Voice and the Jacobean State

> You are the Braine, the Liver, and the Heart
> Of this great Body and the Vitall-part
> Which gave it motion; But we are the Hands,
> Whereby it acts: The Feet, whereon it stands;
> The Bulk and Bones which must the burthens bear;
> And, We with you, may claime to have a share
> In all the sences; and without offence
> In that, which hath been cal'd the Common-sence.

> George Wither: 'The Speech of the Well-affected English' to Parliament, *Opobalsamum Anglicanum* (1646).

Coriolanus has never acquired the privileged place in Shakespearean criticism occupied pre-eminently by *Hamlet* and the Jacobean tragedies. This is, no doubt, the cost of the play's embarrassing frontal political nakedness; political theory is its *raison d'être*, and if we try to set it aside nothing of interest, of plot or character, remains. For this study of power relations in Rome in the earliest days of the republic subsumes, as an inevitable category of those relations, the formidable influence of matriarchy on maleness, militancy and their half-glimpsed shadow, homoeroticism.

What this commanding narrowness argues, however, is still at issue. As late as 1976 the Coleridgean tradition was still being maintained by Philip Brockbank for the New Arden edition, along with an implied critique of functionalist literature, and a mild form of Coleridge's conservativism. For Brockbank, the English theatrical history of production has been truer to Shakespeare's 'wonderful impartiality' than the European. In translation, he suggests, the play may lose its textual 'constraints and ironies', so that the 'propaganda potentials of its political myth can be more manifest'.[1] Yet in another sense the play is, or is coterminous with, its political myth; it is not clear how we distinguish between potential and actual propaganda; while the term 'propaganda', of course, remains blind to its own function as a stigma of other people's priorities.

Other people have been busy with their priorities, and with *Coriolanus*, since the late seventeenth century. In 1681 Nahum Tate's adaptation, *The Ingratitude of a Common-Weale*, took the occasion of the Popish Plot and Exclusion crisis to 'Recommend Submission and Adherence to Establisht Lawful Power, which in a word, is Loyalty' to the crown (A2v). Conversely, the Marxist and anti-militarist version by Bertolt Brecht, designed for East Germany in 1952–3, distorted the text in favor of the plebeians and their tribunes.[2] Rather than observing this with disapproval, the play's potential to excite a political response should perhaps encourage us to revalue it upwards. It is now possible to see the actual adaptations which altered the text as only extreme instances of ideological appropriation, which seems to occur more often for this play than for any other in the canon, with the strong exception of *The Tempest*. Most telling is the way in which *Coriolanus* has functioned outside its own territory, so to speak, as a cultural icon to be summoned as witness in debates apparently having little or nothing to do with Shakespeare. Featured in the nineteenth century by Charlotte Brontë in *Shirley* as a model for industrial ethics, and by George Eliot in *Felix Holt* as a lesson in Victorian electoral politics, *Coriolanus* has reappeared in the late twentieth century as a proof-text for contemporary social theory. So Günter Grass intertwined Shakespeare's play with his own critique of the chicken-livered aestheticism he discerned in Brecht and other left-wing German intellectuals;[3] Nancy Armstrong read the reading of *Coriolanus* in *Shirley* in terms of feminist criticism;[4] Allan Bloom, on the way to showing how 'higher education has failed democracy', incorporated the famous Body fable into his defence of the family, which involves an attack on women's liberation;[5] and Mark Kishlansky used the play to support a revisionist history of seventeenth-century electoral theory and practice with strong contemporary applicability.[6] Evidently, it remains a site of our deepest investments and still most urgent concerns.

But this list of appropriations, precisely by being such, raises an important question, the question of Shakespeare's intentions: what does the text of *Coriolanus* itself have to say about power relations, in ancient Rome and elsewhere, subsequently? It happens that all these interpreters, with the notable exception of Brecht, either assumed that Shakespeare's play was deeply conservative in intent, or were able to assimilate it to some conservative purpose. So Grass introduced his own project, in an address to the Academy of Arts and Letters in Berlin on 23 April 1964, the quatercentenary of Shakespeare's birth, by referring to the play's 'antidemocratic bias', a concept derived from the preface to an (unnamed) modern edition. His project then was to show that Brecht's attempt to reverse this bias in his *Coriolan* was doomed, both by the essence of the play that Shakespeare wrote, and by the posthistory of left-wing movements in the modern world, whose haplessness was for Grass epitomized in the East German industrial uprising of 17 June 1953, which Brecht notoriously had refused to support by any public statement.

This chapter will address the question of essence, as it were, by restating it as the critical concept of the grain, textual or historical, a sly-boots term when applied to *Coriolanus*, which begins with a grain riot. But it is also deeply serious. In one of his most famous pronouncements, Walter Benjamin warned the would-be cultural historian that the cultural history we have received is in more than one way a document of barbarism, concealing the power relations from which all art is produced. But to brush that history against the grain, as Benjamin proposed,[7] implies that we can decide which way the grain goes before we resist it, and indeed whether the grain's direction is determined by 'the text itself' or rather by habit, interpretative traditions, 'common opinion'. I shall here argue, first, that *Coriolanus* was constructed out of material already strongly grained in a certain direction, and that Shakespeare would not have chosen that particular story from Roman history to work with had he not been susceptible to its ideological import; second, that most of the appropriations referred to, along with some not yet mentioned, show distinct signs themselves of having to brush *their* accounts of Shakespeare's play, or the Roman history behind it, against the grain; and third, that it is possible to distinguish between 'impartiality', especially when that implies detachment (the separation of the playwright from local issues and the theater from social agency), and the balanced and nuanced assessment of rightful and wrongful causes, of justice and injustice, that Shakespeare had by this time trained himself to provide, and that had brought him, about five years after James's accession, to his most radical position: a belief that Jacobean England desperately needed to borrow from the strengths, as well as learn from the difficulties, of republican political theory.

To read *Coriolanus*, then, plunges us into the heart of the problems of historicism, old and new. Fifty years ago it was widely if not ubiquitously assumed that disputes about the 'meaning' of a text or its author's intentions could be resolved by recourse to 'history'. It is now equally widely assumed that no such recourse is possible, because, as late twentieth-century scepticism has easily shown, 'history' in that positive sense of actual occurrences has no demonstrable existence beyond its textual witnesses, who necessarily speak, consciously or not, in the service of different agenda; while 'history' as a discipline has likewise been deprived of its claims to objective method. Both positions are, of course, exaggerated, and the case of *Coriolanus* demands a peculiarly exacting poise between them.

As in *Henry V*, Shakespeare's project in *Coriolanus* makes heavy demands on its audience because of the intersection within it of more than one set of 'historical' correlatives. But where *Henry V* required one to juggle fifteenth-century history and the events of the 1590s (with a brief glimpse of Rome at the moment when Essex himself is invoked), *Coriolanus* involves several interdependent moments: the testing of the early Roman republic (in 494 BC) by popular protest and the consequent change in the constitution that provided, through the tribunate, for popular representation; the transmission of this story in written history, whether ancient (Plutarch and Livy) or modern (their Renaissance translators and commentators); and the local, seventeenth-century history that was Shakespeare's own environment. As *Henry V* spoke (in the Folio text) to the crisis of political authority at the end of Elizabeth's reign, *Coriolanus* seems clearly to address another stage of crisis brought to the public attention by the Midlands Rising of 1607, but involving larger questions, of the distribution of power in the state and of the nation's resources. Here too, as with Elizabeth's self-definition as Richard II, there is witness to the analogy from an authoritative source: several times in 1605 and 1606 James himself referred to the opposition leaders in the Commons as tribunes of the people.[8] But the congruence between ancient Rome and early modern England, past and present history, was more deeply theorized, more *structural* than convenient. Only if one perceives how this crucial moment in the development of Rome as a republic marked the convergence of class interests and constitutional theory does the choice of the Coriolanus story seem inevitable for Shakespeare, at this stage of his own development and that of the Jacobean state.

Perhaps because of the undeniability of this topical friction in the play, critics have been eager to deny, instead, that Shakespeare was engaging in a radical critique of the English system. Philip Brockbank, for the Arden edition, admitted the play's 'contemporaneity' but rejected the inference that this was the focus of Shakespeare's intentions. 'It may be true,' he remarked, 'that *Coriolanus* was the work of a "conservative observer" of the contest between James and his refractory parliaments, but there is nothing to indicate that it was prompted by those contests' (pp. 26–7). That concessive 'it may be true' shelters the conviction, though attributed to another,[9] that Shakespeare was *both* conservative and disinterested.

But others have believed him extremely interested–in a conservative direction. Both Gordon Zeefeld and C. C. Huffman, who were primarily responsible for working out the play's relation between Roman and Jacobean politics, infer that Shakespeare, whom they predetermine a supporter of the crown, *must* have been working the analogy to the disadvantage of republican theory. And while much of the evidence for this position is adduced at the level of behavior – the tribunes are corrupt, the plebeians are inconsistent and easily led – it also entails a redescription of the political myth behind the play. So Huffman averred that 'the story Shakespeare chose to dramatize was considered to be...the single instance of failure, that is, of actual armed strife', in Roman republican history (p. 172), and that the establishment of the tribunate, 'a major republican victory praised by many on the Continent...is undercut' by being 'associated with innovation and insurrection' (p. 179). And Zeefeld described it as 'the spectacular failure of representative government', in which, at the play's conclusion, 'popular representation has ceased to exist, and commonwealth as an ideal is as far away as ever' (p. 333). As in previous chapters, I do not mean, by defining the conservative position as 'common opinion', to discount those who have preceded me in disbelieving this story. Anne Barton, for instance, drawing on the implications of Shakespeare's use of Livy, and his assumed use of Machiavelli's *Discourses* on Livy, concluded that Shakespeare 'chose to emphasize what was hopeful, communal and progressive' in the young republic.[10] But the fact remains that these are the minority, and that most continue, as Günter Grass's experience testifies, to believe that the play (and hence Shakespeare) shows an antidemocratic bias. The notion, visible especially in Huffman, that Shakespeare was fighting a continental tradition of political thought, is highly suspicious, for it may be the critic, rather than the playwright, who is here reading against the grain.

Transferring old Rome hither

Let us, then, reopen the question of the political myth with which Shakespeare began, the Coriolanus story itself. To choose a Roman subject at all was, first, to engage in a Jacobean cultural practice. The play would have been seen as colleague with Ben Jonson's *Sejanus* (1603) and *Catiline* (1607), and the anonymous closet play of *Claudius Tiberius Nero*, also in 1607, all of which dramatized the alternatives of republican and imperial systems.[11] This trend became theorized in the revolutionary period, when Andrew Marvell, who certainly followed it in his *Horatian Ode* and elsewhere, produced an attack on the historian Thomas May for doing the same thing. In *On Tom May's Death*, Marvell apparently ventriloquized the voice of authority, speaking through the ghost of Ben Jonson (obviously in real life a user of Roman analogy), to excoriate May for 'transferring old Rome hither':

> Go seek the novice Statesmen, and obtrude
> On them some Romane cast similitude,
> Tell them of liberty, the Stories fine,
> Until you all grow Consuls in your wine.[12]

However we read his ambiguous attitude to May as a historian, Marvell evidently assumed that the primary motive for 'transferring old Rome hither' was to build support for republican principles.

In 1651 Thomas Hobbes made the same assumption, though unequivocally from an anti-republican position. 'As to Rebellion,' he wrote in *Leviathan*:

> one of the most frequent causes of it, is the Reading of the books of Policy, and Histories of the ancient Greeks, and Romans; from which, young men, and all others that are unprovided of the Antidote of solid Reason, receiving a strong, and delightful impression, of the great exploits of warr, atchieved by the Conductors of their Armies, receive withall a pleasing Idea, of all they have done besides; and imagine their great prosperity, not to have proceeded from the aemulation of particular men, but from the vertue of their popular forme of government: Not considering the frequent Seditions, and Civill warres, produced by the imperfection of their Policy. From the reading, I say, of such books, men have undertaken to kill their Kings, because the Greek and Latine writers, in their books, and discourses of Policy, make it lawfull, and laudable, for any man so to do; provided before he do it, he call him Tyrant...From the same books they that live under a Monarch conceive an opinion, that the Subjects in a Popular Commonwealth enjoy Liberty; but that in a Monarchy they are all Slaves...In summe, I cannot imagine, how anything can be more prejudiciall to a Monarchy, than the allowing of such books to be publikely read, without present applying such correctives of discreet Masters, as are fit to take away their Venime. (Part II, Chapter 29)

By protesting against it, Hobbes bore witness to the practice of reading ancient history for structural models of a 'popular forme of government'. And in Hobbes's alternative model, with its emphasis on absolute government embodied in a single person, the success of ancient polities is attributed *not* to their structures but to a heroic and individual militarism – precisely the value that critics of all persuasions agree is embodied in Coriolanus.

'Your voices!' Popular Representation and the Franchise

But Shakespeare's choice was not merely of Roman history generically, but of a phase in that history to which he seems to have been peculiarly addicted. When his *Rape of Lucrece* appeared in 1594, it was framed in an 'Argument' that both historicizes and politicizes a subject otherwise intelligible only in terms of erotics and psychology. Its beginning, which Joel Fineman has declared missing,[13] is as follows:

> Lucius Tarquinius (for his excessive pride surnamed Superbus), after he had... contrary to the Roman laws and customs, not requiring or staying for the people's suffrages...possessed himself of the kingdom, went...to beseige Ardea.

Its ending explains the role of Lucius Junius Brutus in generalizing the rape of Lucrece as a matter of national concern. This has two phases; in the first, Lucrece's own family '*with one consent*. . . all vowed to root out the whole hated family of the Tarquins', a phase interpretable merely as patrician feuding; but subsequently, 'bearing the dead body to Rome, Brutus acquainted the people with the doer and the manner of the vile deed; with a bitter invective against the tyranny of the King, wherewith the people were so moved, that *with one consent* and a general acclamation the Tarquins were all exiled, and the state government changed from kings to consuls' (italics added).[14] This emphasis on the role of 'the people', on 'the people's suffrages', and especially on popular consensus (the repeated 'with one consent') provides the 'Argument', and hence the poem, with a *constitutional* focus of remarkable precision.[15]

In *Julius Caesar* Shakespeare had represented with empathy the beginning of the last phase of the republic and especially the self-contradictions in the rallying-cry, 'Peace, freedom, and liberty', when used as an incitement to tyrannicide. In *Antony and Cleopatra* he had used the end of the republican era to contrast the chilly Roman ethos embodied in Octavius with the opulent freedoms of pagan fertility myth and adult sexuality. In *Coriolanus*, however, he returned to the youth of the republic, being careful to remind his audience of its birth in the expulsion of the Tarquins, by adding a telling detail that was not in North's account. When Tarquinius Sextus attempted to reclaim his kingdom, Coriolanus as an adolescent fought on the side of Rome and, added Shakespeare, 'Tarquin's self he met/And struck him on his knee' (2:2:994–5). This unlikely confrontation between Shakespeare's sixteen-year old (North's 'strippling') and the archetypical tyrannical monarch finds its structural converse when Coriolanus responds to his mother's pleas not to destroy his city, and the text looks back to that first deliverance by upstaging popular protest's traditional appeal to a merrier world in the past: 'A merrier day did never yet greet Rome, / No, not th'expulsion of the Tarquins' (5:4:43–4).[16]

In focusing now on the *second*, confirmatory moment in the history of Rome as a republic, Shakespeare chose a story in which the ideological grain of the material was no less clearly determined than in the story of Lucretia and Lucius Junius Brutus, and more theoretically significant in Renaissance political thought. For the creation of the tribunate did not, despite Zeefeld's assertions, lead to civil war or any destruction other than that of Coriolanus himself; rather, it issued in four and a half centuries of republican government.[17] As Machiavelli had put it in his *Discourses* on Livy (which were translated into English by Philemon Holland in 1600) it was this moment of explicit class tension that strengthened the republican constitution to the point of giving it durability:

In spite of the fact that Rome had no Lycurgus to give it at the outset such a constitution as would ensure to it a long life of freedom, yet owing to *disunione* between the plebes and the senate, so many things happened that chance effected what had not been provided by a lawgiver. So that, if Rome did not get fortune's first gift, it got its second... This came about when the Roman nobility became so overbearing... that the populace rose against them, and they were constrained by the fear that they might lose all, to grant the populace a share in the government.[18]

This last sentence, with its emphasis on the checks and balances that result from the clash of interests in more or less civilized polities, might well stand as a preliminary description of Shakespeare's intentions in staging *Coriolanus*, sometime between the summer of 1607 and the spring of 1610, when James's parliament, continually prorogued in the aftermath of the Midlands Rising, finally reconvened. For whereas in *King Lear* Shakespeare had moved from a posture of social questioning to one of social criticism and even of meliorism *within* the general frame of a constitutional monarchy, in *Coriolanus*, thanks to the incentive of the Rising and what followed, he had evidently followed his own enquiry considerably further. If, as Machiavelli had argued, the patricians were forced by effective popular protest to 'grant the populace a share in the government', such an adjustment in the power relations of the Jacobean state was not, however unlikely, inconceivable; and to dramatize its occurrence in antiquity made the process of conceiving it visible and accessible to others. In *Coriolanus*, for the first time, Shakespeare's audience is invited to contemplate an alternative political system; and, more significantly still, to experience an entire dramatic action devoted to these questions: who shall speak for the commons; what power should the common people have in the system; to what extent is common power compatible with national safety?

Further, Shakespeare returned to that aspect of populism that was most germane to his own role as a popular dramatist – how shall the voice of the people be heard? – with a new and daring focus. The play's second line, with its doubled invitation and exhortation, 'Speak, speak', for the first time allows the people to speak *for themselves* as a political entity, with legitimate grievances, and with a considerable degree of political self-consciousness. Most significantly, the play's center, both in terms of plot and structure, consists in two scenes (for which neither Plutarch nor Livy provided a mandate) in which Coriolanus's achievement of the consulate is made dependent upon the popular voice as a constitutional entitlement. In these two pivotal scenes the word 'voice' is repeated 28 times, almost in mockery of the dramatist's knowledge that an audience's attention is ensured by repetition. As Coriolanus himself puts it, 'Your voices: for your voices I have fought; watched for your voices; for your voices bear of wounds two dozen odd; . . . for your voices have done many things; some less, some more: your voices: Indeed I would be consul' (2:3:125–36). In *Coriolanus*, in other words, the popular has become unmistakably the identified with popular power, expressed in part through tribunal representation, but also, a much more threatening concept, through the franchise. The voices are also votes.

In the late 1980s, these scenes have acquired an extra-literary status, having come to the attention of Mark Kishlansky, an American historian of seventeenth-century English politics. Kishlansky's project was to describe how the old system of parliamentary *selection* in England, that is to say, of uncontested nominations arranged by private agreement among the enfranchised gentry, was gradually displaced by *election*, or a contest for votes. The scenes of Coriolanus' appeal for 'voices', he claims, 'so accurately portray the process by which officeholders were selected in the early seventeenth century that one must conclude that Shakespeare had first-hand experience, either of wardmote selections to the London Common Council or of parliamentary selections themselves. It is rare to have the testimony of so acute an observer.'[19] Shakespeare, then, is said to have recreated 'the central tenets of selection,' namely, the choice of a single candidate, and collective spoken *assent*, rather than *consent*. For whereas consent implies the negotiated support of a single agenda, assent, according to Kishlansky, implied (for we no longer have it) an identity of interests within society, 'unanimity rather than majority' (pp. 7–8).

As with the argument of Zeefeld and Huffman, however, Kishlansky's account of this non-classical episode shows signs of strain, of having to read against the grain. He was forced to acknowledge that these scenes actually reveal 'an under-current of disharmony, an expression of views that would render traditional practice inadequate';

> While one citizen asserted that the people could not deny Coriolanus their voices, another believed that 'we may, Sir, if we will.' One asked the crowd, 'Are you all resolved to give your voices?' He then answered the murmur of discontent; 'But that's no matter, the greater part carries it.' There is even a hint that the individual voice is as important as the collective one: 'He is to make his request by particulars; wherein every one of us has a single honor in giving him our own voices with our own tongues.' (p. 8).

So, Kishlansky was required to argue, Shakespeare simultaneously reflected contemporary electoral practice, imagined its replacement by something closer to the 'democratic' model, and in so doing warned against such change. Shakespeare becomes a prophet of disaster. 'A process of social distinction would give way to one of political calculation, and along the way England would be brought as close to collapse as was Coriolanus'

Rome' (pp. 8–9). We have returned, by a devious route, to the claim that Shakespeare was politically conservative; but determined to show it, perversely, by dramatizing material that could easily (indeed, more easily) encourage a diametrically opposite conclusion. And Kishlansky's argument is also tendentious in what it does *not* observe – the one, striking dissimilarity between Rome in the age of Coriolanus and England in the age of James. For it was precisely at the point of the franchise that the Roman political system, while disenfranchising the entire slave class, admitted that huge group of persons that English electoral law excluded, Sir Thomas Smith's 'fourth sort of men' which 'have no voice nor authoritie in our common wealth.'

Smith's list of the disenfranchised, we remember, included day labourers, copyholders, landless merchants, and all types of artisans[20] – that level of society represented as the plebeians of Shakespeare's Rome, both here and in *Julius Caesar*. But in *Julius Caesar* the carpenter and the cobbler are dismissed in the opening scene as 'idle Creatures' who have mistaken a 'labouring day' for a holiday, and whose transfer from Pompey of the popularity that now makes Caesar such a threat is merely castigated, without further analysis.[21] Here, in the opening scenes of *Coriolanus*, the people are introduced rather as 'mutinous Citizens', who are allowed to speak for themselves; and in so doing present a critique of precisely those assumptions (what James C. Scott calls 'official platitudes') that, in *Julius Caesar* permitted that easy, contemptuous dismissal. It is all the more disturbing, therefore, to see how often the dismissal is *transferred* by modern readers from *Julius Caesar* to *Coriolanus* and assumed, moreover, to be Shakespeare's own position. As early as 1710, Charles Gildon reproached Shakespeare for intending to 'flatter Arbitrary Power' by representing 'the Commons of Rome, as if they were the Rabble of an Irish village';[22] as late as 1964 Günter Grass defined *Coriolanus* as this 'bothersome play' in which Rome's plebeians, 'like London's artisans, are cowardly rats and ignorant dogs'.[23] Yet the evidence for this position (which is, of course, the view of Coriolanus himself) consists solely in the fact that the plebeians twice change their minds about him, the first time under the influence of the tribunes, who incite them to reverse his election as consul, the second under the influence of fear at the news of the Volscian invasion. That Coriolanus is twice persuaded to change *his* mind by his mother, the first time to modify his scorn of the plebeians until they have granted him the consulship, the second time to spare his city, is somehow not subject to the same stigma. One can only assume that Gildon and Grass and everyone in between who shared their view have been, for whatever reason, unable to focus on what Shakespeare actually wrote.

Take, for example, the term and concept 'multitude'. As a numerical sign, it points to the play's most important contrast – that between the many and the one. The plebeians' plurality is registered by their ordinal numbering, and marked by their anonymity, whereas Coriolanus's singularity is marked by his commitment to a *name* as the sign of personal identity and worth, and by Shakespeare's complete omission of the other consul. (To retain a balance of power, the consulate was always double.) But in Shakespeare's culture, as Christopher Hill has shown, the most common term for the many was 'multitude', whose function, especially when governed by 'many-headed', was to imply irrational action by the lower classes.[24] What has many heads can have no single agenda, the composite phrase implied, defying the linguistic logic that ordains that any collective noun must be, in effect, oxymoronic, the many as the one. In the anonymous *Histriomastix Or, The Player Whipt* (1610) a stage direction brings on 'a sort of Russetings and Mechanichalls (Fury leading them) and crying confusedly, Liberty, Liberty, Liberty' (F3v), who are immediately defined as 'this common beast the multitude...in a rebellious land,' (F4r). In *Coriolanus*, by contrast, the citizens themselves are aware that this terminology is invidious, and that Coriolanus has made it so: 'for once we stood up about the corn, he himself stuck not to call us the many-headed multitude' (2:3:15).[25] So says the First Citizen, who knows that 'to make us no better thought of, a little help [from ideology] will serve'. And the Third Citizen develops his insight into a self-mocking observation:

> We have been called so of many; not that our heads are some brown, some black, some abram, some bald, but that our wits are so diversely colored. And truly I think, if all our wits were to issue out of one skull, they would fly east, west, north, south, and their consent of one direct way should be at once to all the points of the compass. (2:3:18–25)

It would be possible to read this passage (humorlessly) as confirming the hegemony's rating. It is also possible to recognize, in the Third Citizen's mention of 'their consent of one direct way', not only an echo of the 'consent' foregrounded in the 'Argument' to *Lucrece* (and specifically denied by Kishlansky) but also the shape of one of the most intractable questions of political theory; in Hobbes's terms (as restated by Foucault), 'the problem of the distillation of a single will – or rather, the constitution of a unitary, singular body animated by the spirit of sovereignty – from the particular wills of a multiplicity of individuals.'[26] It is significant that both Hobbes and Foucault imagined this problem as a giant body, whose troubled shape appears also, of course, in the opening fable of *Coriolanus*. But in the central scenes where the citizens are preparing themselves to vote Coriolanus the consulship and assessing their qualifications to do so, it appears that Shakespeare has not only framed the question of the general will but also its partial solution. The negative implications of 'multitude' are, to be countered, first, by the intimations of majoritarianism ('the greater part carries it', 2:3:42), and second, by individualism: 'We are not to stay all together, but to come by him where he stands, by ones, by twos, and by threes. He's to make his requests by particulars; *wherein every one of us has a single honor, in giving him our own voices with our own tongues*' (2:3:44–9). In the ratifying act of democracy, giving one's voice, casting one's vote, the paradox is reversed and the many become singularly one. Coriolanus, naturally, believes that there is no general will, but rather a 'general ignorance' (3:1:146), and that therefore the voice of the people can be silenced by depriving them of official representation, by cutting out 'the tongues o' th' common mouth' (3:1:22), the tribunes.

This is to make the same mistake as many of Shakespeare's critics, many of whom have identified, consciously or unconsciously, with Coriolanus. (Coriolanus is no more reliable a teacher of political theory than is Theseus on the subject of poetics.) It is also the same *kind* of error as that which claims *Henry VI, Part 2* as an antidemocratic document on the grounds that Jack Cade is represented as a vicious and self-contradictory hypocrite. The presence of Brutus and Sicinius as 'the tongues o' th' common mouth' is proof, rather, of Shakespeare's continued interest in the problem of who shall speak for the people, who here, evidently, require no ventriloquizers because they are not dummies. There is, however, a parody of spokesmanship by Coriolanus himself, reporting on the opening protest against the dearth, which even he calls a petition:

> They said they were an-hungry, sigh'd forth proverbs–
> That hunger broke stone walls; that dogs must eat;
> That meat was made for mouths; that the gods sent not
> Corn for the rich men only. With these shreds
> They vented their complainings...
>
> (1:1:205–208)

By recalling his own use of the 'they say' formula in *Henry VI, Part 2*, Shakespeare warns us against taking at face value the ventriloquist's account, which is here manifestly reductive, reproducing only the 'shreds' of the popular tradition of protest. As for the tribunes themselves, they fully deserve the *moral* opprobium that has been heaped upon them; they are evidently no more genuinely popular leaders than Cade. It is they, not the plebeians, who are the 'tawdry petits bourgeois' of Günter Grass's condemnation, elected officials who exploit their position, despise their constituents, and (reversing the ventriloquist model) put into the people's mouths a more violent message than, left to themselves, would have been forthcoming:

> Assemble presently the people hither:
> And when they hear me say, 'It shall be so
> I'th' right and strength o' the commons,' be it either
> For death, for fine, or banishment, then let them,
> If I say fine, cry 'Fine,' if death, cry 'Death,'
>
> And when such time they have begun to cry,
> Let them not cease, but with a din confus'd
> Enforce the present execution.
>
> (3:3:12–21)

But before we too smugly assume that by making the tribunes unacceptable Shakespeare was warning his nation against classical republicanism, we ought to perceive that modern democracies are riddled with such types, that electoral politics depend on the manipulation of the electorate, and that the tribunes represent, in particular, a noxious form of the left-wing intellectual's dilemma – that leadership, coming from above, is difficult to distinguish from exploitation.

But the point that Shakespeare apparently wished to make was that Rome's plebeians, though they needed the tribunes as a structural device, were not the pathetic nonentities, aimless and inarticulate, with 'thick tongues', that readers from Gildon to Grass have thought they saw. They themselves have the 'gift of gab' that Grass, in rewriting the story at Brecht's expense, attributed solely to 'the Boss', playwright, director, left-wing intellectual.[27] This claim connects with E. P. Thompson's work in recuperating the signs of self-consciously political strategy in working-class protest movements, particularly the 'food riot', so-called in order to denote its participants as sub-rational.[28] Here I wish to focus on Thompson's brilliant phrase for the theory he rejects, the 'spasmodic' economic history that sees in food-centered protests only 'rebellions of the belly'. For it really was no coincidence that Shakespeare began *Coriolanus* with a commoners' protest against a shortage of grain, a focus which, as has often been observed, he achieved by rewriting the history he received from Plutarch and Livy, and condensing two uprisings into one. The result of this condensation was to bring out the deepest social implications of the famous Belly fable told by Menenius Agrippa, which in Plutarch was applied to an uprising that did not have hunger as its cause, and so was severed from its own truth. As Agrippa tells it, he faces not a rebellion *of* the belly, but a rebellion against the Belly by the members of the body politic. But, as almost all modern commentators have had to admit, the famous fable is 'inept'.[29] It does not *apply*. It is manifestly the citizens whose stomachs are grumbling. If the second line of the play ('Speak, speak') introduces the theme of popular expression itself, the third line connects that theme to its primal content, hunger. 'You are all resolved,' says the First Citizen, 'rather to die than famish?' And the response is indeed 'Resolved, resolved'.

But Shakespeare, having identified the undeniably physical content of the citizens' motivation, does not leave them, in the terms that Thompson deplored, clapping their hands spasmodically upon their stomachs. On the contrary, they proceed to discuss the political economy, not without wit, and not without considerable social perspective:

> We are accounted poor citizens, the patricians good. What authority surfeits on would relieve us. If they would yield us but the superfluity while it were wholesome, we might guess they relieved us humanely; but they think we are too dear, the leanness that afflicts us, the object of our misery, is as an inventory to particularize their abundance; our sufferance is a gain to them. Let us revenge this with our pikes ere we become rakes. For the gods know I speak this in hunger for bread, not in thirst for revenge. (1:1:15–15)

For all of its anti-poetic protocols, one could hardly find elsewhere in Shakespeare a passage that more rewards a careful exegesis. The pun on 'rakes' (both the symbol of emaciation and a reminder that this is an agricultural problem) is only the last and weakest in a chain of polysemantics that includes the irony of 'they think we are too dear', the two meanings of 'sufferance' (both pain and pain's passive endurance) and the deep truth that perceives a society's moral vocabulary ('We are accounted poor citizens, the patricians good') as the ideological form of economic difference. But beyond this deep wit and salty desperation lie practical and theoretical insights, fortifying what might otherwise have remained at the discursive level of *Hamlet*'s levelling gravedigger. There is food going to waste in the community that could have been used, 'while it were wholesome', to relieve the famine. 'Superfluity' recalls Lear's unfulfilled promise on the heath to 'shake the superflux' to relieve 'houseless heads and unfed sides' (3:4:35, 30).[29] And the reason for this waste, the first Citizen discerns, is that the patricians *need* the dearth as a physical demonstration of the reality of their own wealth, of economic difference. 'The leanness that afflicts us...is *as an inventory* to particularize their abundance.' Extreme indigence in others is the bottom line in the symbolic computing of personal net worth. So it comes as no surprise that Menenius Agrippa, before he proceeds to the Belly fable, asserts the impossibility of any change in the system:

> For your wants,
> Your suffering in this dearth, you may as well
> Strike at the heaven with your staves as lift them

Against the Roman state, whose course will on
The way it takes, cracking ten thousand curbs
Of more strong link asunder than can ever
Appear in your impediment. For the dearth,
The gods, not the patricians, make it, and
Your knees to them (not arms) must help...
and you slander
The helms o' th' state, who care for you like fathers.
(1:1:67–78)

But if these are hegemony's biggest guns (protest will fail, the gods and the state are at once identical, benevolent, and impervious to change), the plebeians are not deceived. They know the difference between eternal laws and local legislation, and that the latter not only permits change but has recently enacted it to their own disadvantage:

Care for us! True, indeed. They ne'er cared for us yet. Suffer us to famish, and their storehouses crammed with grain; make edicts for usury, to support usurers; repeal daily any wholesome act established against the rich, and provide more piercing statutes daily to chain up and restrain the poor...and there's all the love they bear us. (1:1:80–6)

And those who assume that the plebeians are pacified, as they were in Plutarch, by Menenius Agrippa's fable, have patently ignored the fact that they agree to listen, *provided* he does 'not think to fob off our disgrace with a tale' (1:1:92–3). Even while it is in the telling, their 'petition' for formal representation, as Coriolanus himself reports, is being granted by the Senate.

The entire episode, complete with Agrippa's fable, finds its modern analogy in the late nineteenth century, when Marx himself entered an early challenge to the 'laws' of classical economic theory, and specifically to the principle of fixity in real wages in relation to the gross national product. In *Value, Price and Profit,* written in 1865 and first published in 1898, Marx addressed himself to the 'Citizens' of Europe in the context of an 'epidemic of strikes', to argue against John Weston for the legitimacy and efficacy of group protests in support of higher wages; and his argument was intended to show that wage levels were not fixed by absolute economic laws, but rather by 'the *mere will* of the capitalist, or the limits of his avarice'. 'It is,' wrote Marx, 'an arbitrary limit. There is nothing necessary in it. It may be changed *by* the will of the capitalist, and may, therefore, be changed *against* his will'; and he proceeded to translate macroeconomic concepts back to their primal and most human origins–food and its distribution:

Citizen Weston illustrated his theory by telling you that when a bowl contains a certain quantity of soup, to be eaten by a certain number of persons, an increase in the broadness of the spoons would not produce an increase in the amount of soup. He must allow me to find this illustration rather spoony. It reminded me somewhat of the simile employed by Menenius Agrippa. When the Roman plebeians struck against the Roman patricians, the patrician Agrippa told them that the patrician belly fed the plebeian members of the body politic. Agrippa failed to show that you feed the members of one man by filling the belly of another.[31]

According to Allan Bloom, it was not until after Hobbes and Locke that we became capable (like Marx) of penetrating such 'myths of rulership' as the Belly fable, with its underlying notion of an organicist society joined for the common good.[32] According to Günter Grass, who rewrote the Belly fable yet again, this 'nonsense hallowed by tradition' was not only effective against Shakespeare's plebeians, it was still operative in modern East Germany. 'The barbs of progress cannot pierce its hide.'[33] Against them both, I aver that Shakespeare had not only pierced the fable's hide, he permitted his plebeians to do so as well; and one of the reasons for their insight was the Midlands Rising of 1607.

'No part of common powre?': The Midlands Rising

It has long been taken for granted that Shakespeare's decision to stage the Coriolanus story, and to begin it with a food protest, was motivated in part by the Midlands Rising. But after this historical reference has been pressed into the service of our exercises in dating the plays, it is usually abandoned, as one of 'those cobwebs of topical allusion' which, as Fredric Jameson put it, 'the ahistorical and formalising reader attempts desperately to brush away'.[34] And when, as by E. C. Pettet, the connection between play and event has been taken seriously, the result has been, not surprisingly, controlled by the tradition of Shakespeare's innate conservativism. Thus Pettet concluded that the play 'reflects the natural reactions of a man of substance to a recent mob rising in his country',[35] the Coleridgean position (including the derogatory 'mob') on Shakespeare's social attitudes, exaggerated in this instance, it is assumed, by the self-interest of an increasingly prosperous property owner. I have already demonstrated that these assumptions must now be abandoned. But the Midlands Rising itself now needs to be reinterpreted, and freed from constraints imposed on its meaning by modern historians. In the wake of E. P. Thompson's attractive but misleading thesis, some revisionist historians have produced an account of the Rising that renders it politically innocuous: that is to say, a conservative and ritual social action that is closer to an 'extreme form of petitioning'[36] than a real threat to the system. Derek Hirst's account may be taken as typical:

> The attitude of the authorities also helps to explain why popular disturbances were more akin to demonstrations than violent outbursts. The government balanced denunciation of disorder with a surprising understanding. . . Thus, after the Midland Rising of 1607 against aggressive landlordism in the arable plain, the council issued wholesale pardons to the rioters while fining several landowners in star chamber. . . The behaviour of the poor in the few times of trouble is equally instructive. Whether in agrarian or food riot, the pattern of popular unrest manifests general acceptance of a patriarchal scheme of authority. Protesters invariably first approached the neighboring magistrate to complain about what they saw as anti-social activity, whether by landlords or food traders. Only if rebuffed did the poor act for themselves, and even they never challenged the social order, nor attacked the rich as rich.[37]

In fact contemporary records of the Rising do not themselves support the revisionist account. It is true that the government proceeded against notorious enclosers;[38] and it is also clear that the Rising had certain ritual components, since it began, significantly, on the eve of May Day, 1607, reminding us that festive practices and inversion rituals, suppressed by Puritan-minded local authorities, still functioned as symbols of popular solidarity. It began, too, in Northamptonshire, whose people had three years earlier petitioned the House of Commons to intervene against 'de-population and excessive conversion of tillage into pasture' and early involved Warwickshire (Shakespeare's own county) whose self-named 'Diggers. . . from Hampton Field' had petitioned the king against 'these devouring encroachers'.[39] Yet it quickly ceased to be a local extension of those earlier petitions, and by its rapid spread to other counties began to take on the appearance of an organized rebellion. The rioters were identified as 'levellers' and 'diggers', not, writes David Underdown, 'yet with the revolutionary connotations that the terms acquired forty years later, but it was not an unthinkably long step from levelling fences to levelling social distinctions.' And he cites a written challenge thrown into a Northampton church during the Rising, entitled 'The Poor Man's Friend and the Gent-leman's Plague'.[40] But from the government's perspective, the chief concern was the *spread* of the disturbance, reaching Warwickshire and Leicestershire by late May, and even after the Northampton rising had been put down in June, spreading to Lincolnshire, Derbyshire, Worcester-shire, Oxfordshire and Bedfordshire, with the last two counties, moreover, involved in *revivals* of previously suppressed disturbances.[41]

On 29 May, the Privy Council issued orders to local sheriffs and justices of the peace to disperse any anti-enclosure gatherings. The following day, James issued a proclamation in his inimitably querulous and self-righteous style, complaining that his previous 'lenitie hath bred. . . rather encourage-ment then obedience', and that the protesters 'have presumed to gather themselves in greater multitudes, as well in that County, as in some others adjoyning.' He claimed that from the beginning of his reign he had been ordinarily careful to prevent enclosures, and was even now engaged in extraordinary remedial measures, two claims (though the second contradicted the first) that ought to have prevented 'disordered persons' from taking the law into their own hands, instead of trusting to 'the care and providence of their Sovereigne', behavior which justifies a 'sharper remedie'.[42] Both James's 'care', a term, we remember, invoked by Menenius Agrippa and mocked by the First Citizen, and Hirst's 'surprising understanding' become suddenly inappropriate when, on 8 June, one thousand levellers who had assembled at Newton, Northamptonshire, to dig out enclosures, and who refused to disperse when this proclamation was read to them, were attacked by Sir Anthony Mildmay's soldiery, both cavalry and foot. Fifty of the protesters were killed outright, 'a great many wounded, and many captured and later hanged and quartered, as exemplary punishment.'[43] And on 3 July was issued another proclamation, drafted by Cecil, which even as it reiterates the 'Princely care and providence to preserve our people from decay or dimunition' threatens 'execution (even to present death)' of those who continue to show resistance.[44] Most significantly, James himself here introduced the possibility that the protest had spread 'either by secret combination...or by ill example of the first beginners', two equally threatening alternatives.

While enclosures were the immediate cause of the Rising, the documents of its aftermath indicate that food shortages were also a major issue. The arable price index, it is true, reflects nothing comparable to the catastrophic crop failures of 1596 (the context of *A Midsummer Night's Dream*), when prices of all kinds of grain were more alarming than at any time since 1317; it does, however, show a sharp rise in wheat prices in 1608, and in 1609, when wheat recovered, a corresponding rise in the price of barley, the poor man's grain.[45] But there is other evidence that in 1607 both the authorities and those whom they would restrain made a theoretical connection between enclosures and dearth, even before the signs of the latter were powerful enough to register in the national statistics. On 24 July 1607, a royal proclamation, whose primary agenda was to *revoke* the threats issued three weeks earlier, and to promise pardon to all who would submit before Michaelmas, complained that 'there was not so much as any necessitie of famine or dearth of corne' to excuse the offenders.[46] But in late August 1607, James issued a proclamation against the use of corn for starch, since this practise '(especially in times wherein the plentie of Corne shall not be very abundant) must needs encrease both the scarcitie, and the prices thereof.'[47] In yet another proclamation of 1 June 1608, James addressed complaints of grain hoarding, engrossing, the export of grain, unfair pricing, quality control and even unemployment. He appealed to justices of the peace to ensure 'that the poore may bee served of Corne at convenient and charitable prices', and 'that the richer sort be earnestly mooved by Christian charitie, to cause their Graine to be sold under the common prices of the Market to the poorer sort.'[48] This was the recall of a 'moral economy' with a vengeance. Not surprisingly, the appeal seems to have failed, if one can judge by popular ballads that appeared in November: 'A new ballad exhortinge all synners to require Gods commiseration and mercy for the great famine and plague which at this instant we justly suffer'; and 'A just complaint made by the poore people of England against the covetousnes of gredy fermours whiche cause a Dearth of plentifull thinges – being an old ballad prynted by Yarath James.' And in January 1609, another proclamation prorogued the parliament (for the fourth time, and for a further eleven months) citing the royal reasons: 'forasmuch as the dearth and scarcitie of all kinde of Victuall is at present great, And if it should draw so great a concourse of people hither as the Parliament will bring, it would not onely more increase the prices of al things hereabouts (which are already very high) but also draw many Gentlemen out of their Countreys, where their hospitality will give much reliefe to their poore neighbours.'[49]

We can, then, reasonably infer that when Shakespeare began work on *Coriolanus*, probably in 1609, the issue of the Rising had merged in the public consciousness[50] with the problem of dearth (in both its senses). And while the records indicate that James's policy began and ended in leniency and a corrective, rather than a repressive social policy, they also indicate a stage of panic, with correspondingly draconian language and reactions. There was evidently a public perception, which *Coriolanus* exhibits in its own way, that the country had experienced not a ritual protest but a major test of the government's ability to maintain order, which in turn was structurally connected to its ability to feed its citizens; amd this perception produced at least one other account of the Rising that matches *Coriolanus* in its analysis, and possibly even in its intentions.

As I argued in chapter 2, between official statements (which tend to survive) and direct expressions of the popular voice (which survive only in shreds) there exists another category of documents, in which the system itself records the protests against it. Sometimes, as in contemporary accounts of Robert Kett's rebellion in 1549, the popular voice and its grievances are ventriloquized with the intention of refuting and ultimately silencing them. But in the case of the Midlands Rising, between the royal proclamations and the popular ballads, there happens to survive a pamphlet that intended for itself a mediatorial status. On 21 June, shortly after the Northamptonshire massacre, a clergyman named Robert Wilkinson preached a sermon 'before the Lord Lieutenant of the County, and the rest of the Commissioners there assembled upon occasion of the late Rebellion and Riots in those parts.'[51] And before the end of the year, he published the sermon and dedicated it to Thomas Cecil, earl of Exeter and baron Burleigh, styling himself Cecil's 'late Chaplaine', and directing his admonitions equally at the 'Oppression of the mighty, and Rebellion of the manie' (A3v). Wilkinson appealed to Cecil, precisely because he had been 'meanes for the due execution of justice upon the rebellious, so likewise... to promote the cause & complaints of the expelled, half pined, and distressed poor, that they rebell no more' (A4r). And he read the lesson of the moral economy to 'all states generally, not to grind the faces of the poore (Esa. 3) but the master to wage his servant that he may live; & the work-master so to wage the laborer, that he may live, & the land-lord not to rack, but so to rate his tenant that he may live, *not miserably*' (D2r; italics added).

Like Menenius Agrippa, Wilkinson cited the perennial fable of the body, but with a different allocation of body parts and responsibility:

> I know ye thinke it horrible, that (as in this late Rebellion) Mechanicall men are come to beard Magistrates,... but as it is an ill foot that kicketh at the head, and an ill hand that beateth it, so is it an ill head that wisheth the hand cut off, or diviseth a way to have fewer fingers on the hand, (C4v).

Further, Wilkinson implicitly connected his own body fable to the belly theory of popular protest, confirming the Rising's connection to experience or fears of dearth. His text for the sermon, in fact, was Matthew 4:4, 'Man shall not live by bread alone', for which he produced a remarkably materialist exegesis: 'That man liveth by bread, is inferred out of the very text; for even where [the apostle] saith, "not by bread onely," it followeth of necessitie, that amongst other meanes, yet bread for one' (C2v). 'For,' he continued, 'the belly sayth that bread must be had, and the soule subscribeth... and though reason may perswade, and authoritie command, and Preachers exhort with obedience and patience to sustaine the want of bread, yet for all that, *Venter non habet aures* [the belly has no ears], in case of extreame hunger men will not be perswaded, but they will have bread' (D2v).

And Wilkinson underlines the occasional nature of his chosen text at every turn: 'Because we are fallen into a time, wherein poverty without patience hath much disordred us,' he wrote, 'I have therefore chosen to speak of the hungry temptation, & yet not of the temptation neither... but rather of the answer to it' (B2r). Christ found himself in a place 'where was neither bred nor corn, as may be *now*', precisely that hypothesis that the king's proclamation would two months later deny. But the contemporary version of the temptation is, Wilkinson imagines, socially bivalent. Some the devil 'tempteth to turne bread into stones, that is, to decay the plenty of the earth, as many rich & greedy minded men do *now*; and some he tempteth to turne stones into bread, that is, to use unlawful meanes for their own releife, as the mad & rebelious multitude doth *now*' (B1v). The three-times repeated *now* and the causal construction ('because we are fallen into a time') invite us to situate this sermon centrally in any viable theory of topicality in Jacobean texts; while the astonishing move that makes Christ in the wilderness an appropriate analogy to the Midland Risers as well as to the authorities who put the Rising down is only the first of the essentially *literary* strategies by which Wilkinson invokes sympathy for the insurgents even as he delegitimates their intervention. Later, by an eloquent shifting of personal pronouns, he will move from the denoting the 'mad and rebelious multitude' as 'they' to addressing them as 'yee' and even 'good people', and even to syntactical incorporation with them. Arguing for Job as a model, he advises the Risers that sometimes God, 'for the exercise of *our* patience', will send men to take away our daily bread, 'and no marvell if it be thus now, that the cruell and *tyrannos*, . . . the mighty, and men of authority have the earth in possession' (E3v); and, more startling still, the communal *we* remains when Wilkinson turns to describing how the Risers have abandoned patience for protest: 'yea, bearing is come to bearding, and because of a little want, men have buried their patience as they buried hedges. Yea, we are come to banding. . . & now at last we are come to flat resisting' (F1r).

And in this last construction the radical import of Wilkinson's sermon as a whole and its importance for *Coriolanus* becomes manifest. Even in arguing for what Shakespeare's First Citizen had ambiguously designated 'sufferance', Wilkinson testifies simultaneously to the scale of the Rising, to its efficacy ('A King of three great kingdomes must capitulate with a Tinker', F1r) and, most significantly, to its motives:

> let men set what pretence & colour they will, yet this hath bin from time to time the common proceeding of popular mutinies; first to murmure upon some just cause. . . Afterward. . . they murmured not for want, but for wantoness. . . But. . . their murmuring came to that, that they would change the state,. . . they would have no head at all; right as in the daies of the Judges, wherein 'there was no King in Israell, but every man did what was right in his own eyes' (Judges 17.6). Thus we find in Scripture, thus in [hi]stories, yea and in our owne English stories, and I do not thinke it would have bin otherwise now, unless it had bin worse. First like Adams sonnes they come forth with shovels and spades, like simple men to reduce the earth to her ancient and native tilladge, but afterward they come forth like Tubal-kaines sonnes, armed with swords and weapons of yron. . . First they professe nothing, but to throw downe enclosures, though that were indeed no part of common powre, but afterward they will reckon for other matters. . . and counsell is given to kill up Gentlemen, and they will levell all states as they levelled bankes and ditches: and some of them boasted, that now they hoped to worke no more (F2r–3v).

Not only does this passage defy the assertion of Hirst and others that protesters 'never challenged the social order' as such; it actually identifies the model of rational argument that the protesters are reported (or imagined) to have used. One thing leads to another. From the experience of local hardship ('some just cause'), they can generalize to the injustice of the socioeconomic structure as a whole, and finally imagine a utopian inversion ('they hoped to worke no more') that is ultimately far more threatening than republicanism, more daring even than imagining the body politic without the head. To argue, as a revisionist social history would need to, that Wilkinson's fears were exaggerated is to ignore the work that his sermon was intended to do, to *negotiate* between the authorities and the protesters; and if this model of reasoning had not been available to the Midland Risers before May Day, 1607, it was certainly available to them, in print, by the end of the year.[52]

Perhaps the most crucial phrase in Wilkinson's sermon, however, occurs in his statement that levelling enclosures, though the most justified first stage in the conceptual structure of protest, was 'no part of common powre'. For the phrase itself, by imagining other parts that common power might appropriately subsume, adopts the same strategy as 'not by bread only', which permits the materialist solution 'amongst other meanes, yet bread for one'. More centrally, it destabilizes the standard assumption that the common people had no power at all, nor desire for power, and hence removes from 'common power', and by extension 'commonwealth', their hegemonic self-contradictions. Sir Thomas Smith's constitution had been seemingly unruffled by the giant oxymoron at the heart of the system he described. But between 1583 and 1607 much had occurred to make political theory a matter of broader public interest; amd between 1607 and 1610, while the country was reflecting on the Midlands Rising, 'common power' and 'common wealth' were the lexical signs of an ideology in trouble. In *Coriolanus*, I have suggested, Shakespeare sent them wheeling through the play-text with an interrogatory, repetitive and contradictory force that is unequalled in the canon. The *plot* of *Coriolanus* pits political power and the difficulties of its sharing against that militarist sense of the word 'power' which Coriolanus himself represents, and which he ultimately pits against the state as the rough and ready alternative to constitutional checks and balances; but the play as a whole worries more about the constitution, and how it is possible to define and limit such a previously unspeakable concept as common power.

This brings us back to the political vocabulary of Shakespeare's play. Not only is *Coriolanus* the play whose numerical interest in 'power' is by far the greatest in the canon (thirty-eight appearances, as compared to eighteen in *Richard II*, the closest competitor); but also the *primary* usage, again uniquely, is to denote some version of political, that is to say, structural power. In *Richard II* the majority of citations refer to an armed force. But in *Coriolanus* Shakespeare appears to have committed himself to a view of the semantics of power that is not supposed to have been available in political theory, let alone common usage, until half a century later. Again, the plebeians themselves are apparently aware that the term is problematic. 'We have power in ourselves to do it,' worries the Third Citizen in advance of the consular election, 'but it is a power that we have no power to do' (2:3:4–5). The first two 'powers' refer to their *right* to deny Coriolanus the consulship by withholding their votes; the last to their *inability* to deny those votes for fear of seeming ungrateful for his victory, an ingratitude which would lend substance to the invidious view of the 'multitude' that Coriolanus has already circulated. When the tribunes learn of the positive vote, they berate the plebeians for removing Coriolanus from a position where he had 'no power/But was a petty servant to the state', to 'a place of potency and sway o' th'state' (2:3:188). In turn, Coriolanus will berate the patricians for creating the 'power' of the tribunate, which, like Zeefeld, he sees as producing a constitutional imbalance[53] leading to stalemate:

> When two authorities are up
> Neither supreme, how soon confusion
> May enter 'twixt the gap of both and take
> The one by th'other.
>
> (3:1:109–12)

If one follows the semantics of 'power' to their inevitable conclusion, it is surprising how daring Shakespeare has become. He echoes North in having Coriolanus attribute the policy of free distribution of corn to the democratic model of the Greek city states, where 'the people had more absolute power' (3:1:115) than even in Rome at this stage; but there is nothing in North to provoke the multiple distinctions and confusions that follow. Brutus defends the 'authority' of the tribunes as *representing* 'the part o' th' people, in whose power we were elected theirs' (3:1:209–10). Volumnia reproaches Coriolanus for not having put the 'power' of the consulship 'well on' before depriving the people of theirs. It would have been more strategic, she advises too late, 'if/You had not showed them how ye were disposed/Ere they lacked power to cross you' (3:2:22–3). This lends credit to the tribunes' repeated accusation that Coriolanus 'affects/Tyrannical power' (3:3:2, 65), a charge that conceptually separates power from authority and brings it closer to its sole meaning in the last act, that of the military force without which 'authority' as a concept in political theory is finally empty. In one passage the tribunes announce 'in the name o'th'people / And in the power of us the tribunes' that Coriolanus is banished for 'seeking means / To pluck away [the people's] power' (3:3:96,

100), while a few minutes later it is reported that the patricians take the banishment so hard that 'they are in a ripe aptness to take all power from the people and to pluck from them their tribunes forever' (94:3:24–5). Following this pattern, as power shifts from mouth to mouth, is to experience conceptual instability – a political vocabulary, in short, in process of evolution; But what remains when these indecidabilities have been fully recognized is that ancient history provided precedents for attributing far more power to the common people than seventeenth-century England; and that Shakespeare exploited these precedents to the utmost by refusing to let the matter drop.

In this late play, then, which may have been his last tragedy, Shakespeare provided a remarkably daring analysis of the sociopolitical system, one that also, like Wilkinson's protesters, imagined the body politic without the head, while retaining some of the head's least attractive attributes (the confidence, in particular, of natural superiority) in Coriolanus himself. He clearly shows us plebeians capable of reasoning from one thing to another, from a local corn shortage to economic injustice in general; and, as a consequence of the changes he made in the Roman historical pretext, he shows us that popular, food-centered protest could *work*, since it resulted in the creation of the tribunate. And however disreputable some aspects of these particular tribunes' behavior, there is nothing in the play to challenge that famous interpretation of the tribunate itself which Livy permitted and Machiavelli made a premise of Renaissance political theory. Did Shakespeare, then, imagine that chance, in the shape of the Midlands Rising, might now be offering England what Machiavelli had denoted 'Fortune's second gift', the opportunity to negotiate needed changes in the sociopolitical structure and so to stabilize it?

In order to complete the answer to that question, we need to go forward in time to the spring of 1610, when James's much prorogued parliament was finally recalled to business. It so happens that in the first weeks of debate the body metaphor appears in parliament in a context that itself emphasizes the problem inherent in the term 'common wealth', that is to say, wealth's distribution, with food standing for the national resources. Since the only reason for recalling parliament was the king's need for funds, Robert Cecil, as Treasurer, had an uncomfortable role to play, given what had occurred during the long prorogation, and perhaps contributed to its length. He chose to ask for a supply by alluding to the venerable image of incorporation:

> The king (being the politic head) can receive no other good from the body of this parliament, severed in itself, than the natural head can receive comfort when there is interruption of the passages between the brain and the heart, whereof the best

issue can be no other but the effects of a dead palsy which taketh away motion first and life after.[54]

On 3 March, Sir Edwin Sandys, arguing for the crown, developed the metaphor more carefully as one of distribution and digestion:

What his majesty demandeth, supply and support, [are] things so necessary even for a private person that without them no particular man's estate can subsist. All kings in these cases have ever had recourse to parliament. The sun raiseth vapors before it dissolveth them into showers, the liver draweth nourishment before it distributeth blood to the body. The ocean must be filled by the rivers and the head maintained by the members. The sun doth not ingulf the waters nor the liver engross the blood but distributeth where it want, for natura *abhorret a vacuo*. All kings have had ordinary resort to the bounty of their subjects and the people must be as ready to return to the king as the king is ready to distribute to the people. (2:43)

On 21 March, James himself returned to the metaphor of the body, but in a tone considerably less conciliatory than that of his supporters, and in a medium, since his speech was promptly published, that was generally available to the reading public. 'As for the head of the naturall body,' he said:

the head hath the power of directing all the members of the body to that use which the judgement in the head thinkes most convenient. It may apply sharpe cures, or cut off corrupt members, let blood in what proportion it thinks fit, and as the body may spare.[55]

But the problem was, as every member of both houses must have been aware, that these body fables, whatever their tone, were as 'inept' as the version told by Menenius Agrippa. The national resources have simply not been circulating as the organicist metaphors imply they must, and the people have nothing to return to the king. And, while the Midlands Rising itself is barely alluded to in the debates, it had clearly given rise to a sharpened political consciousness, a more charged political vocabulary, and indeed to a sense of the responsibilities of the House of Commons as representatives not only of the nation at large but especially, perhaps, of those least capable of effective self-representation. Sir Francis Bacon, with his eyes set on the Great Contract which would obviate such debates in the future, saw what was coming and warned against over-explicitness in constitutional relations: 'Questions which concern the power of the king and the liberty of the subject,' Bacon protested, 'should not be textual, positive and scholastical, but slide in practice silently and not be brought into position and order.'[56] But the king warned the Commons not to 'meddle' with his 'power of government', for, he said, 'If a king be resolute to be a tyrant, all you can do will not hinder him' (p. 103). And the opposition leaders whom he had accused of creating a tribunate[57] in England for their turn cited Magna Carta, the 'ancient liberties' and the common law, all of which were, they claimed, 'plainly set forth to be for restraining great and mighty men from wronging or oppressing the common people' (p. 196).

As the debates wore on the concept of the popular, and of popular representation, emerged into lexical audibility and some theoretical clarity. The king desired the Commons to distinguish between genuinely popular grievances and their own, and 'not to buzz those things into the people's heads which they never thought grievous,' (2:61), a warning that might equally have applied to Robert Wilkinson and William Shakespeare. And on 14 November, at a conference between the Lords and the Commons, Northampton finally articulated that version of the body fable that was most appropriate to the dissentious tone of this parliament and the national crisis that led up to it. 'Some say,' he began, 'that the king must begin to relieve himself out of the riches of his own best means and not to depend only upon the supplies of state':

> The like quarrel was made once to the belly, as we read in the Roman histories, by all other parts, for that it engross'd and consumed whatsoever could be gained by the providence and industry of other parts, but finding by experience that upon their envious conspiracy to abstain from offices enjoined by the law of nature for the feeding of that spring which by the timely distribution of nourishment to every part conserves the body, not the belly only but the head, the feet, the arms, the legs, and every part that first began the quarrel fell into decay, they fell again to their old offices and grew very much ashamed of the mutiny.[58]

This speech confirms the intuition that Shakespeare's version of the body fable comes late in the discursive formation begun by the Midlands Rising and ending, in February 1611, with the collapse of the Great Contract and the dissolution of parliament, which was not to meet again until the spring of 1614. Implicitly, in Northampton's version, the king has become the belly of the state, however much he himself insisted on the head's authority; and although there is no textual indication that Shakespeare was aware of Northampton's speech, or the earl of Shakespeare's play, our interpretation of both is richer if we assume a horizontal force field of connections between them, an intertextuality authorized by historical circumstances, and by the intensity of the concerns that revitalized old metaphors and carried them, on the popular circuits, from mouth to mouth and from mind to mind.

Two days later, Samuel Lewknor, speaking for the opposition, declared that it is 'now a fit time to speak plainly and let the King know the voice of his commons'. For, and like Shakespeare and Wilkinson, he puts words into their mouths:

> They complain already that such are their extremities as they are fallen into a gulf of necessity, that they are the anvils whereon all sorts of people do strike. Alas, what gain is this, when the benefit that the King has by a subsidy comes out of the tears of the people?. (Foster, 2:333–34).

So the term 'commons' shifts downwards in the social register, from the third estate generally to the underclasses, to incorporate that 'fourth sort of men' whom the constitution, as defined by Sir Thomas Smith, had utterly excluded. It was no doubt with some sense of where his eloquence had taken him that Lewknor closed his speech by requesting 'that no evil exposition' be made of anything he said, and that it had not been motivated by any 'affectation of popularity' (2:335).[59] But his words, along with those of Wilkinson and Shakespeare, had entered the discursive formation whose beginning was the Midlands Rising, and whose conclusions, in the slow evolution of political practice, we today take for granted. And if Shakespeare's play appeared in London in late 1609 or early 1610, he too might have hoped, not only that 'no evil exposition' might be made of it (a hope that went unfulfilled), but that the theater, as well as the pulpit and parliamentary bench, might 'speak plainly and let the King know the voice of his commons'; at the very least, if the few require the support of the many, 'the price is, to ask it kindly'.

Post-scripting: The Victorians and Their Readers

In 1849, after the collapse of the Chartist movement, Charlotte Brontë produced a novel that would, in effect, pass judgement on the Industrial Revolution and the working-class movements thereby generated, by a retroactive focus on the Luddite or frame-breakers riots thirty years earlier.[60] In *Shirley*, moreover, she not only read 1849 through the lens of 1819, but both of them through the lens of 1609–10 (and hence also of 494 BC); for a crucial scene of evaluation is staged by way of a theatrical reading of *Coriolanus*, in which the readers are, respectively, Caroline Helstone, a young English woman of democratic sympathies, and a young factory-owner of partly Belgian origin, Robert Moore, whose treatment of his workers Caroline wishes to improve. It was Caroline who proposed the exercise; and Robert responded, evidently, by identifying both with

Coriolanus himself and with the Coleridgean view of what we should look for in Shakespeare:

> The very first scene in 'Coriolanus' came with smart relish to his intellectual palate, and still as he read he warmed. He delivered the haughty speech of Caius Marcius to the starving citizens with unction; he did not say he thought his irrational pride right, but he seemed to feel it so. Caroline looked up at him with a singular smile.
>
> 'There's a vicious point hit already,' she said; 'you sympathize with that proud patrician who does not sympathize with his famished fellow-men, and insults them: there, go on.' He proceeded. The warlike portions did not rouse him much; he said all that was out of date, or should be; the spirit displayed was barbarous, yet the encounter single-handed between Marcius and Tullus Aufidius, he delighted in. As he advanced, he forgot to criticize; it was evident he appreciated the power, the truth of each portion; and, stepping out of the narrow line of private prejudices, began to revel in the large picture of human nature...
>
> Coriolanus in glory; Coriolanus in disaster; Coriolanus banished, followed like giant-shades one after the other...With the revenge of Caius Marcius, Moore perfectly sympathized; he was not scandalized by it, and again Caroline whispered, 'There, I see another glimpse of brotherhood in error.'[61]

There could scarcely be a more deft display of two modes of reading; the one responding to traditional concepts of heroism and of literature's transcendence ('stepping out of the narrow line of private prejudices') the other critical, pragmatic and analogical in its procedures, requiring not sympathetic identification but application. Tragic heroism is to be displaced by enlightened managerial strategy. Her question, 'And have you felt anything in Coriolanus like you?' if answered affirmatively, requires a negative judgement on both parties in the identification: 'you must not be proud to your workpeople; you must not neglect chances of soothing them, and you must not be of an inflexible nature, uttering a request as austerely as if it were a command' (p. 105). But Caroline also adds (anticipating Christopher Hill and E. P. Thompson) that she cannot 'help thinking it unjust to include all poor working people under the general and insulting name of "the mob", and continually to think of them and treat them haughtily.' To which Robert replies, with masculine condescension: 'You are a little democrat, Caroline: if your uncle knew, what would he say?' (p. 105)

In this astonishing passage, Brontë configured a challenge to received opinion infinitely bolder than that which the novel finally endorses. Caroline is not the female protagonist of choice, but is displaced by the titular heroine Shirley, of considerably higher social standing; and the issue of hunger ('famished fellow-men') is removed from the socioeconomic sphere and rendered a psychological problem in Caroline's emotionally produced anorexia. If any character is the vehicle of Brontë's opinions it is presumably Shirley, who herself uses the term 'mob' without a qualm, and who delivers a violent attack on opinions like Caroline's, or those of 'Hiram Yorke, the Reformer of Briarfield':

> All ridiculous, irrational crying up of one class, whether the same be aristocrat or democrat...all arraying of ranks against ranks, all party hatreds, all tyrannies disguised as liberties, I reject and wash my hands of (pp. 414–15).

It is true that the lesson that Caroline read out of Coriolanus (of whose name hers, mysteriously, is the female anagram) is eventually learned empirically by Robert after a Luddite riot in his plant. He nearly goes bankrupt, and then spends several months in Birmingham observing working-class indigence at close quarters. 'I went,' he tells Yorke in the chapter subtitled 'A Confessional', 'where there was want of food, of fuel, of clothing; where there was no occupation and no hope...I saw what taught my brain a new lesson, and filled my breast with fresh feelings' (p. 616). Yet his account of this 'new lesson' is expressed in terms of personal integrity rather than social meliorism:

> I have no intention to profess more softness or sentiment than I have hitherto professed; mutiny and ambition I regard as I have always regarded them: I should resist a riotous mob just as heretofore...Something there is to look to, Yorke, beyond a man's personal interest:...beyond even the discharge of dishonouring debts. To respect himself, a man must believe he renders justice to his fellow-men. (p. 616)

And even the spectre of industrial hardship is finessed away by a tragicomedic resolution: the providential repeal of the Orders in Council which, he claims, will permit him in the future to 'take more workmen; give better wages; lay wiser and more liberal plans' (p. 733) and buy a house for Caroline and himself.

It is this domestic perspective which, as Nancy Armstrong recognized, registers *Shirley* a reliable witness as to how the bourgeois fiction of the nineteenth century did its own political work, by creating a sensibility in which 'authority is internalized and subjectivity itself becomes a self-regulating mechanism'.[62] I cannot understand, however, how Armstrong could read the scene of reading of *Coriolanus* as a *suppression* of the political content of the play by this new subjectivization. The very male/female dialectic that Armstrong observes as the most crucial factor of this scene works against the association of the female principle with subjectivity, since it is Robert who operates at the transcendental, transhistorical level and Caroline who insists on the political and class dimensions of the tragedy.[63] In fact, that it is *not* essentially a male/female dialectic is confirmed by the later debate between Yorke, who takes Caroline's position on the relation of Moore to his workers, and Shirley who defends the heroic individualism of the industrialist ('one against two hundred') and regards the 'advoca[cy] of liberty' expressed in terms of class as 'dangerous nonsense'.

It is not Caroline, either, who teaches Robert to step 'out of the narrow line of private prejudices' into 'the large picture of human nature', but Robert who discovers that picture for himself; the narrative line leaves uncertain, even, whether the narrator believes unquestioningly in the universalist critical tradition, or whether it might not even be the case that, for readers of Robert's perspective, the large picture is itself a product of a prejudicial theory of literature. What matches Caroline's interpretive strategy, after all, is Brontë's own decision: to write a fable of industrial relations that is triply layered in historical retrospect and proceeds by historical analogy, a method to which the frontal presentation of *Coriolanus* is at once the key and the professional statement of intent. That Caroline is reduced to a minor voice in the authorial repertory, as Brontë progressively softens the 'democratic' message, was perhaps an inevitable consequence of the genre's expected readership and primarily romantic plot conventions. But to deny her voice its function is to reduce the individual woman to her gender (and hence to be complicit in precisely that novelistic appropriation that Armstrong, presumably, intended her analysis to disempower). It is also to miss the acuity of Brontë's reading of *Coriolanus* and the demands it makes upon the political consciousness, demands which the scene of reading reiterates by updating it for the Victorians.

If *Shirley*, then, rediscovers *Coriolanus* as a fable for the mid-nineteenth century and the problems of Chartism, George Eliot found it equally pertinent to those producing the second Reform Bill of 1867, which in *Felix Holt* she chose to represent under the figure of the first Reform Bill of 1832. Published by the Tory publisher John Blackwood in June 1866, and subtitled *The Radical*, Eliot's novel features, in apparent contrast, an artisanal hero who is proud of his working-class origins, and who actually finds himself leading a violent riot, for which he is imprisoned. Yet Eliot's agenda was actually far more conservative than Brontë's. The entire novel is devoted to the task of reconceiving radicalism in precisely those interior, subjective, moral terms that, for Armstrong, characterize the period's most successful fiction. Initially defined perjoratively – 'a Radical was no gentleman'[64] – the term is further stigmatized by being adopted by wealthy Harold Transome (who will also become Felix's rival in love); and George Eliot's own position is only slightly caricatured in an early statement delivered at Treby Manor by 'the glib Christian':

> Reform has set in by the will of the majority – that's the rabble, you know; and the respectability and good sense of the country, which are in the minority, are afraid of Reform running on too fast. (p. 188).

In 1866, the issue of the few versus the many, and hence of crowd control, is unmistakably also, as it was in *Coriolanus*, the issue of electoral politics and the franchise. Unlike the actual context of *Shirley*, when the Chartists were doomed by their isolation, the period of *Felix Holt's* composition saw a new and surprising alliance between the Radical group in parliament headed by John Bright and Richard Cobden and the new trade union movement, the former pushing for a further reduction of the property qualification, the latter demanding complete manhood suffrage.

Felix Holt's own credo is delivered, therefore, as a rewriting of *Coriolanus* to suit the circumstances. On nomination day, in a chapter which opens under a Shakespearean epigraph ('His nature is too noble for the world') (3:1:254) that is to say, Menenius Agrippa's view of Coriolanus, Felix finds himself taking a heroic stance in the market-place, as the rhetorical opponent of a trade union speaker, who is arguing against Gladstone's limited Reform bill and for all of the demands of the People's Charter of 1838: 'universal suffrage, and annual parliaments, and the vote by ballot, and electoral districts' (p. 397). Significantly, this populist speech connects the issue of the franchise both with the ancient trope of liberty and with popular protest's primal fact, the fact of hunger:

> the greatest question in the world is, how to give every man a share in what goes on in life...Not a pig's share, not a horse's share, not the share of machine fed with oil only to make it work and nothing else...that's a slave's share; we want a freeman's share, and that is to think and speak and act about what concerns us all, and see whether these fine gentlemen who undertake to govern us are doing the best they can for us. They've got the knowledge, say they. Very well, we've got the wants. There's many a one who would be idle if hunger didn't pinch him; but the stomach sets us to work. There's a fable told where the nobles are the belly and the people the members. But I make another sort of fable. I say, we are the belly that feels the pinches, and we'll set these aristocrats, these great people who call themselves our brains, to work at some way of satisfying us a bit better. (p. 396)

Rewriting Menenius Agrippa's fable so as to make it no longer inept, but on the contrary an apt rationale for manhood suffrage, by connecting the primal urge to eat with the rational need to contribute rationally to the decision-making process that regulates, if not drives the economy, this unnamed speaker does for the popular voice in 1865–6 what Shakespeare and Wilkinson did for it in 1607–10: render it articulate. The difference would seem to be, however, that Eliot chose that version of social ventriloquism that allows the people to speak for themselves not in order to mediate class difference but merely to reinforce it.

For Felix Holt proceeds to express George Eliot's own doctrine that personal change, through education, should replace the demand for institutional or constitutional change. As he had earlier redefined the meaning of his radicalism to the Nonconformist Lyon, who reminded him of what the name once meant ('Root-and-branch man, as they said in the great times when Nonconformity was in its giant youth'), he is a Radical, yes, but one who wants 'to go to some roots a good deal lower down than the franchise', p. 368). And here, in the forum, Felix (like Shakespeare) exposes the term 'power' to its own dialectical play:

> I want the working man to have power. I'm a working man myself, and I don't want to be anything else. But there are two sorts of power. There's a power to do mischief – to undo what has been done with great expense and labour, to waste and destroy, to be cruel to the weak... That's the sort of power that ignorant numbers have... It's another sort of power that I want us working men to have, and I can see plainly enough that our all having votes will do little towards it at present... I hope we, or the children that come after us, will get plenty of political power some time. But I should like to convince you that votes would never give you political power worth having while things are as they are now, and that if you go the right way to work you may get power sooner without votes. (p. 399)

'We have power in ourselves to do it,' said Shakespeare's First Citizen, 'but it is a power that we have no power to do.' Whatever meliorism, then, is to be aimed for, Felix declares, 'must come out of human nature – out of men's passions, feelings, desires' (p. 400), which in turn will only be improved by sobriety and education. The argument for patience is familiar; going the right way to work is, evidently, going *back* to work (as the artisans were sent packing in the first scene of *Julius Caesar*) and leaving behind the false and intoxicating holiday air of nomination day, with its temporarily legal but nonetheless dangerous public assemblies. And it is no surprise, therefore, to find Eliot beginning her chapter on the insurrection with a quotation from *Julius Caesar* ('Mischief, thou art afoot') while the crowd itself is described by the narrative voice in the familiar contemptuous terms:

> At present there was no evidence of any distinctly mischievous design. There was only evidence that the majority of the crowd were excited with drink, and that their action could hardly be calculated on more than those of oxen and pigs congregated amidst hootings and pushings. (p. 421)

It is to avoid the 'blind outrages of this mad crowd' that Felix intervenes for the second time, and, thinking to distract them from the worst, *assumes* the role 'of a mob-leader' (p. 425). Nothing could be clearer. Eliot hereby anticipated one of the strategies of the conservative historiography of popular protest, whereby behind any insurrectionary event there must be imagined the directing (in this case, misdirecting) leadership of members of an educated class who are merely exploiting the unrest for their own, quite different purposes.

We scarcely need the confirmation she herself supplied in 1867, when, in response to an invitation by Blackwood to respond to the Second Reform Bill (and to Disraeli's 'address to the working men' defending it), Eliot published her own *Address to Working Men, by Felix Holt*, in which she again rewrote the fable of the body in defence of her argument for organic growth rather than organized demand for change. Starting from the premise (that was also Menenius Agrippa's) that we all live with 'the law of no man's making, and which no man can undo,'[65] and having as its objective the prevention of any *further* structural change, the address makes two astonishing claims: the first, that the organic health of England is posited on the class structure; the second, that the real wealth of the country consists in those intangible cultural treasures that only the upper classes possess: treasures 'of knowledge, science, poetry, refinement of thought, feeling, and manners, great memories and the interpretation of great records, which is carried on from the minds of one generation to the minds of another' (p. 621). 'Well,' she wrote, 'taking the world as it is':

> no society is made up of a single class: society stands before us like that wonderful piece of life, the human body, with all its various parts depending on one another, and with a terrible liability to get wrong because of that delicate dependence. (p.615)

Nothing is to be gained, therefore, but social disease, by 'any attempt to do away directly with the actually existing class distinctions and advantages, as if everybody could have the same sort of work, or lead the same sort of life (which none of my hearers are stupid enough to suppose)' (pp. 616–17). And, by the same token, it is dangerous to imagine one could wrest from the privileged classes their monopoly of the cultural treasures which, above all, are the markers of class distinction:

> Do anything which will throw the classes who hold the treasures of knowledge – nay, I may say, the treasure of refined needs – into the background, cause them to withdraw from public affairs, stop too suddenly any of the sources by which their leisure and ease are furnished,...[and] you injure your own inheritance and the inheritance of your children...If the claims of the unendowed multitude of working men hold within them principles which must shape the future, it is not less true that the endowed classes, in their inheritance from the past, hold the precious material without which no worthy, noble future can be moulded...here again we have to submit ourselves to the great law of inheritance (pp. 622, 626).

The encouragement to self-education and self-improvement is, therefore, nakedly qualified. Here, and not in *Shirley*, is the move explicitly made to appropriate 'all cultural materials' and to turn them 'into works of high culture', into that 'document of barbarism' that Benjamin warned us against when he encouraged the practice of reading against the grain. In Eliot, the grain of social prejudice is set not, as Armstrong argued (p. 219), by a feminized discourse that reinscribes authority in a domestic discursive frame, but by a female intellectual speaking through *two* male pseudonyms for the natural foundations of patrician culture which, as she evidently realized, alone gave access to the corridors of power.

For both Charlotte Brontë and George Eliot (as also for Coleridge and Hazlitt) the dominant stage Coriolanus would have been John Philip Kemble's representation of him as an aristocratic hero destroyed by a mean and ludicrous populace. Prophetically, Kemble's adaptation of the play appeared for the first time in February 1789, three months before the French Estates General met at Versailles, to be followed in July by the storming of the Bastille; but he continued in the role through 1817, when Coleridge was planning his Shakespeare lectures. Significantly, his version *omits* the Belly fable, and the accompanying social analysis. In 1820 William Hazlitt had based a pro-plebeian review on Edmund Kean's unsuccessful attempt, to break the mould and show Coriolanus as a neurotic; and in the same year George Cruikshank, the political cartoonist, ironically portrayed George IV himself as Kemble's Coriolanus, proudly repelling the proponents of electoral reform, among whom are visible Cruikshank himself and his publisher William Hone.[66] These facts survive to remind us, yet again, how urgent it was for the shapers of nineteenth-century culture from above to interpret Shakespeare's play in a way that protected their social structures from further abrasion from below. Now that history has disproved their convictions, their version of *Coriolanus* also can be put in its place.

7

'Thought is Free': *The Tempest*

Popular men,
They must create strange monsters and then quell'em
To make their arts seem something.

Ben Jonson, *Catiline* (3:1:104–6)

In *Felix Holt: The Radical*, the novel in which George Eliot elaborated her theories of class structure, electoral politics and the deep connections between cultural and political conservativism, her hero, as well as her narrator, cites Shakespeare. In fact, Shakespeare is brought into contest with Milton, as if they were ideologically opposed. In the interview alluded to in the last chapter, between Felix and Mr Lyon, the Nonconformist minister, Felix is reminded of the older meaning of radicalism, of 'the great times when Nonconformity was in its giant youth', the years of the Puritan revolution, and responds by redefining radicalism as sending its roots 'a good deal lower down than the franchise'.[1] What then develops is a debate on priorities, on the relative importance of inner and outer change. As Lyon sees the problem, 'there is a work within which cannot be dispensed with; but it is our preliminary work to free men from the stifled life of political nullity, and bring them into what Milton calls "the liberal air", wherein alone can be wrought the final triumphs of the Spirit.' As Felix sees it, no amount of political liberation or consciousness-raising will have any melioristic effect while the common man remains the common man: . . . while Caliban is Caliban, though you multiply him by a million, he'll worship every Trinculo that carries a bottle. I forget, though – you don't read Shakespeare, Mr. Lyon' (pp. 368–69).

This exchange aptly introduces the problem posed by *The Tempest*, not only for this study, but for all of Shakespeare's audiences, directors, readers and critics. What does it mean to be Caliban? This question goes far beyond Shakespeare studies in cognitive range and geographical application; upon its answering more depends, even, than on what we make of *Coriolanus*; and here, as has not been the case with *Coriolanus*, while the dominant tradition of interpretation has agreed, more or less, with George

Eliot, its control over the play has been strongly challenged in the twentieth century by a counter-interpretation, in which Caliban, not Prospero, is the rightful spirit at the play's center. And it was precisely the dominance of the dominant tradition that Other accounts of *The Tempest* were designed to resist. I refer here, of course, to appropriations of the play and its central symbols by African and Caribbean writers, partly in response to the provocation delivered by Octave Mannoni's *Psychologie de la Colonisation*, published in Paris in 1950 as a response to the Madagascan uprising of 1947–8. For where Mannoni, correctly diagnosing the uprising as a sign of the death of French colonialism and the birth of African nationalism, reread *The Tempest* as an allegory of colonial relations, and particularly of the psychology of colonial master and slave,[2] his successors effectively reversed the allegory in favor of anti-colonial polemic. Yet for Aimé Césaire, George Lamming and Roberto Fernández Retamar,[3] as also for their commentators,[4] the project was always a reversal, a transgressive reading against the grain that Western cultural and political history had engraved on their lives and their countries.

Not surprisingly, I question their central assumption, that Shakespeare's play was fully complicit in a mythology of benevolent colonialism, of the foreign conqueror's right to the land and labour of native peoples supposedly less civilized than himself. In the list of *Dramatis Personae*, Caliban is introduced in terms that might seem to settle his value for all time, 'a salvage and deformed slave'; yet every director has to decide for himself what Caliban shall look like. 'Slave' is, we learn, Prospero's term for Caliban, and accurate in that endless work without wages has been imposed upon him. Miranda's term is 'villain' (villein) which was also Cornwall's term for the servant who intervened against the blinding of Gloucester. 'Monster' is Stephano's term, born of mistaking Caliban and Trinculo, under a single cloak, for a creature with four human legs. But Caliban's own name is a symbolic anagram of race, an allusion to Montaigne's essay 'Of the Cannibales', and at least for Montaigne and his translator Florio virtually an honorific.

Also, simply at the level of character and action there are facts about Caliban and his master that are difficult to square with the critical convention of bestializing the former and idealizing the latter. We learn that Caliban loves music, has learned English, speaks as good poetry as the playtext has to offer, and knows something about the laws of inheritance. 'This island's mine, by Sycorax my mother, / Which thou tak'st from me' (1:2:333–4). Even Coleridge, in his lectures of 1811–12, before the pressures of post-Waterloo England showed him 'the springs of the vulgar in politics' in this play, had responded to the evidence of Caliban's sensibility. And for every intimation of something valuable in Caliban that cannot be controlled stigmatically, there is an aspect of Prospero not fully compatible with ideas of benevolent, providential government. In the 1920s, Lytton Strachey's 'irreverent eye' had already seen him 'as an unpleasantly crusty personage, in whom a twelve year's monopoly of the conversation had developed an inordinate propensity for talking.'[5] And, as Stephen Orgel observed for the new Oxford edition, such scepticism is also to be found in post-World War II productions in Britain.[6]

Orgel continued this line of interpretation, moreover, by focusing on non-characterological problems in the text: the magus's association, by way of his long quotation from Ovid's Medea, with an unmistakably sinister concept of magic; the incompleteness of his reconciliatory and regenerative plan, since Antonio refuses to repent, and nurture will not stick to Caliban's nature; and the startling interruption of the betrothal masque when Prospero recalls the conspiracy of Caliban and his mates. This disruptive moment Orgel connected to his own earlier work on the Jacobean masque as merely the illusion of power, rather than power's effective form in the symbolic order. Yet despite his stress on the play's 'ambivalences', Orgel concluded that it remains at heart benevolent, and so reinscribed the critical enterprise within what he rightly denoted 'Prospero's view' of its meaning.

The inference that Prospero's perspective is the commanding one, the one closest to Shakespeare's own attitude, is structurally related to beliefs that the Thesean aesthetic governs *A Midsummer Night's Dream* and that the politics of Coriolanus sufficiently explain the play that bears his name; but in *The Tempest* the inference is supported, apparently, by autobiographical gesture: Prospero's resignation of his magic, Shakespeare's farewell to the stage. This attractive notion was already in circulation when Dryden produced his Restoration adaptation; it was undoubtedly reinforced, rather than contradicted, by the fact that *The Tempest* has pride of first place in the Folio edition of Shakespeare's *Works*; and it tends to override the factual question of whether, and how much, Shakespeare contributed to *Henry VIII* or *All is True*. The premise that this play is in some sense Shakespeare's last 'Will and Testament' needs, however, to be treated with a certain caution. It does not require us to set Shakespeare himself up as a benevolent spiritual father, asserting the rightful primacy of mind over matter, art over nature, the philosopher over the slave.

It seems inarguable that, by keying his play both to pamphlets describing the colonialist ventures of James's England, and to Montaigne's utopian essay 'Of the Cannibales', Shakespeare intended a contribution to a philosophical debate on colonialism and race relations that was already surfacing in the Europe of his day. Yet it does no dishonour to the anti-colonialist argument to suggest that *The Tempest* speaks to a still more expansive set of problems. Following the focus, though not the opinions of George Eliot, I assume that Caliban has always represented, as well as the racial Other, those underclasses of whose low nature and inclinations Felix Holt is certain. When Shakespeare turned back to the territory of fantasy he had not re-entered since *A Midsummer Night's Dream*, he retained as an essential constituent of that fantasy the idea of the lowest common denominator, unaccommodated man, the base at the bottom of the superstructure. But in Caliban, as was not true even of Bottom, and certainly not of the Roman plebeians, this idea is rendered in absolute, mythic, terms. To show that he had not forgotten his earlier sociopolitical analyses, the text of *The Tempest* is filled with the ideologemes of popular culture; but they now reverberate as echoes from another world of more or less realistic mimesis. In *The Tempest*, instead, we move in the territory of philosophical allegory.

One can perhaps see this coming, by way of the increasingly non-realistic 'romances'. In *The Winter's Tale*, especially, the popular tradition had resurfaced in clearly festive terms, signalled by Perdita's unserious imitation of 'Whitsun pastorals' (4:4:134); the subversive impulse in the popular tradition was there divided between pre-Homeric trickster and Elizabethan clown, Autolycus whose ballads are hawked as trinkets, the shepherd's son whose echoes of Lear's fool ('I was a gentleman born before my father' 5:2:148–9) are confidently ludic, whose social satire is authorized by unexpected gentrification. Controlling them both is the premise of fictionality embedded in the play's title, 'a winter's tale' being proverbial for popular fictions in the oral tradition; while allegory's coming is announced by Time's appearance as master of ceremonies, in the long midway breach that makes nonsense of chronological realism.

In *The Tempest*, from the start, the allusions to popular culture come from the more threatening territory of protest and resistance. The play opens with a challenge from below: the Boatswain announces that physical danger from the elements makes nonsense of social hierarchy, and equates personal worth with the willingness to work.[7] But the equation between waves and rioters – 'What care these roarers for the name of King?'[8] – is one that objectifies elemental turmoil, while relegating the political to mental (metaphorical) space.

Likewise, *The Tempest* reintroduces one of the central problems of populism: what is the role of education in political society, and what does it contribute to social justice? Caliban's famous statement, so often quoted in anti-colonialist polemic – 'You taught me language, and my profit on it is, I know how to curse,' – clearly relates also to the vexed status of literacy in the history of popular protest. Shakespeare's Jack Cade had confusedly grasped hegemony's central dilemma – that while the educational system and its central symbol, *the book*, normally works to keep the underprivileged unenlightened, it occasionally produces, precisely by making them articulate, effective popular spokesmen. Caliban has also learned the power of the book, and instructs Stephano and Trinculo to begin their insurrection by seizing Prospero's library; yet because we also know that the books are those of a Neoplatonic magus, that their content is literally magic, the political point is raised to a level of high abstraction.

What Shakespeare did *not* do in *The Tempest* was done for him in a nakedly political appropriation of his play, the late nineteenth-century adaption by Ernest Renan, *Caliban: Suite de La Tempête*, published in Paris in 1878 in the aftermath of the Paris Commune. As Robert Fernández Retamar observed in his own *Caliban*, Renan was one of those French humanists who savagely denounced the Commune, and who believed that the future lay with a philosophical elite who would govern the world by possessing the secrets of science.[9] Rewriting *The Tempest* according to this agenda, Renan represented Caliban as a French populist *citoyen*, who leads a successful insurrection against Prospero, but who, once in power, gradually finds himself adopting the beliefs and alliances of the deposed aristocracy. Significantly, Renan's agenda could only be accomplished by removing both master and slave from their insular, allegorical space and by returning them to Italy, where Caliban's monstrosity disappears in 'cette grande école de canaille populaire qui s'appelle Milan' (p. 18); and where Shakespeare's Caliban knows only that Prospero's books are the mysterious source of his power, Renan's Caliban knows precisely how the social structure is supported by an elitist, obscurantist education:

War against books! They are the worst enemies of the people. Those who possess them hold power over their equals. The man who knows Latin rules other men. Down with Latin![10]

And in an important statement of his own principles of interpretation and adaptation, Renan put into the mouth of Ariel an account of his own move to realism:

I will explain it to you...It is Alonzo and those like him who were susceptible to our magic...When Alonzo saw the tempest, he believed that the waves speak, that the winds growled, that the tempest murmured, that the thunder, that 'deep and dreadful organ-pipe,' reproached him in its deep voice for the crime which he had committed against you. The people admit nothing of the kind...The magic no longer works. Revolution, that is realism.[11]

Despite or because of his extreme antidemocratic bias, Renan provides remarkable insight both into *The Tempest* and into the critical tradition, which has deeply invested in the play's projection of idealisms – neoplatonism, providentialism, benevolent rule, the redemptive power of forgiveness.[12] Renan's nineteenth-century conviction that all idealisms are magic (that is to say, ideological phantasms that the underclasses have become immune to) reveals the unspoken equation in *The Tempest* between art and ideology and, more important, that Shakespeare leaves it unspoken. 'What is to be done,' Renan's Ariel asks (in *Caliban* he is explicitly idealism's representative) 'when the people have become positivists?' But *Caliban* itself makes positive what *The Tempest* only makes conceivable; and it shows more clearly than can *The Tempest* alone, or in contrast to the earlier plays, the political implications of a realist mimesis that is here, unmistakably, avoided.

Must we, then, draw the conclusion that after *Coriolanus*, in which Shakespeare challenged the very structure of his society, he retreated to the philosophical aristocracy of which, according to Coleridge, he had always been a member? Is the allegorical ambience of *The Tempest* precisely the sign of the 'prevalence of the abstracting and generalizing habit' that Coleridge saw in Hamlet and himself, the habit not only of doing philosophy but of aiming it against the 'general' in the other sense? Not necessarily; for by the same autobiographical ruse that invites the conflation of Shakespeare's attitudes and 'Prospero's view' *The Tempest* warns us against that easy assumption of superiority, and suggests that Prospero, and hence Shakespeare himself, are not the masters of all they command, but the slaves of peculiar circumstance.

By having his Caliban open the 'Suite' with a soliloquy on liberty and the inalienable rights of man, Renan's *Caliban* also underlines *The Tempest's* insistence on ideas of freedom and servitude. In Shakespeare's play, however, it is impossible to prove (though not to claim) how the Master–Slave dialectic connects to historical circumstances. While it is possible to align the play with developments in James's England, and particularly with the increasing emphasis on political liberties that appears in the records of the 1610 parliament, the fact remains that Shakespeare virtually prohibits a topical response like that produced (I assume) by *Coriolanus*. And as in the 1610 parliament Sir Francis Bacon had warned that 'questions which concern the power of the king and the liberty of the subject should not be textual, positive and scholastical, but slide in practice silently',[13] Shakespeare slid into the text of *The Tempest* a discourse of liberty and servitude that is, if not silent, deeply mysterious. For not only is Caliban a slave to Prospero, but so also is Ariel, whose servitude is in no sense penal; and in the epilogue, so vital to the assumption that Prospero speaks for Shakespeare himself, he too claims to be on the wrong side of the Master–Slave dynamic, likely to end his days in a penal colony:

> I must be here confin'd by you
> Or sent to Naples...
> Now I want...
> Spirits to enforce, Art to enchant;

And my ending is despair,
Unless I be reliev'd by prayer,
Which pierces so, that it assaults
Mercy itself, and frees all faults.
As you from crimes would pardon'd be,
Let your indulgence set me free.

What can this mean (beyond the conventional actor's appeal for applause) if not that Shakespeare, at the end of his career, found himself in the carceral space of his own intelligence and its limits, partly self-imposed, partly the constraints of time, place, profession and belief. The effect of the Epilogue, then, is to situate the Master–Slave dynamic *within* the problematic of intellectual freedom, which also includes artistic independence, the question of agency, and, in a religious context, which the Epilogue certainly invokes, the role of the 'Will' – Shakespeare's personal signature. But to broaden the question does not necessarily weaken the force of any component; and for Shakespeare, in his own time, place, and especially as a popular dramatist, the premise of thought's freedom would have retained a sociopolitical charge.

In 1601, in the wake of the Essex rebellion, one of the many published comments on that event was E. Nisbet's *Dialogue or A Familiar Communication containing the first Institution of a Subject, in allegiance to his Soveraigne*. It is only nominally a dialogue, in the sense that the outcome has already been decided by the title, while the contributions of each speaker (a father and his son) and their respective claims to authority, have been equally predetermined by age, relationship and the educational premise. At times that relationship sounds more like that of priest to catechumen; and the pamphlet would be utterly undistinguished in its confirmation of patriarchal ideology were it not for one detail: that in the course of the son's education in hegemony he cites, with a hopeful curiosity, a question that would seem to endanger the governing hypothesis – that political insubordination will always fail because surveillance is total.

Shall not Thought be free? (p. 23)

Mysteriously attributed here to John 4:14, whereas in fact it has not biblical but proverbial origins, the phrase appears twice in Shakespeare's canon. Once, in *Twelfth Night*, when Maria is teasing Sir Andrew Aguecheek (1:3:68):

Now, Sir, 'thought is free'; I pray you, bring your hand to the buttery bar and let it drink.

and once in *The Tempest*, where also in the context of drunken festivity, Stephano sings a popular song:

> Flout 'em and cout 'em,
> And scout 'em and flout 'em;
> Thought is free.
>
> (3:2:119–21)

It is worth noting that Caliban already knows this song, and complains that it is sung to the wrong tune, whereupon Ariel, who has been invisibly observing the group as they plan their revolt against Prospero, supplies the right one. He therefore gives approximately the same answer (though rendered musically) to the question ('Shall not Thought be free?') as was given by the father in Nisbet's pamphlet, who advised his son that thought is always exposed to God: 'he need not goe farre for an informer' (p. 25). For Ariel's presence in the air is the ultimate representation of surveillance.

In Sir John Hayward's notorious *Life* of Henry IV, to which Shakespeare's company was connected at least by association, the bishop of Carlisle, who represents the voice of order and moderation, speaks against the deposition of Richard as follows: 'It is a common saying, thought is free: free indeede from punishment of secular lawes, except by worde or deed it breake foorth into action: Yet the secret thoughts against the sacred maiesty of a Prince, without attempt, without endeavour, have been adiudged worthy of death.'[14] The political context of this 'common saying', and its evident absorption by a tradition of resistance, is unmistakable in Hayward's text even as its speaker, ventriloquizing the popular tradition, attempts to deny its optimistic claim: that there is always an interior freedom (a Will) immune from external coercion. Shakespeare passes this popular wisdom on, not, as one might have supposed, to Caliban, but to Stephano, 'a drunken butler'.

But there it stands, nevertheless, the common saying released by the common players on to the stage at Whitehall in the spring of 1613, and probably at the Blackfriars, as Dryden attested in the preface to his own adaptation, *The Tempest, or The Enchanted Island* (1674). The thought that thought is free must have been always on Shakespeare's mind when he wrote for the Elizabethan and Jacobean stages, knowing that his own powerful work was contributing to what was thinkable. When Prospero aligns his 'so potent Art' with Medea's magic – calling forth 'mutinous winds' and opening the graves of history to let out their sleepers – he speaks perhaps for Shakespeare, who may also have wished to abjure such 'rough magic' (5:1:42–51) as renders baseless, if not actually rends, the visionary social fabric (4:1:151). If so, he surely confessed as much to the *other* temptation, to impose on resistant human material an idealized, fantastic, allegorical resolution.

When Dryden adapted the *The Tempest* for Restoration audiences, his prologue assumed that Prospero, at least as magician, was Shakespeare's self-characterization:

> But Shakespeare's Magick could not copy'd be,
> Within that Circle none durst walk but he.
> I must confess t'was bold nor would you now
> That liberty to vulgar wits allow
> Which works by Magick supernatural things:
> But Shakespeare's pow'r is sacred as a Kings.
>
> (ll. 19–24)[15]

But even as he established metaphorically an alliance between playwright and ruler, Dryden recorded it as an act of 'bold' social inversion, implying that Shakespeare's own wit was profoundly *vulgar*, claiming for itself the *liberty* to *work*, by magic, on the structure of his world. In the subsequent history of Shakespeare's reception, these are the terms and issues in Shakespeare's plays that have gone insufficiently recognized, while the sacredness of his power, and all of the exclusions that implies, has been at the center of the enterprise.

Notes

Foreword: Hindsight

[1] See Samuel Schoenbaum, *William Shakespeare: A Compact Documentary Life* (Oxford, 1977), pp. 227–32.

[2] Edward Bond, *Bingo: Scenes of Money and Death* (London, 1974), p. ix: 'Shakespeare created Lear, who is the most radical of all social critics. But Lear's insight is expressed as madness or hysteria. Why? I suppose partly because that was the only coherent way it could have been expressed at that time. Partly also because...you understand so much about suffering and violence...and yet live in a time when you can do nothing about it.'

[3] See, for example, J. A. Sharpe, *Early Modern England: A Social History 1550–1760* (London, 1987), pp. 198–224, who while regretting the 'lack of precision' showed by 'highly–placed observers...when describing their social inferiors', and carefully drawing distinctions based on estimated income, nevertheless himself falls back on 'The Common People' as the title for this section of his analysis.

[4] The larger estimate is by Derek Hirst, *The Representative of the People? Voters and Voting under the Early Stuarts* (Cambridge, 1975), pp. 104–05; what Hirst called the 'conservative estimate' is by J. H. Plumb, 'The Growth of the Electorate in England from 1600 to 1715', *Past and Present* 45 (1969), 90–128. In fact, Plumb's 'conservative' estimate was consistent with his liberal historiography, whereas Hirst belongs to that 'revisionist' movement in early modern history that seeks to replace, as explanations of the past, class conflict and large ideological agenda with local patterns of cause and motivation. Thus where Plumb saw 'the puritans' as lobbying for a wider franchise as part of their interest in reform (p. 94) Hirst saw 'the self-interested intervention of an outside gentleman who was looking for support in his bid for a seat' (p.44)

[5] Sir John Spelman, *A View of Printed Book Intituled Observations* (Oxford, 1643), sig. D2. Cited by Hirst, *The Representative of the People*, p. 29.

[6] I refer to the potential disenfranchisement, through either economic controls or voter registration, of the underclasses in modern democracies.

[7] Terry Eagleton, *William Shakespeare* (Oxford, 1986), p. 1.

[8] Eagleton, *William Shakespeare*, p. 1.

[9] John Dryden, 'An Essay of Dramatick Poesie', in *Works*, 20 vols, Vol. 17, eds Samuel Monk *et al* (Berkeley and Los Angeles, 1971), p. 35.

[10] John Milton, Preface to *Samson Agonistes* (1671); italics added. This is not the place to investigate Milton's social attitudes, which though always anti-authoritarian were only at rare moments democratic; but his play itself, interestingly, undoes these prefatory statements by making only the 'vulgar' spectators in the bleachers survive the catastrophe in the Philistine 'Theater'.

[11] Samuel Taylor Coleridge, *Lectures 1808–1819 on Literature*, ed. R. A. Foakes, in *Collected Works*, ed. Kathleen Coburn, Vol. 5 (London, 1987), Part 2, pp. 272–3.

[12] The *Champion* for 21 December 1818 published a report of this lecture which blended praise with reproach for political turncoatism (published in *Lectures*, pp. 275–6). In a previous lecture on *The Tempest* delivered on 6 February 1818, Coleridge had, according to the *Courier*, interpreted the figure of Caliban 'as an original and caricature of Jacobinism', provoking Hazlitt to write an attack on Coleridge's new politics, and on the impropriety of including them in his lecture. See *Lectures*, p. 110.

[13] See notes taken at the lecture of 6 February 1818 by H. W. Cawardine (*Lectures*, p. 119): 'Self-sustained – deriving his genius immediately from heaven – independent of all earthly or national influence... Least of all poets antients or modern does shakespear appear to be coloured or affected by the age in which he lived – he was of all times – & countries.'

[14] See John Payne Collier's shorthand notes of the 1811–12 lectures, *Lectures*, p. 442.

[15] See also Coleridge's defence in *The Courier* of Robert Southey, his partner in early radical enthusiasms, for the pirated publication of his *Wat Tyler* in February 1817: '*Wat Tyler* is a *Poem*, and a *dramatic* Poem, and... it is both unfair and absurd to attribute to the Poet, as a man, all the sentiments he puts in the mouth of his characters... We do not pretend that *John Ball* was neither more nor less to Mr. Southey than *Jack Cade* to Shakespeare. But we do affirm, that though his boyish *leaning*... was in favour of the rebels, as more under intolerable oppressions, yet that the greater part of the speeches were even then designed to be read by imagined oppressors, not by the oppressed.' See *Essays on His Times*, ed. David Erdman, in *Collected Works*, Vol. 3 (London, 1978), Part 2, pp. 457–8.

[16] That Coleridge's ideas were widely circulated in America long before they were taken up by I. A. Richards and thence by New Criticism is indicated by the publication history. His *Complete Works* were published in New York in 1853, 'with an Introductory Essay upon his Philosophical and Theological Opinions', and reissued in 1854, 1860, 1863, 1868, reprinted in 1884.

[17] R. C. Churchill, *Shakespeare and his Betters* (London, 1958), p. 123.

[18] Lawrence W. Levine, *Highbrow/Lowbrow: The Emergence of Cultural Hierarchy in America* (Cambridge, Mass., 1988), p. 73.

[19] Levine, *High-brow/Low-brow*, pp. 64–6.

[20] Brents Stirling, *The Populace in Shakespeare* (New York, 1949), p. 85. Stirling's footnotes provide the best guide to his predecessors on this topic.

[21] It is sometimes hard to recognize Stirling as a liberal, especially when he warms to the task of demonstrating that Shakespeare's commoners exhibit 'a collective halitosis of democracy in action' (p. 66), firmly asserting that none but 'mechanics' or artisans have this characteristic; how could he so conveniently forget Sonnet 103, and the 'breath that from my mistress reeks'?

[22] Coleridge, 'The Statesman's Manual', in *Lay Sermons*, ed. R. J. White, in *Collected Works*, Vol. 6, pp. 35–8. Coleridge planned three 'lay sermons', the first to the 'clerisy', an alliance of the ruling and professional classes, the second to the 'Higher and Middle Classes on the Existing Distresses and Discontents', and the third to the labouring classes, with the goal of unmasking 'our Incendiaries', the radical spokesmen like William Cobbett and John and Leigh Hunt. The last, the only work of his he 'had meant to be popular', was never produced.

1 Caviar or the General: Hamlet and the Popular Theater

[1] This chapter will deal, inevitably, with the differences between Folio and Quarto texts as a sign of *Hamlet's* existence in the real world of Elizabethan theatre; but where textual divergence is not at the centre of the argument, references, for the sake of simplicity, are to the new Arden edition: *Hamlet*, ed. Harold Jenkins (London and New York, 1982).

[2] E. K. Chambers, *The Elizabethan Stage*, 4 vols (Oxford, 1923); Alfred Harbage, *Shakespeare's Audience* (New York, 1941).

[3] Ann Jennalie Cook, *The Privileged Playgoers of Shakespeare's London, 1576–1642* (Princeton, 1981).

[4] See Martin Butler, *Theatre and Crisis 1632–1642* (Cambridge, 1984), who, in an appendix, 'Shakespeare's unprivileged playgoers', notes that if 'the total playhouse capacity for the 1590s and 1630s appears to have been somewhere in the region of 50,000 spectators per week, in the 1610s considerably more... virtually *every single one* of Cook's 52,000 privileged...would have had to be going to the theatres every week to have kept them full' (p. 297).

[5] Walter Cohen, *Drama of a Nation: Public Theater in Renaissance England and Spain* (Ithaca and London, 1985), p. 168.

[6] Perry Anderson, *Lineages of the Absolutist State* (London, 1974).

[7] The balance has been recently shifted away from Cook's position by Andrew Gurr's judicious *Playgoing in Shakespeare's London* (Cambridge, 1987), required reading for anyone interested in the social composition of Shakespeare's audiences.

[8] Lawrence Levine, *Highbrow/Lowbrow: The Emergence of Cultural Hierarchy in America* (Cambridge, Mass., 1988), p. 56.

[9] T. J. Clark, *The Painting of Modern Life: Paris in the Art of Manet and His Followers* (New York, 1985), p. 234.

[10] As partly collected in Chambers, *Elizabethan Stage*, 4:259–351.

[11] Virginia Gildersleeve, *Government Regulation of the Elizabethan Drama* (1908, repr. Westport, Conn., 1975), p. 15.

[12] Chambers, *Elizabethan Stage*, 4:316–17.

[13] Patrick Collinson, *Archbishop Grindal 1519–1583* (Berkeley and Los Angeles, 1979), p. 203.

[14] If so, one wonders why, in 1591, the popularity of the theaters grew 'to the great hurte and destruction of the game of beare bayting and lyke pastymes' (Chambers, 4:397).

[15] Florio was discovered in the retinue of Shakespeare's patron, the earl of Southampton, as early as 1594. See Charlotte Stopes, *The Life of Henry, Third Earl of Southampton, Shakespeare's Patron* (Cambridge, 1922), pp. 68–9.

[16] Montaigne, Michel, 'Of the Institution and Education of Children; to the Ladie Diana of Foix, Countess of Gurson', in *Essays*, tr. John Florio (1603), 3 vols (London, 1910, Everyman), 1:190.

[17] Thomas Heywood, *Apology for Actors* (1611), f. 3r.

[18] Sir William Davenant, 'Preface to *Gondibert*' (1650), in *Critical Essays of the Seventeenth Century*, ed. J. E. Spingarn, 3 vols (Bloomington, Ind., 1957), 3:47.

[19] Michel Foucault, *Power/Knowledge: Selected Interviews and Other Writings 1972–1977*, ed. Colin Gordon (New York, 1980), pp. 97–8.

[20] See Leonard Tennenhouse, *Power on Display: The Politics of Shakespeare's Genres* (New York and London, 1986), p. l.

[21] Stephen Greenblatt, 'Invisible bullets', in *Shakespearean Negotiations: The Circulation of Social Energy in Renaissance England* (Berkeley and Los Angeles, 1988), pp. 21–65, especially p. 65. In his introduction, however, Greenblatt somewhat modified his earlier idea of containment, and recognized that 'particular and local pressures' might have affected Shakespeare's theater.

[22] Dover Wilson, ed., *Hamlet* (Cambridge, 1934), pp. 181–2.

[23] Steven Mullaney, *The Place of the Stage: License, Play, and Power in Renaissance England* (Chicago, 1988), pp. 26–59.

[24] *Shakespeare's Plays in Quarto*, eds Michael Allen and Kenneth Muir (Berkeley and Los Angeles, 1981), p. 594.

[25] Philip Edwards, ed., *Hamlet, Prince of Denmark* (Cambridge, 1985), p. 132.

[26] See Chambers, *Elizabethan Stage*, 2:37.

[27] *Shakespeare's Plays in Quarto*, p. 631.

[28] Harold Jenkins, ed., *Hamlet* (London, 1982), p. 471.

[29] Montaigne, 'Of Custome, and how a received law should not easily be changed', in *Essays*, tr. Florio, 1:118–19. On the importance of Montaigne, see also Jonathan Dollimore, *Radical Tragedy: Religion, Ideology and Power in the Drama of Shakespeare and his Contemporaries* (Chicago, 1984), especially pp. 16–19.

[30] Stephane Mallarmé, 'Notes sur le Théâtre', *Revue Blanche* (Paris, 1 November 1866), in *Oeuvres Complètes* (Paris, 1945), p. 1564.

[31] James Joyce, *Ulysses* (Harmondsworth, 1968), p. 187.

[32] Daniel Sibony, '*Hamlet*: A Writing-Effect', *Yale French Studies*, 55–6 (1957), pp. 53–93, which expands on hints in Lacan's notorious 'Desire and the Interpretation of Desire in *Hamlet*', ibid., 11–52.

[33] Geoffrey Hartman, 'The Interpreter: A Self-Analysis', *New Literary History*, 4 (1972–3), 213–27; reprinted in *The Fate of Reading* (Chicago and London, 1975), pp. 3–19.

[34] J. M. Nosworthy, *Shakespeare's Occasional Plays* (London, 1965), pp. 171–82.

[35] André Gide, *Pages de Journal 1929–1932* (Paris, 1934), pp. 108–9: 'A-t-on fair valoir, en explication du caractère de Hamlet, que celui-ci revient d'une université allemande? Il rapporte dans son pays natal des germes d'une philosophie étrangère; il a plongé dans une métaphysique dont le 'to be or not to be' me paraît le remarquable fruit. Tout le subjectivisme allemand, je l'entrevois déjà dans le célèbre monologue. Au retour d'Allemagne, il ne peut plus vouloir; il ratiocine. Je tiens la métaphysique allemande pour responsable de ses irresolutions. De ses maîtres de là-bas, son esprit a pris la clef des champs de la spéculation abstraite; qui, si spécieusement, au champ de l'action se superpose.'

[36] Hamlet was born on the same day that old Hamlet defeated Fortinbras, which was also the day that the gravedigger became sexton, which was, as he tells Hamlet in Act 5, Scene 1, thirty years ago. This retroactive dating, deeply symbolic, cannot be explained away as Shakespeare's vagueness, or in terms of the way the illiterate 'remember' dates.

[37] It is important to note, however, that some of the emphasis on bookishness and student culture survives in the first, abbreviated Quarto.

[38] Lawrence Stone, *The Crisis of the Aristocracy 1558–1641* (Oxford, 1965), p. 331.

[39] Cited in Stone, *Crisis*, p. 331.

2 The Peasant's Toe: Popular Culture and Popular Pressure

[1] Sir Thomas Smith, *De Republica Anglorum* (1583), ed. L. Alston (Cambridge, 1906), p. 46.

[2] Peter Burke, *Popular Culture in Early Modern Europe* (New York, 1978), p. 28.

[3] Peter Burke, 'Popular Culture in Seventeenth-Century London', in *Popular Culture in Seventeenth-Century England*, ed. Barry Reay (New York, 1985), p. 32.

[4] Burke, *Popular Culture*, p. 24.

[5] See, for instance, Roger Chartier's careful study of the French popular press, *The Cultural Uses of Print in Early Modern France*, tr. Lydia Cochrane (Princeton, 1987), especially pp. 145–82: 'Publishing Strategies and What the People Read, 1530–1660'.

[6] Burke, 'Popular Culture in Seventeenth-Century London', p. 46.

[7] Brian Manning, *Village Revolts: Social Protest and Popular Disturbances in England, 1509–1640* (Oxford, 1988), p. 187.

[8] *Acts of the Privy Council*, 1591–92, ed. J. R. Dasent (London, 1901), 22:550.

[9] See Richard Wilson, '"A Mingled Yarn": Shakespeare and the Cloth Workers', *Literature and History*, 12 (1986), p. 174. Wilson derives his version from D. J. Johnson, *Southwark and the City* (Oxford, 1969), p. 227.

[10] Manning, *Village Revolts*, pp. 207–8 (italics added). He derives his emphasis from Mayor William Webbe's letter to the Treasurer, Burghley, summarized in W. H. Overall, ed., *Remembrancia: Analytical Index to...Archives of the City of London, 1579–1664* (London, 1878), pp. 474–5. It adds to the confusion that Manning manifestly misdates the skirmish as occurring on 11 July 1591, an error of both month and year; while Wilson accepts Johnson's redating to 11 June 1592 (too early for the solstice) and asserts, in defiance of Dasent, that the Privy Council ban on the theater really occurred on 19 June.

[11] The Privy Council apparently believed that the mayor of London, William Webbe, also sympathized with the apprentices. See Dasent, ed., *Acts of the Privy Council*, 23:19: 'certaine examynacions taken by the Lord Maiour of London... have ben very partiallie taken and to favorably in theire behalfe.'

[12] Hanspeter Born, 'The Date of *2, 3 Henry VI*', *Shakespeare Quarterly*, 25 (1974), pp. 323–34.

[13] This opinion is somewhat undermined by Wilson's own statement that the Southwark disorder ended 'seventy-five years of urban peace', a statement incompatible, also, with Manning's statistics.

[14] E. K. Chambers, *The Elizabethan State*, 4 vols (Oxford, 1923), 4:319. The occasion referred to was the scandal over *The Isle of Dogs*, a collaborative play for which Ben Jonson and the actors were imprisoned.

[15] If the 'harey the vj' mentioned by Henslowe as a 'ne' play performed at the Rose on 3 March 1592 was *Henry VI, Part 1*, and if it was chronologically the first in the trilogy but the second in composition, then *Henry VI, Part 2* could have been played in London in late 1591. That *Part 1* was in existence by 8 August 1592 is attested by Thomas Nashe's *Pierce Pennilesse*, entered in the Stationers' Register on that date. The New Oxford *Textual Companion*, eds Stanley Wells and Gary Taylor (Oxford, 1987), p. 111, 'presumes' that *The First Part of the Contention* (their preferred title) was written first, in 1591, and that all parts were completed by March 1592.

[16] E. P. Thompson, 'The Moral Economy of the English Crowd in the Eighteenth Century', *Past and Present*, 50 (1971), 76–136.

[17] Perry Anderson, *Arguments within English Marxism* (London, 1980), p. 56.

[18] John Walter and Keith Wrightson, 'Dearth and the Social Order in Early Modern England', in Paul Slack, ed., *Rebellion, Popular Protest and the Social Order in Early Modern England* (New York, 1984), p. 128.

[19] Diarmaid MacCulloch, 'Kett's Rebellion in Context', in *Rebellion, Popular Protest and the Social Order*, p. 50.

[20] R. B. Dobson, *The Peasants' Revolt of 1381* (London, 1970), p. 40.

[21] See, for several instances, Brents Stirling, *The Populace in Shakespeare* (New York, 1949), 131–50; but compare also Abraham Cowley, *The Civil Wars*, ed. Alan Pritchard (Toronto, 1973), 2:493–6, where the chain is reversed, leading backwards from the 1640s to 'Kets, and Cades, and Tylers', and the emphasis falls on the ignorance and blindness of the 'endlesse multitude' 'that hether groap'd their way' from 1381.

[22] George Puttenham, *The Arte of English Poesie* (1589), p. 218.

[23] Richard Bancroft, *A Survey of the Pretended Holy Discipline* (London, 1593), pp. 8–9.

[24] See Stirling, p. 135, who thinks, improbably, that Shakespeare, too, might simply have been confused.

[25] As the *Anonimalle Chronicle* put it, 'Teghler's demands included the centralization of the laws, the abolition of outlawry, that the possessions of the church, beyond that needed for the church's sustenance, should be redistributed among the commons, that both secular and clerical 'lordship' should be abolished, except for the king himself and a single archbishop, and that 'there should be no more villeins in England...but that all men should be free and of one condition.' See Dobson, *Peasants' Revolt*, pp. 164–5.

[26] Alexander Neville, *De furoribus Norfolciensium Ketto Duce* (London, 1575, 1576, 1582), p. 141. See also *Norfolkes Furies, or A View of Ketts Campe*, tr. Richard Woods (London, 1615), and *The History of the Rebellion in Norfolk* (London, 1751), a different translation. An alternative account by Nicholas Sotherton, which survives only in manuscript, was published by Barrett Beer, '"The commoyson in Norfolk, 1549": a narrative of popular rebellion in sixteenth-century England', *Journal of restieval and Renaissance studies* 6 (1976) 73–99.

[27] See Charles Hobday, 'Clouted Shoon and Leather Aprons: Shakespeare and the Egalitarian Tradition', *Renaissance and Modern Studies*, 23 (1979), pp. 63–78.

[28] *Certayne causes gathered together, wherin is shewed the decaye of England, onely by the great multitude of shepe, to the utter decay of householde keping mayntenaunce of men, dearth of corne, and other notable dyscommodityes approved by syxe olde Proverbes* (London, 1548). Evidently, the work of this pamphlet could have been largely accomplished by the title-page alone.

[29] This ballad was listed in the Stationers' Register for 12 November 1608.

[30] See Rosamond Faith, 'The "Great Rumour" of 1377 and Peasant Ideology', in *The English Rising of 1381*, ed. R. H. Hilton and T. H. Aston (Cambridge, 1874), pp. 63–4. Faith connects this belief to the legend of King Offa, who had once (quondam) granted the peasants liberties and privileges, as well as with the insistence of the 1381 insurgents against the abbot of St. Albans that a 'charter of liberties' existed somewhere in the abbey.

[31] See Manning, *Village Revolts*, p. 223.

[32] Pierre Macherey, *A Theory of Literary Production*, tr. Geoffrey Wall (London, 1978), 265 (italics added).

[33] Thomas Cooper, *An Admonition to the People of England* (London, 1589), p. 156.

[34] See, for example, the full title of Woods' translation: *Norfolkes Furies, or A View of Ketts Campe: Necessary for the Malecontents Of our Time, for their instruction, or terror; and profitable for every good Subject, to incourage him. . .to stand faithfully to maintayne his Prince and Countrey, his Wife and Children, goods, and Inheritance.*

[35] See Beer, ' "The commoyson in Norfolk, 1549" '; and Perez Zagorin, *Rebels and Rulers, 1500–1660*, 2 vols (Cambridge, 1982), 1:210: 'The protector's well-known sympathy with peasant grievances undoubtedly helped to raise expectations that something would be done about them.' The rebellion discredited Somerset and contributed to his fall in October 1549.

[36] James C. Scott, *Weapons of the Weak: Everyday Forms of Peasant Resistance* (New Haven and London, 1985), p. 331.

[37] Robert Crowley, *The Way to Wealth* (London, 1550). See Boyd Berry, 'On the language of the "Commonwealth of the Plowman"', *Renaissance Papers* (1987), 15–17.

[38] Edmund Spenser, *Poetical Works*, eds J. C. Smith and E. De Selincourt (Oxford, 1912), p. 453.

[39] Cited in Dobson, *Peasants' Revolt*, pp. 390–1.

[40] Irving Ribner, *The English History Play in the Age of Shakespeare* (London, 1957, 1965), p. 108.

[41] Walter Cohen, *Drama of a Nation: Public Theater in Renaissance England and Spain* (Ithaca and London, 1985), pp. 227–8.

[42] References are to the New Arden edition, ed. Andrew S. Cairncross (Cambridge, Mass., 1957).

[43] All of these elements are preserved, and rather carefully, in the 1594 Quarto, *The First Part of the Contention*; in fact, although Salisbury's speech is reduced from 27 lines to 8, the effect of the 'they say' formula is proportionately increased.

[44] Edward Hall, *The Union of the two noble and illustrate famelies of Lancastre and York* (London, 1542, 1548, 1550), 2:2.

[45] See Dobson, *Peasants' Revolt*, pp. 133–4, 155, 157, 184. The attack on written records was, however, selective, since at St Albans the rebels also pinned their faith in the 'charter of liberties' supposed to exist somewhere in the abbey archives.

[46] Scott, *Weapons of the Weak*, p. 319.

[47] See L. W. Conolly, *The Censorship of English Drama 1737–1824* (San Marino, 1976), pp. 97–8.

3 Bottom's Up: Festive Theory

[1] *The Diary of Samuel Pepys*, eds Robert Latham and William Matthews, 11 vols (Berkeley and Los Angeles, 1979), 3:208.

[2] Although Pepys's editors conclude that by 1660 he was 'clearly an Anglican by habit and sentiment' (*Diary*, 1:xviii), he was educated first at Huntingdon grammar school (of which Oliver Cromwell was an alumnus) and subsequently,

following the path of John Milton, at St Paul's School and at Puritan Cambridge. One of his cousins, Richard Pepys, became Cromwell's Lord Chief Justice of Ireland; and Pepys himself recorded in his *Diary* for 1 November 1660 his embarrassment when one of his old school-fellows 'did remember that I was a great roundhead when I was a boy' (1:280).

[3] See R. A. Foakes, ed., *A Midsummer Night's Dream* (Cambridge, 1984), 12–17.

[4] References are to the New Arden edition: *A Midsummer Night's Dream*, ed. Harold Brooks (London, 1979).

[5] Jan Kott, *The Bottom Translation* (Evanston, Ill., 1987), pp. 29–68.

[6] H. H. Furness, ed., *A Midsommer Nights Dreame*, New Variorum Edition (1895, repr. New York, 1966), p. 75. How prolific were the efforts of the old historical allegorizers can be seen from the seventeen pages of annotation that Furness had to provide for this single passage.

[7] See also Louis Montrose, '"Shaping Fantasies": Figurations of Gender and Power in Elizabethan Culture', *Representations*, 2 (1983), p. 80, on the 'last and most extravagant phase' of the cult of virginity. Montrose mentions the 'sacred Temple of the Virgins Vestal' that was featured in the 1590 Accession Day pageant.

[8] See Montrose, p. 80, citing John Nichols, *Progresses and Public Processions of Queen Elizabeth*, 3 vols (1823; rep. New York, 1966), 118–19.

[9] Theodore Leinwand, '"I believe we must leave the killing out": Deference and Accommodation in *A Midsummer Night's Dream*', *Renaissance Papers*, 1986, pp. 17–21.

[10] *Calendar of State Papers Domestic*, 1603–10, Vol. 28, art. 64, p. 373 (misplaced and misdated). For accounts of the Oxfordshire rising, see Buchanan Sharp, *In Contempt of All Authority: Rural Artisans and Riot in the West of England, 1586–1660* (Berkeley, 1980), pp. 39–40; John Walter, 'A Rising of the People? The Oxfordshire Rising of 1596', *Past and Present*, 107 (1985), 90–143.

[11] See Yves-Marie Bercé, *Fête et Révolte: Des mentalités populaires du XVIe au XVIIIe siècle* (Paris, 1976), especially pp. 55–92, 'Les Fêtes Changées en Révolte'. The fullest description of the Romans happening is by Le Roy Ladurie, *Carnival in Romans*, tr. Mary Feeney (New York, 1979). Reversing Bercé's thesis, François Laroque argued, in relation to *Henry VI, Part 2*, that Jack Cade's *jacquerie* turned into a carnival. See 'Shakespeare et la fête populaire: le carnaval sanglant de Jack Cade', in *Réforme, Humanisme, et Renaissance*, 11 (1979), 126–30.

[12] Brian Manning, *Village Revolts: Social Protest and Popular Disturbances in England, 1509–1640* (Oxford, 1988), p. 208.

[13] See Manning, *Village Revolts*, pp. 209–10. Apparently here too, reversing the situation in 1592, one of the authorities sided with the insurgents; in this instance it was Sir Michael Blount, lieutenant of the Tower, who resisted Mayor John Spencer's attempts to restore order, and who was later accused of conspiring to support the Earl of Hertford's claim to the throne.

[14] *A Students Lamentation that hath sometime been in London an Apprentice, for the rebellious tumults lately in the Citie hapning: for which five suffred death on Thursday the 24. of July last. Obedientia servi Corona* (London, 1595), B1r. Significantly, this pamphlet cannot help connecting the apprentice riot to 'peasant

ideology': 'Of Jacke Straw, Will Daw, Wat Tiler, Tom Miller, Hob Carter and a number more such seditious inferiour ringleaders...what hath been the end....All these at the beginning would be Reformers, & wrongs forsooth they went about to right: but when they had got head, what wrong did they not count right?' (B2v–3r).

15 Buchanan Sharp, *In Contempt of All Authority*, p. 31. See also p. 37, for the indictment of a weaver for seditious words in November 1596. The plight of the weavers in 1595 was protested by Thomas Deloney in a published letter. See Frances Consitt, *The London Weavers Company* (Oxford, 1933), pp. 312–16. I owe this reference to Arthur Kinney.

16 See John Walter, 'A "Rising of the People"? The Oxfordshire Rising of 1596', *Past and Present*, 107 (1985), 90–143.

17 See, for instance, John W. Draper, 'The Queen Makes a Match and Shakespeare a Comedy', *Yearbook of English Studies*, 2 (1972), 61–7; Steven May, '*A Midsummer Night's Dream* and the Carey-Berkeley Wedding', *Renaissance Papers* (1983), 43–52; and, for a non-marital occasion, Edith Rickert, 'Political Propaganda and Satire in *A Midsummer Night's Dream*', *Modern Philology*, 21 (1923), 53–153, who connected the play to an entertainment given for the queen by Edward Seymour, earl of Hertford, and hence to the problem of the earl's secret marriage to Lady Katherine Grey, whose child, declared illegitimate by the angry queen was, Rickert thought, obliquely represented in the changeling boy.

18 On the office of the Master of the Revels, see Virginia Gildersleeve, *Government Regulation of the Elizabethan Drama* (1908, repr. Westport, Conn., 1975).

19 C. L. Barber, *Shakespeare's Festive Comedy: A Study of Dramatic Form and Its Relation to Social Custom* (Princeton, 1959).

20 Compare Edmond Malone, *The Plays and Poems of William Shakespeare*, 10 vols (London, 1790), 2:464: 'Some, however, have thought that "the nine men's morris" here means the ground marked out for a morris dance performed by nine persons.'

21 On the hobby-horse, compare Malone, 9:307: 'Amongst the country may-games there was a hobby-horse, which, when the puritanical humour of those times opposed and discredited these games, was brought by the poets and ballad-makers as an instance of the ridiculous zeal of the sectaries.'

22 Victor Turner, *From Ritual to Theatre* (New York, 1982), p. 9.

23 Victor Turner, *The Ritual Process: Structure and Antistructure* (Chicago, 1969), p. 176.

24 Victor Turner, *Dramas, Fields, and Metaphors: Symbolic Action in Human Society* (Ithaca, 1974), p. 35.

25 Robert Weimann, *Shakespeare and the Popular Tradition in the Theater*, ed. Robert Schwartz (Baltimore, 1978, 1987).

26 Mikhail Bakhtin, *Rabelais and his World*, tr. Helene Iswolsky (Boston, 1968, Bloomington, 1984), p. 21.

27 See Peter Stallybrass and Allon White, *The Politics and Poetics of Transgression* (London, 1986), pp. 12–22.

28 For an extended defense of this as the intended staging, see Thomas Clayton, '"Fie What a Question's That If Thou Wert Near a Lewd Interpreter": The Wall

Scene in *A Midsummer Night's Dream*', *Shakespeare Studies*, 7 (1974), 101–23.

[29] George Puttenham, *The Arte of English Poesie* (London, 1589), p. 43.

[30] Barber, *Shakespeare's Festive Comedy*, p. 120: 'Shakespeare does not make himself accountable for exact chronological inferences.'

[31] Louis Adrian Montrose, '"*Shaping Fantasies*"'.

[32] Frankie Rubinstein, *A Dictionary of Shakespeare's Sexual Puns and their Significance* (London, 1984), p. 17.

[33] John Milton, *Colasterion*, in *Complete Prose Works*, ed. D. M. Wolfe *et al.* (New Haven, 1953–82) 2:2:57.

[34] See R. Howard Bloch, *The Scandal of the Fabliaux* (Chicago and London, 1986): 'In the counting of the vagina and the anus we recognize the accounting of the poet who plays upon the homophone of *con* [cunt] and *conte* [tale]... The debate between adjacent body parts is, at bottom, that of the jongleur who, in addressing his audience, manages to make *cons* and *culs* speak' (p. 106).

[35] See Jack Lindsay, tr., *The Golden Ass* (Bloomington and London, 1932), p. 22; and, for an extension of Shakespeare's interest in Apuleius, J. J. M. Tobin, *Shakespeare's Favorite Novel* (Lanham, Md., 1984), especially pp. 32–40.

[36] Bakhtin, *Rabelais and his World*, p. 78.

[37] Leinwand, p. 22.

[38] E. K. Chambers, *The Elizabethan Stage*, 4 vols (Oxford, 1923), 4:318.

[39] Alexander Neville, *Norfolkes Furies, or A View of Ketts Campe: Necessary for the Malecontents Of our Time, for their instruction, or terror; and profitable for every good Subject*, tr. R[ichard] W[oods], (London, 1615), B2r (italics added).

4 Back by Popular Demand: The Two Versions of *Henry V*

[1] In this chapter, where the history of the play-text and the divergences between Quarto and Folio are at the center of the argument, references are to the facsimile *First Folio of Shakespeare*, prepared by Charlton Hinman (New York, 1968), and *Shakespeare's Plays in Quarto*, eds Michael Allen and Kenneth Muir (Berkeley and Los Angeles, 1981).

[2] See *Film Scripts One*, eds George P. Garrett, O.B. Hardison, Jr, and Jane R. Gelfman (New York, 1971), p. 40. But compare also Dover Wilson, ed., *Henry V* (Cambridge, 1947), viii: 'Happening to witness a performance by Frank Benson and his company at Stratford in August or September 1914, I discovered for the first time what it was all about. The epic drama of Agincourt matched the temper of the moment, when Rupert Brooke was writing *The Soldier* and the Kaiser was said to be scoffing at our 'contemptible little army' which had just crossed the Channel, so exactly that it might have been written expressly for it.'

[3] Lily B. Campbell, *Shakespeare's 'Histories': Mirrors of Elizabethan Policy* (San Marino, Calif., 1947; repr. London, 1964), pp. 255–305; E. M. W. Tillyard, *Shakespeare's History Plays* (New York, 1944, repr. 1947), pp. 304–14. Tillyard took a less sanguine view of *Henry V* than Campbell, regarding it as a routine and formulaic performance without the energies invested in the two parts of *Henry IV*.

[4] For a larger analysis and critique of the 'theme of England', as promoted by Tillyard and by Olivier's production, see Graham Holderness, *Shakespeare's History* (New York, 1985), pp. 18–26, 184–200.

[5] See, for instance, Stephen Greenblatt, 'Invisible Bullets', in *Shakespearean Negotiations: The Circulation of Social Energy in Renaissance England* (Berkeley and Los Angeles, 1988), pp. 21–65; Jonathan Dollimore and Alan Sinfield, 'History and Ideology: the Instance of *Henry V*', in *Alternative Shakespeares*, ed. John Drakakis (London, 1985), pp. 206–27; and Larry S. Champion, '"What Prerogatives Meanes": Perspective and Political Ideology in *The Famous Victories of Henry V*', *South Atlantic Review*, 53 (1988), pp. 1–19, which provides an account of Shakespeare's most important source 'as either a glorification of monarchy or as an attack on its corruption, egocentricity, and militaristic monomania' (p. 14), depending on the spectator's own position. Earlier sceptical readings were primarily characterological in focus, including even that of Gerald Gould, who in the immediate aftermath of World War I revolted against the 'more hideous "Prussianisms" with which Shakespeare has endowed his Henry'. See 'A New Reading of *Henry V*', *English Review* (1919), p. 42.

[6] For the Quarto, I have used *Shakespeare's Plays in Quarto*, eds Michael J. B. Allen and Kenneth Muir (Berkeley and Los Angeles, 1981); for the 1623 Folio, *The First Folio of Shakespeare* (New York, Norton Facsimile edition, 1968).

[7] Gary Taylor, ed., *Henry V* (Oxford, 1984), p. 7 (italics added).

[8] See *Film Scripts One*, p. 134: the film's final words are as follows:

Small time: but in that small, most greatly lived
This star of England: Fortune made his
sword: and for his sake
In your fair minds let this acceptance take.

[9] It is sometimes assumed that the Folio text, though not deriving from a promptbook, represents an acting version, and that, on the basis of Choric references to staging, especially to the 'wooden O' of the fifth Chorus, it was designed for the new Globe theater built in 1599; but it is equally assumed in other instances (such as *Hamlet*) that the Folio text was sometimes or always abridged in actual performance.

[10] See A. W. Pollard, *Shakespeare's Folios and Quartos: A Study in the Bibliography of Shakespeare's Plays, 1594–1685* (London, 1909); W.W. Greg, ed. *The Merry Wives of Windsor* (Oxford, 1910); his theory was refined in *Two Elizabethan Stage Abridgements* (Oxford, 1923).

[11] Peter Blayney, 'Shakespeare's Fight', referring to Francis Beaumont and John Fletcher, *Comedies and Tragedies* (London, 1647), Sig. A2r.

[12] Since Moseley did not in fact base his edition on these theatrical transcriptions, but rather, as he insists, on authorial manuscripts, he himself had nothing to gain by establishing the social legitimacy of the practices here described.

[13] J. H. Walter, ed., *King Henry V* (Cambridge, Mass., 1954), xxxv.

[14] Alfred Hart, *Stolne and Surreptitious Copies: A Comparative Study of Shakespeare's Bad Quartos* (Melbourne, 1942), p. 130.

[15] Evelyn May Albright, 'The Folio Version of *Henry V* in relation to Shakespeare's Times', *PMLA*, 42 (1928), 722–56. This contributed to a long and intemperate argument between herself and Ray Heffner, who preferred to separate Shakespeare from politics. On Albright's side, see 'Shakespeare's *Richard II* and

the Essex Conspiracy', *PMLA*, 42 (1927), 686–720; and 'Shakespeare's *Richard II*, Hayward's *History of Henry IV* and the Essex Conspiracy', *PMLA*, 46 (1931), 694–719; For Heffner's rebuttal, see 'Shakespeare, Hayward and Essex', *PMLA*, 45 (1930), 754–80, an essay which nevertheless contains invaluable information about Hayward's involvements with Essex.

16 See the confession of Sir Gilly Merrick, Essex's steward, on 5 March 1601, *Calendar of State Papers Domestic*, 1598–1601, Vol. 278, art. 78, p. 575.

17 In Stanley Wells and Gary Taylor, *Modernizing Shakespeare's Spelling with Three Studies in the Text of Henry V* (Oxford, 1979). See also, for earlier versions of this theory, H. T. Price, *The Text of Henry V* (Newcastle-under-Lyme, 1920); Gerda Okerlund, 'The Quarto Version of *Henry V* as a Stage Adaptation', *PMLA*, 49 (1934), 810–34; and W. W. Greg, *The Shakespeare First Folio* (Oxford, 1955).

18 For alternative, unpersuasive explanations for the problem posed by a text without the Choruses, see G. P. Jones, op. cit., and W. D. Smith, 'The *Henry V* Choruses in the first Folio', *Journal of English and Germanic Philology*, 53 (1954), 38–57, who sought to prove that the Choruses were a later addition, that the allusion in the fifth prologue was not to Essex but to Lord Mountjoy, who took over his commission. This argument was refuted by R. A. Law, 'The Choruses in *Henry V*', *University of Texas Studies in English*, 35 (1956), 11–21.

19 In Taylor's single-volume edition of the play the casting hypothesis remains unqualified, but the 'simplification in the direction of patriotism' theory is greatly expanded to include a whole series of omissions. See *Henry V*, p. 12. The contradiction between this perceived pattern and its supposed motives – reducing the cast – is hereby exacerbated.

20 *The Mirror for Magistrates*, ed. Lily B. Campbell (Cambridge, 1938; repr. New York, 1960), p. 8.

21 See Elizabeth Story Donno, 'Some Aspects of Shakespeare's Holinshed', *Huntington Library Quarterly*, 50 (1987), 229–47.

22 See W. W. Greg, ed., *Sir Thomas More* (Oxford, 1911), xiii-xv. The date of this note has been much disputed, and its full documentation here would be disproportionate to its importance; but for a recent analysis of the problem, especially as it concerns Shakespeare's involvement in this play, see Scott McMillin, *The Elizabethan Theatre and The Book of Sir Thomas More* (Ithaca, 1986), where Tilney's intervention is dated 1592–3.

23 See Margaret Dowling, 'Sir John Hayward's Troubles over his *Life of Henry IV*', *The Library*, 4th. ser., 11 (1930), 212–24; F.J. Levy, 'Hayward, Daniel, and the Beginnings of Politic History in England', *Huntington Library Quarterly*, 50 (1987), pp. 1–34.

24 The terms of the Order are recorded in the Stationers' Register for 4 June. Its primary focus was the suppression of the current craze for inflammatory verse satire, and the restriction on histories (and on plays) merely restated earlier legislation. Yet it is hard to believe that that restatement was not motivated by the current scandal about Hayward's *History*, given the Order's timing, and the involvement of Archbishop Whitgift himself in the suppression of Hayward's book.

25 Fulke Greville, *The Life of the Renowned Sir Phillip Sidney* (London, 1653), p. 239.

26 See John Racin, 'The Editions of Sir Water Ralegh's *History of the World*', *Studies in Bibliography*, 17 (1964), 199–209; and Leonard Tennenhouse, 'Sir

Walter Ralegh and Clientage', in *Patronage in the Renaissance*, eds Stephen Orgel and Guy Fitch Lytle (Princeton, 1981), pp. 235–58.

[27] Tennenhouse, p. 235: 'The *History* failed as an act of clientage because, following the death of its original patron, it was subjected to a tendentious reading by the King.'

[28] Edward Hall, *The Union of the two noble and illustrate famelies of Lancastre and York ... proceeding to the reign of the high and prudent prince King Henry the Eighth, the indubitable flower and very heir of the said lineages* (London, 1548).

[29] John Stow, *The Chronicles of England, from Brute unto this present yeare of Christ, 1580* (London, 1580), iiiir.

[30] For reactions against Tillyard's over-emphasis on providentialist history as the only historiography available, see H.A. Kelly, *Divine Providence in the England of Shakespeare's Histories* (Princeton, 1957); Holderness, *Shakespeare's History*, pp. 14–39.

[31] Raphael Holinshed, *Chronicles of England, Scotland and Ireland* (London, 1587), 2:1570, 1576. The fable's darker meaning is made especially available by Holinshed's description of the earlier state of the frogs, as 'living at libertie in lakes and ponds, would needs (as misliking their present intercommunitie of life) with one consent sue to Jupiter for a king.' This behaviour is further identified as 'longing after novelties'. The two appearances of 'libertie' in this passage are, therefore, diametrically opposed to each other.

[32] William Camden, *The Historie of the Princesse Elizabeth*, tr. R. Norton, 4 parts (London, 1630), 4:192–33. Compare also John Chamberlain, whose letters during 1599 kept Dudley Carleton informed of every stage of Essex's affairs. On 1 March 1599, Chamberlain remarked, 'The erle of Essex is crased, but whether more in body or minde is doubtfull', and, some sentences later, reported on the scandal over Hayward's *History*: 'Here hath ben much descanting about yt, why such a storie shold come out at this time, and many exceptions taken, especially to the epistle ... dedicated to the erle of Essex.' *Letters of John Chamberlain*, ed. Norman McLure, 2 vols, (Philadelphia, 1939), 1:69–70. In both Camden's view and Chamberlain's, it was the *timing* or 'untimely' aspect of Hayward's book, in the context of the greater scandal that Essex was creating, that rendered it subject to the conspiracy theory.

[33] See Roy Strong, *The Cult of Elizabeth: Elizabethan Portraiture and Pageantry* (London, 1977), pp. 46–55.

[34] See Richard McCoy, '"A dangerous image": the Earl of Essex and Elizabethan chivalry', *Journal of Medieval and Renaissance Studies*, 13 (1983), 313–29.

[35] William Camden, *Annales* (London, 1625), p. 718.

[36] Camden, *Historie*, 4:127.

[37] Chamberlain, *Letters*, 1:67. The allusions are to Horace, *Epistles*, 1:2:14, 16 ('Whatever folly the kings commit the Greeks must suffer for'; 'the Greeks are transgressing both inside and outside the city'). Their anti-heroic tone is the mirror image of Cockson's epic engraving, as well as of Chapman's translations of the *Iliad* (*Seaven Bookes* and *Achilles Shield*) that were dedicated to Essex in 1598.

[38] *Historical Manuscripts Commission, Penshurst*, ed. C. L. Kingsford, 2:132, 146, 169.

[39] Rowland Whyte to Sir Robert Sidney, *Historical Manuscripts Commission, Penshurst*, 2:435.

[40] See McCoy, p. 325, citing *Acts of the Privy Council*, 30 August 1600, ed. John Roche Dasent (London, 1905), new series xxx, pp. 619–20.

[41] *Calendar of State Papers Domestic*, 1598–1601, Vol. 275, art. 28, pp. 450–51. Cited by Ray Heffner, 'Shakespeare, Hayward and Essex', *PMLA*, 45 (1930), 761.

[42] *Calendar of State Papers Domestic*, 1598–1601, Vol. 278, art. 63, p. 567.

[43] Thomas Birch, *Memoirs of the Reign of Queen Elizabeth*, 2 vols (London, 1754), 2:450.

[44] Compare Albright, 'The Folio Version', p.734, on the connection between this stress on numbers and the figures later cited in testimony about the rebellion.

[45] The classic text here was Virgil, *Georgics*, 4:67–87, a passage traditionally supposed to have figuratively described the struggle for power between Octavian and Antony.

[46] Jonathan Dollimore and Alan Sinfield, 'History and Ideology: The Instance of *Henry V*', in *Alternative Shakespeares*, ed. John Drakakis (London, 1985), p. 220. Their reading of the play, however, hews the neo-marxist critical line that literature can only critique ideology unknowingly.

[47] Albright, 'The Folio Version', pp. 732–3.

[48] Cited in Charlotte Stopes, *Henry, Third Earl of Southampton* (Cambridge, 1922), pp. 248–9.

[49] That the beehive speech survived in the Quarto, while the cynical negotiations of the first scene disappear, is further testimony to the relation between abridgement and a simpler form of patriotism. As a set piece, whose objective is to present the organicist theory of a united commonwealth, the beehive speech, with one salient exception, would have looked impeccable. That exception appears in the two lines wherein Shakespeare admitted the humanitarian aspect of that legislation from which, in Holinshed's account, the bishops were so eager to distract the king. The parliament of 1414 had proposed a bill to the effect that 'the temporal lands devoutly given, and disordinately spent by religious and other spiritual persons' should be appropriated by Henry to provide not only for national defence but also for relief of the poor. Their presence in the sociopolitical system is registered in the Folio account of the hive, where the monarch surveys 'the poore Mechanicke Porters, crowding in/ Their heavy burthens at his narrow gate:' (TLN 347–8). In a speech otherwise reported in the Quarto with exceptional fidelity, these two lines significantly disappear.

[50] The most powerful recent statement of this position is Joel Fineman's *Shakespeare's Perjured Eye* (Berkeley and Los Angeles, 1986), pp. 26–7, 289–96.

[51] Anne Barton, 'The King Disguised: Shakespeare's *Henry V* and the Comical History', in *The Triple Bond*, ed. Joseph G. Price (University Park, Pa., 1975), p. 97.

[52] George Puttenham, *The Arte of English Poesie* (1589) (Menston, Scolar Press facsimile, 1968), pp. 214–15.

[53] Chamberlain, *Letters*, 2:120 (italics added).

[54] See Mervyn James, 'At a Crossroads of the Political Culture: The Essex

Revolt, 1601', in *Society, Politics and Culture* (Cambridge, 1986), pp. 416–65.

5 '*What matter who's speaking?*': Hamlet *and* King Lear

1 This returns us to the issue raised in chapter 1 (p. 16), that although the evidence for performance before 'the two Universities of Cambridge and Oxford' is provided, paradoxically, by the abridged first Quarto, not the second, the longer version may well have been performed in full before academic audiences.

2 *Shake-speares Sonnets* (London, 1609), G3r.

3 Stephen Booth, ed., *Shakespeare's Sonnets* (New Haven and London, 1977), p. 342.

4 J. E. Tanner, *Constitutional Documents of the Reign of James I 1603–1625* (Cambridge, 1930), p. 25.

5 Barry Coward, *The Stuart Age* (London and New York, 1980), p. 104.

6 Elizabeth died on 24 March 1603. James's accession was announced on 27 March. His order for Southampton's release was signed on 5 April. See Charlotte Stopes, *The Life of Henry, Third Earl of Southampton* (Cambridge, 1922), pp. 258–9; and, for a paraphrase of the sonnet's message, G. P. V. Akrigg, *Shakespeare and the Earl of Southampton* (London, 1968), p. 255.

7 A connection between *Hamlet* and the Essex rebellion continues to be suspected by readers of various persuasions. For J. Dover Wilson, *The Essential Shakespeare* (Cambridge, 1935), pp. 104–7, Hamlet is Shakespeare's last, tragic, portrait of Essex, whom he had earlier represented as Henry V. For Mervyn James, 'At a Crossroads of the Political Culture: The Essex Revolt', in *Society, Politics and Culture* (Cambridge, 1986), p. 460, *Hamlet* is 'the classic statement of the problem of choice in a multi-cultural situation', the problem faced by Essex. I much prefer the second formulation, not least because its cultural, rather than characterological, linkage is compatible with a view of Hamlet as, in part, Shakespeare's own persona (and dilemma) as the playwright/intellectual; yet there are aspects of Hamlet, most obviously his rank, less obviously his role as a failed political leader, that must have been suggestive of Essex after February 1601.

8 Samuel Daniel, *Complete Works*, ed. A. B. Grosart, 5 vols (New York, 1963), 2:297. On Daniel's relation with Essex, and their consequence for the *Civil Wars*, see Joan Rees, *Samuel Daniel* (Liverpool, 1964), pp. 126–9. Daniel, who had rushed to offer James *A Panegyrike Congratulatory* as he stepped over the border into England, also addressed a verse epistle (1:219) to Southampton consoling him for his imprisonment as a test of personal worth.

9 Michel Foucault, 'What is an Author?', in *Language, Counter-Memory, Practice*, tr. Donald Bouchard and Sherry Simon (Ithaca, 1977), p. 138.

10 Michel Foucault, *The Archeology of Knowledge*, tr. A. M. Sheridan Smith (New York, 1972), pp. 122.

11 Jacques Lacan, 'The Freudian Thing', in *Ecrits: A Selection*, tr. Alan Sheridan (New York, 1977) pp. 123, 125.

12 Lacan, 'The Mirror Stage as Formative of the Function of the I as Revealed in Psychoanalytic Experience', in *Ecrits: A Selection*, p. 7.

[13] Lacan, 'The Subversion of the Subject and the Dialectic of Desire', in *Ecrits: A Selection*, pp. 306–7.

[14] Lacan, 'Desire and the Interpretation of Desire in *Hamlet*', *Yale French Studies*, 55/56 (1977), pp. 50–2.

[15] Louis Althusser, *Pour Marx* (Paris, 1965) p. 188; *For Marx*, tr. Ben Brewster (London, 1977), pp. 184–5.

[16] Again, this is consciously or unconsciously obscured by the translator, who produces instead the nonsensical 'If we abstract *from* men in these means of production'.

[17] Geoffrey Hartman, 'The Interpreter: A Self-Analysis', *New Literary History*, 4 (1972) p. 227.

[18] Robert Weimann, *Shakespeare and the Popular Tradition in the Theater* (Baltimore and London, 1978), p. 130.

[19] The term 'playwright', of course, retains that mediatory status between manual and intellectual work, at the level of a cultural pun.

[20] Weimann, *Shakespeare and the Popular Tradition*, p. 180.

[21] As Naomi Wood pointed out to me, the first ('Bad') Quarto of the play offers a version of the quintessential soliloquy, 'To be or not to be', that implies a stronger social criticism designed for the popular stage. In place of 'the oppressor's wrong, the proud man's contumely,/The pangs of despised love, the law's delay,/ The insolence of office', the reader/audience of the first Quarto playtext is asked to consider what it is like to be 'scorned by the right rich, the rich cursssed of the poore?/The widow being oppressed, the orphan wrong'd, The taste of hunger, or a tirants raigne' (Diiv-Eir). The last phrase in particular connects with the 'tyrants crests' of Sonnet 107; and the soliloquy as a whole sounds considerably more materialist, less metaphysical, than its counterpart in the readerly version of 1604.

[22] The term 'digger', along with 'leveller', was already in circulation in 1607 at the time of the Midlands Rising. See Roger Manning, *Village Revolts* (Oxford, 1988), pp. 231, 235.

[23] Edmond Malone, *The Plays and Poems of William Shakespeare*, 10 vols (London, 1790), 9:387.

[24] For an explanation of how the 1587 edition was in fact prepared not by Holinshed, who died in 1580, but by a team of antiquaries, William Harrison, Abraham Fleming, Francis Boteville and John Stow, see Elizabeth Story Donno, 'Some Aspects of Shakespeare's Holinshed', *Huntington Library Quarterly*, 50 (1987), pp. 229–47.

[25] Raphael Holinshed, *The Chronicles of England, Scotland, and Ireland* (London, 1587) 2:1546.

[26] See *Tottel's Miscellany (1557–1587)*, ed. H. E. Rollins, 2 vols (Cambridge, Mass., 1965), 1:167. The poem was entitled 'The lover accusing hys love for her unfathfulnesse, purposeth to live in libertie'. It has since been attributed to Vaux.

[27] Loggets was decreed unlawful by a statute of Henry VIII (33.c 9).

[28] See my contention in 'The Very Name of the Game: Theories of Order and Disorder', *South Atlantic Quarterly*, 86 (1987), pp. 521–2; this view of the radical

semantics of 'revolution' is shared by Michael Hattaway, 'Rebellion, Class Consciousness and Shakespeare's 2 *Henry VI*', *Cahiers Elizabéthains*, 33 (1988), pp. 13–14.

29 See Steven Mullaney, 'Lying Like Truth: Riddle, Representation, and Treason', in *The Place of the Stage: License, Play, and Power in Renaissance England* (Chicago, 1988), pp. 119–20.

30 Lacan, 'Desire and the Interpretation of Desire in *Hamlet*', p. 33.

31 For a simplified account of Lacan's interest in equivocation in the psychoanalytic experience, see Stuart Schneiderman, *Jacques Lacan: The Death of an Intellectual Hero* (Cambridge, Mass., 1983), pp. 116–22.

32 Cited in J. P. Kenyon, *The Stuarts* (Glasgow, 1958, rev. 1970), p. 35.

33 See Frederick von Raumer, *History of the Sixteenth and Seventeenth Centuries, Illustrated by Original Documents*, 2 vols (1835), 2:207. Gary Taylor reprints the king's hunting itinerary from November 1604 to December 1605 in '*King Lear* and Censorship', in Gary Taylor and Michael Warren, *The Division of the Kingdoms* (Oxford, 1984), p. 104. And in 1608, Nicholas Breton's pamphlet, *A Murmurer*, indicates that the king's hunting had already become a popular grievance, occasioning the 'murmuring' against which Breton argued: 'Doeth he hunt and delight in Dogges? better to nourish dogs,/who shew but their nature...then to maintain those monsters of men, that contrary to the nature of men, will murmure at the welfare of their Master' (B6r/v). That Lear was a hunter was, however, already traditional.

34 As in Hamlet's mention of the 'late innovation' that had forced the players to travel, Gloucester's references (in 1:2:106–7) to these 'late eclipses in the sun and moon', encouraged a sense of contemporaneity, given that England had experienced eclipses of the moon and sun in September and October 1605 respectively.

35 See Glynne Wickham, 'From Tragedy to Tragi-comedy: *King Lear* as Prologue', p. 36.

36 See my *Censorship and Interpretation* (Wisconsin, 1984), pp. 64–73.

37 *Journals of the House of Commons*, 1:315.

40 See especially Paul Delaney, '*King Lear* and the Decline of Feudalism', *PMLA*, 92 (1977), 429–40; Rosalie Colie, 'Reason and Need: *King Lear* and the "Crisis" of the Aristocracy', in R. L. Colie and F. T. Flahiff, eds, *Some Facets of King Lear* (Toronto, 1974), pp. 189–216, an application of Lawrence Stone's theories which pits old aristocrat Lear against new man Edmund, yet attempts to locate both in 'a profound critique of habits of quantification induced by a commercial revolution' (p. 190).

39 Kenyon, *The Stuarts*, pp. 8, 37.

40 See Elizabeth Reid Foster, ed., *Proceedings in Parliament, 1610*, 2 vols (New Haven, 1966), pp. 103, 105.

41 Paul Slack cites, among various types of vagrants recorded, 'counterfeit Bedlams'. See 'Vagrants and Vagrancy in England 1598–1634', *Economic History Review*, 27 (1974), p. 364.

42 Richard Strier, 'Faithful Servants: Shakespeare's Praise of Disobedience', in *The Historical Renaissance: New Essays on Tudor and Stuart Literature and Culture*, eds Heather Dubrow and Richard Strier (Chicago, 1988), p. 199.

[43] See Samuel Schoenbaum, *William Shakespeare: A Compact Documentary Life* (Oxford, 1977), pp. 227–32.

[44] For the most extensive discussion of the Fool's prophecy and its relation to earlier forms of protest, including the *Piers Plowman* tradition, see Joseph Wittreich, Jr, *'Image of that Horror': History, Prophecy, and Apocalypse in King Lear* (San Marino, 1984), pp. 60–74. Wittreich refutes the position of P. W. K. Stone (in *The Textual History of "King Lear"* (London, 1980, pp. 119–21) that the prophecy should be discarded as non-Shakespearean on qualitative grounds and, because it is clearly topical, assumed to have been added 'for a purely theatrical purpose', probably by an actor.

[45] James Agee and Walker Evans, *Let Us Now Praise Famous Men* (Boston, 1939, repr. 1960), xviii.

[46] See Laurence Bergreen, *James Agee: A Life* (Harmondsworth, 1984) p. 164.

[47] For a subtle account of *Let Us Now Praise Famous Men* that attempts to relate its aesthetic and political parameters, and to explain its strangenesses as postmodernism *avant la lettre*, see T. V. Reed, 'Unimagined Existence and the Fiction of the Real: Postmodernist Realism in *Let Us Now Praise Famous Men*', *Representations*, 24 (1988), pp. 156–76. It says something about Foucault's notion of a discursive formation that Agee's work, which received, as Reed points out (p. 173), its first full recognition during the civil rights movement of the 1960s, is now being rediscovered again.

[48] Leah Marcus, *Puzzling Shakespeare* (Berkeley and Los Angeles, 1988), p. 238

[49] This allusion was noticed simultaneously by T. V. Reed, 'Unimagined Existence', p. 156, further supporting the notion that cultural paradigm shifts are marked by mysterious coincidences.

[50] See Martin Heidegger, 'The Origin of the Work of Art', in *Reach of Mind: Essays in memory of Kurt Goldstein* (New York, 1968).

[51] Jacques Derrida, 'Restitutions of the truth in pointing [pointure]', in *The Truth in Painting*, tr. Geoff Bennington and Ian McLeod (Chicago, 1987), pp. 255–82.

6 *'Speak, speak!'*: The Popular Voice and the Jacobean State

[1] Philip Brockbank, ed., *Coriolanus* (London, 1976), p. 84.

[2] See Margot Heinemann, 'How Brecht read Shakespeare', in *Political Shakespeare*, eds Jonathan Dollimore and Alan Sinfield (Manchester, 1985), pp. 221–3, for Brecht's own statements of purpose.

[3] Günter Grass, *The Plebeians Rehearse the Uprising*, tr. Ralph Manheim (New York, 1966).

[4] See Nancy Armstrong, *Desire and Domestic Fiction: A Political History of the Novel* (New York and Oxford, 1987), pp. 215–19.

[5] Allan Bloom, *The Closing of the American Mind* (New York, 1987), pp. 110–11.

[6] See Mark Kishlansky, *Parliamentary Selection: Social and Political Choice in*

Early Modern England (Cambridge, 1986).

[7] See Walter Benjamin, 'Theses on the Philosophy of History', in *Illuminations*, ed. Hannah Arendt, tr. Harry Zohn (New York, 1969), p. 256. The phrase has subsequently become canonized in Terry Eagleton's *Against the Grain* (London, 1986).

[8] See W. Gordon Zeefeld, '"Coriolanus" and Jacobean Politics', *Modern Language Review*, 17 (1962), pp. 327–8; and C. C. Huffman, *Coriolanus in Context* (Lewisburg, 1971), pp. 147–50.

[9] The reference is to Richard Garnett, 'The Date and Occasion of "The Tempest"', *Universal Review*, 3 (1889), 565–66.

[10] Anne Barton, 'Livy, Machiavelli, and Shakespeare's *Coriolanus*', *Shakespeare Survey*, 38 (1985), p. 129. For other comparable positions, see Kenneth Muir, 'In Defence of the Tribunes', *Essays in Criticism*, 4 (1954), pp. 331–3; R. B. Parker, '*Coriolanus* and "th'interpretation of the time"' in *Essays in Honour of G. R. Hibbard*, ed. J. C. Gray (Toronto, 1984), especially pp. 266–8; and Jonathan Dollimore, *Radical Tragedy: Religion, Ideology and Power in the Drama of Shakespeare and his Contemporaries* (Chicago, 1984), pp. 218–30.

[11] There would follow Thomas May's lost play of *Julius Caesar* in 1616, Bolton's *Nero Caesar, or Monarchie depraved*, published anonymously in 1624, and Massinger's *Roman Actor*, also about Nero, in the following year.

[12] Andrew Marvell, *Poems and Letters*, ed. H. M. Margoliouth, rev. Pierre Legouis, 2 vols (Oxford, 1971), 1:95.

[13] Joel Fineman, 'Shakespeare's *Will*: The Temporality of Rape', *Representations*, 20 (1987), 26.

[14] James M. Tolbert, 'The Argument to Shakespeare's "Lucrece": Its Sources and Authorship', *University of Texas Studies in English*, 29 (1950), 77–90, believed that the 'Argument' was non-Shakespearean, and constructed by someone else from parts of Livy, Thomas Cooper's *Thesaurus Linguae Romanae et Britannicae* and 'the unidentified source of the story as told in *Cooper's Chronicle* (1549). This not only seems an unnecessarily complicated hypothesis but also begs the question of why Shakespeare, if he did not write it, *permitted* this historical framing of his poem in the 1594 edition. Southampton, to whom he dedicated it, and who was part of the Essex conspiracy, would have seen the point.

[15] See also Michael Platt, '*The Rape of Lucrece* and the Republic for which it stands', *Centennial Review*, 19 (1975), pp. 59–79, reprinted in his *Rome and Romans According to Shakespeare* (rev. ed. Lanham, Md., 1983), pp. 13–51: 'The rape...is the middle of an action whose beginning is 'kings' and whose end is 'consuls,' (p. 20).

[16] Another echo occurs when Macbeth moves towards regicide with 'Tarquin's ravishing strides' (2:1:56), a phrase that registers the interchangeability in that play of anointed king and tyrant, male and female. And in *Henry V*, the Constable of France warns that Henry's misspent youth should rather be interpreted as 'the outside of the Roman Brutus,/Covering discretion with a coat of folly,' (2:4:37–38, 36–38), thereby alluding to the feigned madness with which Lucius Junius Brutus concealed his plans to free Rome from Tarquin oppression.

[17] Compare, however, Richard Greneway's attempt, in the *Proeme* to his 1598 translation of Tacitus, to compress the republican era in the interest of claiming its

instability: 'The citie of Rome was in the beginning governed by Kings. Libertie and the Consulship L. Brutus brought in. The Dictators were chosen but for a time:. . .neither had the Consularie authoritie or the Tribunes or the souldiers any long continuance:. . .Pompey and Crassus quickly yeelded to Caesars force: Lepidus and Antonie to Augustus: who entitling himselfe by the name of Prince, brought under this obedience the whole Romane state, wearied and weakened with civill disorders.' Quoted in G. Bullough, *Narrative and Dramatic Sources of Shakespeare*, 8 vols (1957–74), 5:144–5.

18 Machiavelli, *Discorsi*, tr. Leslie J. Walker, S. J. (Harmondsworth, 1979), p. 111. See the excellent discussion of this passage, and its implications for Machiavelli's thought, by Victoria Kahn, *Journal of Mediaeval and Renaissance Studies*, 18 (1988), pp. 1–19.

19 Kishlansky, *Parliamentary Selection*, pp. 4–5. Though he would broaden the term 'revisionist' to include every historian who aims to mark an advance in knowledge and precision, Kishlansky himself takes that sceptical view of the Whig interpretation of history that, in English historiography, defines a particular kind of revisionism.

20 Sir Thomas Smith, *De Republica Anglorum* (1583), ed. L. Alston (Cambridge, 1906), p. 46. Freemen could vote in London and gradually in other urban centres. 'What this might mean in practice,' wrote Derek Hirst, *The Representative of the People? Voters and Voting Under The Early Stuarts* (Cambridge, 1975) is exemplified by Dover, which admitted 319 freemen between 1603 and 1624, including 9 laborers, 9 fishermen and 18 sailors. Oddly, he describes this development as giving 10% of the franchise to the 'urban proletariat' (p. 95). Yet he also cites (p. 108) George Wither's critique of the Long Parliament in 1646 (*Opobalsamum Anglicanum*) which states clearly those who did *not* have a voice, 'the cobbler and the smith, tapsters, chamberlains and ostlers', could nevertheless the lobbied 'To move their customers who had a voice.'

21 Compare Richard Wilson, '"Is this a holiday?"' Shakespeare's Roman Carnival,' *ELH*, 54 (1987), pp. 31–44, who, as in his treatment of *Henry VI, Part 2* in relation to the feltmakers' uprising in 1592, reads 'the first scene acted at the Globe [i.e. the opening scene of *Julius Caesar*]. . .as a manoeuvre in the campaign to legitimize the Shakespearean stage and dissociate it from the subversiveness of artisanal culture' (p. 33).

22 Charles Gildon, *Remarks on the Plays of Shakespeare in Works of Shakespeare*, ed. Rowe, vol. 7 (London, 1710), pp. 362–3.

23 Grass, *The Plebeians Rehearse the Uprising*, xii.

24 See Christopher Hill, 'The Many-Headed Monster', in *Change and Continuity in Seventeenth-Century England* (Cambridge, Mass., 1975), pp. 181–204; and Jonathan Dollimore, *Radical Tragedy*, pp. 223–6.

25 See also Coriolanus's complaint that the Senate has 'given Hydra here to choose an officer,. . .the horn and noise o' th' monster's' (3:1:92–4). It must be acknowledged that the playtext includes one stage direction 'Enter a rabble of Plebeians with the Aediles' (3:1:179), although in the scene of confusion that follows it is hard to distinguish one disordinate group from another.

26 Michel Foucault, *Power/Knowledge* (New York, 1980) p. 97.

27 Grass, *The Plebeians Rehearse the Uprising*, p. 31.

[28] E. P. Thompson, 'The Moral Economy of the English Crowd in the Eighteenth Century', *Past and Present*, 50 (1971), 76–136.

[29] Philip Brockbank, ed. *Coriolanus*, p. 38; and see also: Andrew Gurr, '"Coriolanus" and the Body Politic', *Shakespeare Survey*, 28 (1975), 63–9; Thomas Sorge, '"Body Politic" and "Human Body" in *Coriolanus*: Ein Beitrag zur Commonwealth-Thematik bei Shakespeare,' *Shakespeare Jarhbuch*, 115 (1979), pp. 89–97; Robert S. Miola, *Shakespeare's Rome* (Cambridge, 1983), pp. 167–8;

[30] We might note in this connection that in 1986 President Reagan deferred funds allocated by the Congress for transporting surplus food to homeless people, despite the fact that the transportation costs, $28 million, were a fraction of the $365 million spent annually to store this food in limestone caves in Kansas and elsewhere. See Jonathan Kozol, *Rachel and her Children: Homeless Families in America* (New York, 1988), pp. 59–60.

[31] Karl Marx, *Value, Price and Profit*, in Karl Marx and Frederick Engels, *Collected Works*, Vol. 20 (New York, 1985), pp. 104, 106. See also *The Condition of the Working-class in England*, *C.W.*, Vol. 4 (New York, 1975), p. 510, where Engels complains of Dr Andrew Ure, 'the most furious enemy of the Unions', who had cited the belly fable in his Philosophy of Manufactures (London, 1835), p. 282; and adds, 'A pity that the English working-men will not let themselves be pacified so easily with thy fable as the Roman Plebs, thou modern Menenius Agrippa!' I owe this additional evidence of the fable's 'modern' vitality to Peter Stallybrass.

[32] Bloom, *The Closing of the American Mind*, pp. 110–11.

[33] Grass, *The Plebeians Rehearse the Uprising*, pp. 80–1.

[34] Fredric Jameson, *The Political Unconscious* (Ithaca, 1981), p. 34.

[35] E. C. Pettet, '*Coriolanus* and the Midlands Insurrection of 1607', *Shakespeare Survey*, 3 (1950), 39.

[36] See Buchanan Sharp, *In Contempt of All Authority: Rural Artisans and Riot in the West of England, 1586–1660* (Berkeley, 1980), p. 42.

[37] Derek Hirst, *Authority and Conflict: England, 1603–1658* (Cambridge, Mass., 1986), p. 51. I wish to record, however, that Hirst subsequently felt that his position was overstated.

[38] See especially Edwin F. Gay, 'The Midland Revolt and the Inquisitions of Depopulation of 1607', *Transactions of the Royal Historical Society*, New Series, 18 (1904), 195–244. The most extensive account of the Revolt is by John E. Martin, *Feudalism to Capitalism: Peasant and Landlord in English Agrarian Development* (London, 1988), pp. 161–215.

[39] See James F. Larkin and Paul L. Hughes, eds, *Stuart Royal Proclamations*, 2 vols (Oxford, 1973), 1:153, n.1; and Martin, *Feudalism to Capitalism*, p. 163, who cites the Warwickshire petition from J. O. Halliwell, ed., *The Marriage of Wit and Wisdom* (London, 1846), pp. 140–1.

[40] See David Underdown, *Revel, Riot and Rebellion: Popular Politics and Culture in England 1603–1660* (Oxford, 1985), p. 115.

[41] See Andrew Charlesworth, ed., *An Atlas of Rural Protest in Britain 1548–1900* (Philadelphia, 1983), pp. 33–4.

[42] See 'A Proclamation for suppressing of persons riotously assembled for the laying open of Inclosures, 30 May 1607', in *A Booke of Proclamations* (London, 1609), p. 139.

[43] Larkin and Hughes, *Stuart Royal Proclamations*, p. 155, n.2.

[44] *A Proclamation signifying his Majesties pleasure aswell for suppressing of riotous Assemblies about Inclosures, as for reformation of Depopulations. 28 June 1607*, in *A Booke of Proclamations* (London, 1609), p. 140.

[45] See Joan Thirsk, *The Agrarian History of England and Wales (1500–1640)*, 8 vols (Cambridge, 1967) 4:820. I am grateful to Derek Hirst for reading the message of these figures to me. See also Martin, *Feudalism to Capitalism*, who argues that whereas in national terms harvests were good until 1607, from the 1590s onwards the Midlands 'experienced a chronic scarcity of grain', and that by April 1607 'the peasantry would have been aware that even harder times were on the way, owing to the meagre condition of the coming harvest' (pp. 161–3).

[46] Larkin and Hughes, *Stuart Royal Proclamations*, 1:161.

[47] Larkin and Hughes, *Stuart Royal Proclamations*, 1:163.

[48] *Orders Appointed by his Majestie to be straigtly observed for the preventing and remedying of the dearth of Graine and other Victuall. June 1, 1608* (London, 1608), p. 13.

[49] Larkin and Hughes, *Stuart Royal Proclamations*, 1:202.

[50] One can be confident of using this phrase when proclamations are involved, since their very function is to bring to public consciousness a particular aspect of governmental policy. Indeed, these proclamations were collected and republished in *A Booke of Proclamations* in 1609, a move interpreted by the Commons as a statement of royal intent to *govern* by proclamation while suspending parliamentary process.

[51] Robert Wilkinson, *A Sermon Preached at North-Hampton the 21 of June last past, before the Lord Lieutenant of the County, and the rest of the Commissioners there assembled upon occasion of the late Rebellion and Riots in those parts committed. Pro.22.2 The rich & the poore meete together, the Lord is the maker of them all* (London, 1607). The existence of this document was briefly noted by Brents Stirling, *The Populace in Shakespeare* (New York, 1949), p. 107, who, however, saw it merely as proof of social unrest that would have stirred Shakespeare to law-and-order activity. See also Martin, *Feudalism to Capitalism*, pp. 163, 176, 179, who, however, assumes that Wilkinson's sermon 'reflects the thinking of the government'.

[52] If Wilkinson really intended his sermon to be bipartisan, he must have assumed that at least some of the Risers were literate.

[53] Zeefeld, '"Coriolanus" and Jacobean Politics', pp. 323–4.

[54] See Elizabeth Read Foster, ed., *Proceedings in Parliament: 1610*, 2 vols, (New Haven, 1966), 2:10–11.

[55] *The Kings Majestie's Speach To the Lords and Commons...on Wednesday the xxi of March, Anno Dom. 1609* (London, 1610), B2.

[56] Foster, *Proceedings*, 2:98.

[57] The term 'tribunes' was still being used pejoratively for the opposition leaders in the Commons on 16 June 1614, when Sir Ralph Winwood wrote to Dudley Carleton: 'Never saw so much faction and passion as in the late unhappy Parliament. . . The impositions were the great grievance, also a speech of the Bishop of London taxing the Commons with sedition, and the Kings messages were thought to abridge the liberty of the House. The break-neck was some seditious speeches which made the King impatient, and it was whispered to him that they would have his life and that of his favourites before they had done, on which he dissolved them. Four of their tribunes, Sir Walter Chute, Christopher Neville, Hoskins and Wentworth, are sent to prison. . .' See *Calender of State Papers Domestic*, James I, Vol. No. 77.

[58] Henry Howard, Earl of Northampton, Lord Privy Seal, in Foster, *Proceedings*, 1:268.

[59] See also Kenneth Muir, 'Shakespeare and Lewkenor', *Review of English Studies*, 7 (1956), 182–3.

[60] As Joseph Kestner points out, *Protest and Reform: The British Social Narrative by Women 1827–1867* (Madison, 1985), Brontë 'sent for the files of the Leeds *Mercury* for 1812–1814 to do research' (p. 127). The immediate cause of the Luddite Rebellion in Yorkshire was the trade war between England and Napoleonic France, which on England's side was initiated by the Orders in Council of 1811, limiting the markets for English cloth. And the Luddites themselves were not merely resisting modernization via mechanization, but intended their protest to demonstrate also workers' solidarity and resistance to wage reductions. See Asa Briggs, 'Private and Social Themes in *Shirley*', *Bronte Society Transactions*, 13 (1958) 203–19, who notes that government brought in an army against the Luddites 'as large as that which Wellington was leading' against Napoleon, a sign of the significance of the social and political issues that were thought to be at stake.

[61] Brontë, Charlotte, *Shirley*, ed. Herbert Rosengarten and Margaret Smith (Oxford, 1979), pp. 103–4.

[62] Armstrong, *Desire and Domestic Fiction*, p. 217.

[63] Armstrong herself cites (p. 166) E. P. Thompson's arguments in 'The Moral Economy of the English Crowd', yet does not comment on Caroline's attack on the perjorative use of 'mob', or Shirley's acceptance of the term. Since she refers to Coriolanus as a 'Roman emperor' (p. 217), it appears that the full political dimensions of the Shakespearean text and its Roman pretexts were beyond her purview.

[64] George Eliot, *Felix Holt, The Radical*, ed. Peter Coveney (Harmondsworth: Penguin, 1972), p. 187.

[65] See *Felix Holt*, ed. Coveney, Appendix A, p. 613.

[66] See Hilary and Mary Evans, *The Man who Drew the Drunkard's Daughter: the Life and Art of George Cruikshank 1792–1878* (London, 1978) pp. 38–9. They speculate (p. 37) that the unusually dignified representation of George IV, whom Cruikshank usually depicted as a sodden debauchee, may have reflected the fact that George and his brother were paid by the Crown in 1820 not to depict the new king in any 'immoral circumstances'. If so, Cruikshank incorporated his resistance to bribery by including himself among the protestors. I owe this information to Brian Parker.

7 'Thought is Free': *The Tempest*

[1] George Eliot, *Felix Holt: The Radical*, ed. Peter Coveney (Harmondsworth, 1972), p. 368.

[2] Mannoni's ideas were also applied to English colonialism. See Philip Mason, *Prospero's Magic: Some Thoughts on Class and Race* (London, 1962), a deeply ambivalent statement by a colonial employee who defended Mannoni's psychology (and the need for the 'firm hand' of paternalistic government) while seeing himself, with distaste, in Prospero.

[3] Aimé Césaire, *Une Tempête: D'Après 'la Tempête' de Shakespeare – Adaptation pour un théâtre nègre* (Paris, 1969); George Lamming, *The Pleasures of Exile* (1960; New York, 1984) and *Water with Berries* (New York, 1971); Roberto Fernández Retamar, 'Caliban. Notes Toward a Discussion of Culture in Our America', first published in Spanish in *Casa de Las Américas*, 68 (1971), tr. Lynn Garafola *et al.*, *Massachusetts Review*, 15 (1974).

[4] For accounts of these anti-colonialist interpretations, see Charlotte H. Bruner, 'The Meaning of Caliban in Black Literature Today', *Comparative Literature Studies*, 13 (1976), 240–53; and Rob Nixon, 'Decolonizing, Revaluing: Caribbean and African Appropriations of *The Tempest*', *Critical Inquiry* 14 (1987), pp. 557–78. For an account of anti-colonial appropriations in Britain, see Trevor R. Griffiths, '"This Island's Mine": Caliban and Colonialism', *Yearbook of English Studies*, 13 (1983), 159–80.

[5] Lytton Strachey, *Books and Characters* (1922), p. 68.

[6] Stephen Orgel, ed., *The Tempest* (Oxford, 1987), 82–7.

[7] The social implications of this challenge did not escape Coleridge, who in the 1611–12 lectures speaks of the Boatswain as pouring forth 'his vulgar mind' 'when the bonds of reverence are thrown off'. See Samuel Taylor Coleridge, *Lectures 1808–1819*, ed. R. A. Foakes, Vol. 5 in *Collected Works*, 16 vols (Princeton, 1987), p. 520.

[8] References will be to the New Arden edition: *The Tempest*, ed. Frank Kermode (Cambridge, Mass., 1954).

[9] Retamar, *Caliban*, p. 16.

[10] Renan, *Caliban*, p. 48: 'Guerre aux libres! Ce sont les pires ennemis du peuple. Ceux qui les possèdent ont des pouvoirs sur leurs semblables. L'homme qui sait le latin commande aux autres hommes. A bas le latin!'

[11] Renan, *Caliban*, pp. 69–70: 'Voici comme je l'explique...C'est que Alonzo et les siens etaient accessible à nos charmes...Quand Alonzo vit la tempête, il crut que les vagues parlaient, que les vents grondaient, que la tempête murmurait, que le tonnerre, cet orgue profond et terrible, lui reprochait de sa voix de basse le crime qu'il avait commis contre toi. Le peuple n'admit rien de tout cela...La magie ne sert plus de rien. La révolution, c'est le réalisme.'

[12] For evidence that this view (that is to say, Prospero's view) was critical orthodoxy, see the protest against it (first published in 1969) by Harry Berger, Jr, 'Miraculous Harp: A Reading of Shakespeare's *Tempest*' in *Second World and Green World: Studies in Renaissance Fiction Making* (Berkeley and Los Angeles,

1988), pp. 147–85. For evidence of its persistence, see John S. Mebane, 'Metadrama and the Visionary Imagination in *Dr. Faustus* and *The Tempest*', *South Atlantic Review*, 53 (1988), pp. 25–45, where the claim is made that 'only those who possess a capacity for this kind of vision can respond to Prospero's magical art or participate in the harmonious order that it helps to establish' (p. 34). What is needed to sustain the idealist interpretation is explicitly stated: 'interpersonal faith'.

[13] See Elizabeth Read Foster, ed., *Proceedings in Parliament. 1610*, 2 vols (New Haven, 1966), 2:103.

[14] Sir John Hayward, *Life of Henry IIII* (London, 1599), pp. 102–3.

[15] For a fine account of Dryden's adaptation, and the difference between its political analysis and that implied by *The Tempest*, see Katharine Maus, 'Arcadia Lost: Politics and Revision in the Restoration *Tempest*', *Renaissance Drama*, 13 (1982), pp. 189–209; and for an account of magic in *The Tempest* as political mystification see Curtis Breight, '"Treason doth never prosper": The Tempest and the Discourse of Treason', an unpublished paper to which I owe this chapter's epigraph.

Index